TRENT

TRENT

What Happened at the Council

JOHN W. O'MALLEY

THE BELKNAP PRESS OF
HARVARD UNIVERSITY PRESS
Cambridge, Massachusetts
London, England
2013

Library of Congress Cataloging-in-Publication Data
O'Malley, John W.
Trent : what happened at the council / John W. O'Malley.
p.   cm.
Includes bibliographical references (p.   ) and index.
ISBN 978-0-674-06697-7 (alk. paper)
1. Council of Trent (1545–1563).   I. Title.
BX8301545   .043   2013
262'.52—dc23   2012023978

For Clare O'Reilly

With gratitude to Giles of Viterbo,
who, long dead though he was,
introduced Clare and me to each other
on Achill Island a half-century ago

History with its flickering lamp stumbles along the trail of the past, trying to reconstruct its scenes, to revive its echoes, and to kindle with pale gleams the passions of former days.

Winston Churchill, eulogy for Neville Chamberlain
November 12, 1940

Contents

TRENT

Introduction

Trent rings a bell, but faint and muffled is the sound. A church council? Against Luther and the Protestants? For many the bell tolls ominously, intimating regression, repression, and the dreaded Counter Reformation. Even for Roman Catholics the bell rings with distant sound and indistinct tone: some stoutly maintain that Trent was the council that wrought all the bad things from which Vatican Council II saved them in the twentieth century, others that Trent created all the good things of which Vatican II then robbed them. Such are the prevailing clichés about the council. Yet even the clichés suggest that Trent, whatever it was, was important. In fact, anyone with the slightest interest in the cultural and religious history of early modern Europe has heard of it and been indoctrinated, subtly or not so subtly, into either a positive or a negative assessment.

"Trent" was indeed a church council that met, not surprisingly, in the city of Trent, located in the Adige River valley just south of the Dolomite Mountains, on the route to the Brenner Pass. It was much closer to Innsbruck than to Rome.[1] The city, although in present-day Italy, owed its political allegiance to the Count of Tyrol, a title held from 1519 to 1521 by the Holy Roman Emperor, Charles V, and after that by his brother, Ferdinand. It was more immediately subject to the overlordship of the local bishop. Trent hosted the council in three distinct periods that stretched over eighteen years—1545–1547, 1551–1552, and 1562–1563. The name of the city in Latin is Tridentinum, hence the English adjective Tridentine.

At the time of the council Trent was incomparably smaller than today's lively metropolis. It counted only about seven or eight thousand inhabitants, of which almost all were Italian-speaking. Trent's winters were long and severe, its summers often heavy and hot, a great trial (not to mention a health threat) for those at the council used to more temperate climes and less dramatic shifts in temperature. The curious bedfellows of tedium and tension also took their toll on the physical well-being and emotional equilibrium of the council's participants.

As the number of prelates attending the council grew, the problem of providing food and lodging in this small city grew accordingly. Lodging became especially difficult because rooms had to be found not only for the bishops but also for their sometimes large retinues, which in a few cases might mean 20 to 30 persons or even many more. The entourage of Cardinal Ercole Gonzaga, the principal papal legate for the last period of the council, comprised 160 persons, and that of Cardinal Charles de Guise, 80.[2]

Provision also had to be made for the theologians advising the bishops, who at times outnumbered them, for occasional princely visitors, and of course for the "orators" (envoys or ambassadors) of the great rulers, who certainly did not come unaccompanied. During the last period, for instance, the envoy of the Portuguese crown had an entourage of 80. By that time the council swelled the town's population by well over 2,000 people. Besides providing food and lodging for all these visi-

FIGURE 1 Map of Italy showing major cities and indicating the distance between Rome and Trent.

tors, the town also had to find fodder for the horses on which they arrived, which itself became a major problem.

Somehow the town managed to accommodate these numbers, but with great difficulty, inconvenience, discomfort, and grumbling on the part of all concerned. Prices skyrocketed. There were other problems. Unlike today, the city was then a cultural backwater, which meant it did not possess the library resources adequate for a gathering such as the council, which had to cope with such serious historical and theological issues.

In comparison with the other problems besetting the council, however, these were almost negligible. The others were so many and so great that it seems a miracle the council ever happened at all and was finally brought to conclusion. War, the threat of war, and the seemingly inexorable onslaught against Christendom's eastern frontier by the forces of the Ottoman Turks, "the infidel," made the council a perilous enterprise. Even during cease-fires the rivalries among the great rulers and the high stakes the council held for them obstructed the council's attempts to move forward on its business.

These extraordinary circumstances meant that, compared with other councils, attendance by bishops was until the third period notably small. Although in the mid-sixteenth century the Catholic episcopate numbered close to 700 members, the council opened with only 29 prelates. The second period, 1551–1552, opened with only 15. In neither of these periods did the number ever reach 100.

The council attained its peak membership during the third period, 1562–1563, when by the second year around 200 were steadily present. During the summer of that year, the number rose for a short time to as high as 280—not a mean achievement, given the troubled times. Most bishops who came to one of the periods of the council stayed for its duration, but others arrived, stayed a while, and then departed—maybe to return, maybe not. A decade and a half separated the opening of the first period from the opening of the third, which meant very few prelates present at the former were alive or well enough to participate in the latter. The long span between the beginning and the end of the council resulted in an extraordinarily large cast of participants, making it difficult to keep track even of the major personalities. The three popes who convoked the three periods (Paul III, Julius III, and Pius IV), the two emperors (Charles V and Ferdinand I), and the two kings of France (Francis I and Henry II) emerge, of course, with clarity, as does, in the last period, the king of Spain, Philip II. The more important papal legates also emerge clearly—Giovanni Maria Del Monte and Marcello Cervini for the first period, Marcello Crescenzio for the second, and Ercole Gonzaga, Girolamo Seripando, Ludovico Simonetta, and especially Giovanni Morone for the third.

But there were other important players, including three who had the rare experience of participating in all three periods—Seripando, the theologically skilled superior general of the Augustinian order for the first two periods and, as mentioned, papal legate for the third; the Jesuit Diego Laínez, who served as a papal theologian for the first two and who appeared as superior general of his order at the third; and Alfonso Salmerón, also a Jesuit, papal theologian for all three.

From the ranks of the Spaniards, small in comparison with the Italians, came forth powerful personalities such as, during the first period, Cardinal Pedro Pacheco and, during the second and third, Archbishop Pedro Guerrero. When the French finally arrived in the middle of the third period, they were led by Cardinal Charles de Guise, who from the first moment of his appearance assumed a powerful leadership role and commanded a sometimes grudging respect. If Morone deserves credit for finally bringing the council to conclusion, he could hardly have done so without the cooperation of de Guise.

There were many others, as the chapters that follow make clear, but why for the first two periods was attendance so sparse? Bishops had their reasons (or excuses) for not going to the council. Skepticism that the council would ever meet, or that, once it met, the pope really wanted it to succeed, ranked high among them. Given such problems, given the turbulent political and religious situation, and given the commitment in time and resources that participation in the council required, it is remarkable that so many bishops in fact came to Trent when the council actually got under way and promised to be viable. In that regard no comparable sixteenth-century gathering was so successful.

What is surprising for us today, however, is that, despite the wording of official documents, there seemed to be no expectation that all bishops would go. Monarchs were in the first instance responsible for determining, at least in general terms, the make-up of the delegation from their domains, and they seemed satisfied with a restricted number. The popes themselves often met sluggish response from the bishops of the Papal States and from other bishops resident in Rome (sometimes a hundred or more) when they applied pressure on them to attend. But they clearly did not expect them all to go.

Except when they were papal legates, the cardinals of the Curia stayed in Rome, which meant only five or six cardinals, at most, were at Trent at any given time. They were needed in Rome for consultation in "consistories," that is, for regular meetings as a body to offer the pope their advice on serious matters *(causae majores).* In the sixteenth century this collegial system was gradually changing, but popes were still constrained to make use of it and were reluctant to act against the opinion of a strong majority.[3]

Northern Europe was badly under-represented even in the last period, and the Italians massively over-represented. Participating at one time or another over the course of the two years of that period, 1562–1563, were 195 Italian prelates, 31 Spanish, 27 French, 8 Greek (prelates from Venetian overseas territories), 3 Dutch, 3 Portuguese, 3 Hungarian, 3 Irish, 3 Polish, 2 German, 1 Czech, and 1 Croatian.[4] Factionalism was inevitable.

"Italian" is of course a misleading term, because Italy was made up of a number of political units, of which some, such as the Republic of

Venice and the Grand Duchy of Florence, were large, wealthy, and of independent mind. Even more important, one of the largest and richest, the Duchy of Milan, was part of the Habsburg domains, as was the Kingdom of Naples. Despite the fact that the council was initially called to deal principally with the German situation, German prelates were virtually absent from Trent except during the second period (1551–1552), when their number reached a mere 13.[5]

Monarchs sent envoys to the council. The envoys, officially known as "orators," enjoyed ambassadorial rank. Some were clerics, some laymen. They had the right to be present at all the working sessions, where they had seats of honor. Although their numbers were small, they exerted considerable influence. This was especially true of those representing the great powers—the empire, France, and, for the last period, Spain.

The Council of Trent was not a sacristy affair. Its outcome held deep political consequences for the future of Europe, a fact of which the monarchs of the era were keenly aware. They had no intention, therefore, of sitting idly by. They tried by every means they could muster to affect its outcome. The story of the Council of Trent is perforce as much a political as a theological and ecclesiastical story.

It would be wrong, however, to reduce the participation of the laity in the Council of Trent to nothing more than political expediency. Such expediency was surely operative, but also important, sometimes principally, was concern for the good of the church. Rulers knew they were not bishops, but they were convinced of the tradition that taught them that they shared with bishops a responsibility for the church's welfare. Upon no one did that responsibility fall more heavily and traditionally than on the emperor. Both Charles V and his successor, Ferdinand I, felt it and did their utmost to live up to it. They and other lay rulers were often more intent on church reform than was their papal counterpart.

Complicating matters almost beyond resolution was the fact that the pope was not simply the chief pastor of the church but also a secular prince, ruler of the Papal States, a large territory that comprised about a third of the Italian peninsula and stretched northeast from just south of Rome almost to Venice. It was difficult for everybody, including the popes themselves, to keep these two responsibilities distinct—because they were in so many ways not distinct. The successor of Saint Peter was in every sense of the word a monarch, with army, navy, prisons, police force, and diplomatic corps. Thus he felt that, like every other monarch, he had to maintain a court of a certain magnificence, which was chronically difficult to finance. The popes needed every source of money they could lay their hands on.

Despite the difficulties, however, and the persistent impact on the deliberations of outside forces, the level of discussion at the council was high. There were ignorant bishops at Trent, but many, especially the Spanish bishops and those from the religious orders, had good theological educations. A number of bishops were experts in canon law. Although perhaps relatively unschooled in formal theology, the canonists were trained to frame official statements in cautiously precise terms.[6] The theologians who assisted the bishops were professionals drawn from prestigious universities or equivalent institutions. The overwhelming majority of these were from the mendicant orders. For all the limitations of the Scholastic theology of the period, its practitioners were skilled in the art of examining evidence and facing it squarely.[7]

The city itself, a highly unlikely location for such a gathering, was chosen only after lengthy and acrimonious negotiation among the parties concerned. Anxiously following the council from afar, the three popes who reigned during its three periods never once set foot in it. They kept a close eye on Trent through special couriers and the regular, fairly efficient postal system. Couriers needed usually three days to carry information and instructions by horseback some 400 miles between the two cities, and the regular post took at least two days longer. If the pope happened to be in Bologna, the second-most important city in the Papal States and the most prosperous, communication took about half that time.

The most effective way in which the popes controlled the council was by endowing their legates who presided at the council with absolute discretion as to which topics were to be put on the agenda. *Proponentibus legatis* ("as the legates propose") was the technical term for this provision in the council's procedures. There were, therefore, no "motions from the floor." Bishops and rulers challenged this much-resented provision, but to no avail.[8]

The legates received frequent and firm directives from the popes, which at the council sparked the sardonic observation that, unlike at other councils where the Holy Spirit descended upon the bishops from on high, at Trent he arrived in the mailbag from Rome.[9] Sometimes, of course, the messages either from or to the pope were urgent, yet, as mentioned, even with a special courier a minimum of six days was required for the exchange of inquiry and reply.[10] The letters were often long, with sensitive parts in code. They reveal that the relationship between the pope and his legates was often testy, sometimes much worse. The tight rein the popes tried to keep on the council was not, therefore, a joking matter. It created intensely bad feeling inside and outside the council chambers.

For the popes the council was an expensive affair. First place among the costs was the generous monthly stipends to the legates for their personal expenses and those related to their office. Next came the subsidies for the living expenses of prelates at Trent who came from poor dioceses, especially in southern Italy. In the last period of the council over one hundred bishops received papal subsidies. Although the popes believed, correctly, that having a large number of Italians at the council was to their advantage, in only a few isolated instances did they use their financial clout directly to influence voting patterns. But the bishops knew where their support came from and were more than inclined to act accordingly. Even so, some spoke and voted in ways not designed to please their benefactor. The papal subventions must be put into perspective: the French crown, for instance, also provided financial support for French prelates at Trent.

The popes had to bear other expenses as well, such as salaries for council officials and for musicians for the solemn liturgies. Papal expenditure during the final two years of the council climbed to somewhere around 18 percent of the annual papal budget. Not surprisingly, for this reason as well as for others, Pope Pius IV during the last period of the council urged the legates again and again to bring it to the earliest possible conclusion.[11]

In 1975 Hubert Jedin (1900–1980), emeritus professor of church history at the University of Bonn and perhaps the most distinguished Catholic church historian of the twentieth century, published the fourth and final volume of his history of the Council of Trent. It was the fruit of a lifetime of research and writing dedicated to the subject.[12] Jedin's *Geschichte des Konzils von Trient* put our understanding of the council on a newly comprehensive and solid basis. It continues to be the first point of reference for all scholarship related to the council.

Strange though it may seem, we were until Jedin still caught in the grips of two incompatible classics from the seventeenth century, both written by Catholic priests. Paolo Sarpi's *Istoria del Concilio Tridentino* interpreted Trent as a tragic story of the failure of true reform to carry the day and the triumph of papal abuse of power. Although Sarpi was a Venetian, he published the book pseudonymously in London in 1619 to avoid censorship. Not until almost forty years later did the Jesuit Sforza Pallavicino undertake a papally encouraged rejoinder in his two-volume *Istoria del Concilio di Trento*.[13] Important though Pallavicino's work is, it lacks the verve and brilliance of Sarpi's. The two trajectories launched by these two publications continue to influence scholarship, but Jedin's history was a giant step in moving us beyond that impasse.[14]

Few are those, however, who have made their way through Jedin's four formidable volumes. The first two were translated into English in 1957 and 1961. They aroused considerable interest because they appeared just as Vatican Council II (1962–1965) was about to get under way. Many people wanted to know the relationship between these two councils, especially once Vatican II began to be dubbed "the end of the Counter Reformation," just as Trent was considered its embodiment. But then interest flagged, and Jedin's final two volumes, not published in German until 1970 and 1975, respectively, were never translated into English. In the meantime scholars from Western Europe continued to write books and articles about the council intended for specialists. Among the most important is Alain Tallon's *La France et le Concile de Trente (1518–1563),* published in 1997. It attempts to balance a French perspective with a historiography on the council dominated by Germans, who according to Tallon were little comprehending of French policy vis-à-vis the council and unsympathetic to it.[15]

Partly because of the excellence of Jedin's *Geschichte* and his many other writings on the council, scholarship especially in Italy has increasingly turned away from the council itself to its implementation and aftermath.[16] The best of this scholarship makes a clear distinction between Trent and *Tridentinismo* ("Tridentinism"), that is, between what the council actually enacted and how its enactments were afterward interpreted. The distinction clarifies how the council grew into a myth beyond the reality of the event itself.[17] If Jedin moved us beyond one impasse, this more recent scholarship, little of which is available in English, has raised further questions about the impact and meaning of "Trent."[18]

With this small book I make no big claims. The Council of Trent was an extraordinarily complex event, and its aftermath even more complex. Jedin himself, tempted at times to lay down his pen because of that complexity, confessed that he felt he was "playing the pitiful role of the amateur."[19] Entire books have been written on virtually every issue I touch upon, which means that in the following pages I gambol blithely through minefields. Omission and simplification are inevitable. But since no such overview of the council exists, I believe a book like mine is needed, and that is why I decided to write it.

My intention is simple: to provide an introduction to the council that will be accessible to the general reader and perhaps helpful even to the professional historian and theologian. In it I hope to put to rest a few of the myths and misunderstandings that abound about the Council of Trent.[20] I lay out the context in which the council took place, the problems it faced, the solutions it adopted. I provide a framework for understanding the council as a single, though extraordinarily complex, event. The council had an internal logic of sorts that configured its seemingly scattered and uncoordinated elements. Once that logic is grasped, the many and seemingly discrete decisions the council took can be seen to fit into a generally coherent pattern.

I am, like everybody today who writes about the Council of Trent, deeply indebted to Jedin. He was the master who led the way. In the course of the many decades that have elapsed since the 1930s, when Jedin first began writing on the council, his work, not surprisingly, has shown its limitations.[21] Still, it has in the main withstood the test of time remarkably well. Without him I could not possibly have written this book. I am indebted as well to the many scholars who have followed in the path he blazed. I am further indebted, of course, to the magnificent edition of primary documents related to the council published over the course of a century by the Görres Gesellschaft, the distinguished learned society founded in 1876 by German Catholic scholars.[22] The final volume in the series appeared only in 2001.

Luther set the agenda for the council. His challenge to the church was twofold. Its origin, as well as its center, was an idea—an idea about how we are saved, namely, "by faith alone" and not by "works," not by our own striving. That insight, though based upon his study of Saint Paul, was for him not so much an abstract doctrine to which one gave intellectual assent as the answer to personal anguish. That fact helps explain the passion with which he professed it and the language in which he expressed it. Found by Luther in "Scripture alone," this truth soon led him further—to new definitions of the sacraments, for instance, and to an utter repudiation of the papacy, which he in time came to see as the Anti-Christ.

Luther's second challenge was a practical one, a cry for reform of various ecclesiastical offices and religious practices. He first effectively hurled this challenge in 1520, just before his excommunication, in his famous "Appeal to the Ruling Class," whose first edition of four thousand copies sold out within five days. This summons to action of the emperor and the German nobility echoed and added to the many grievances voiced by devout Christians for well over a century. His grievances, like theirs, were for the most part directed against the popes and the papal Curia, commonly considered the root of the evils. The popular slogan ran, "Reform Rome and you will reform the world."

Although Luther may have set the agenda, Pope Paul III (1534–1549), who convoked the council, and Emperor Charles V (1519–1555), who for twenty years had been the most persistent advocate for it, were more directly responsible for the binary character of the task the bishops at Trent determined upon. The pope and the emperor agreed in a generic way that both of Luther's challenges had to be met, but that is where the agreement ended. The pope envisaged the council as principally a response to the doctrinal issues raised by Luther and "the Lutherans," a generic term that for a long time included other Reformers like Zwingli and Karlstadt.

Paul and many others interpreted those issues as just some old heresies in new dress, which could therefore be easily disposed of. By the time the council met, he had for all practical purposes given up hope of reconciliation with the Reformers. The Lutherans were to be condemned, and, with little more ado, the council could quickly conclude its business. The council needed to be much more circumspect about reform, however, which was an issue best handled by the pope himself, particularly when it touched upon his court, the Curia.

The Holy Roman Emperor was traditionally recognized as the Protector of the Church, a role emperors took seriously, as did Sigismund at the Council of Constance in the early fifteenth century. Charles V's stake in Trent was even greater than Sigismund's in Constance because he felt that it held the key to political stability and religious peace in the empire. His agenda for the council, which he felt was his prerogative to promote, was almost diametrically opposed to the pope's. He believed some measure of reconciliation with the Lutherans was possible. He feared a condemnation of Luther's teaching as sealing the divisions irreparably, and he therefore tried to delay the council's dealing with doctrine.

A practical man, Charles believed that the real problem was reform. Just as the unreformed condition of the church had, in his analysis, caused the Lutheran crisis, a reform of the church was the first, most urgent, and absolutely indispensable step in resolving it. During the third period of the council, his successor, Ferdinand, shared the same convictions and tried to make them operative at Trent.

The agenda of the council was thus set amid a fundamental conflict of priorities over "the uprooting of heresies" and "the reform of the clergy and the Christian people," as the council itself designated these two goals. This double agenda persisted throughout the council's long course, well after the deaths of the pope and the emperor who principally established it. Under these two headings all of the council's enactments can be gathered. In the early months of 1546, the prelates at Trent —only a few more than the meager numbers who opened the council the previous December—agreed that they would deal with doctrine and reform alternately: first, a decree on doctrine, and then a decree on some aspect of reform. The council proceeded according to this rhythm until it finally concluded on December 4, 1563.

"Doctrine and reform." Put in such abstract terms, the agenda sounds global, without delimitation, as if it comprehended every aspect of Catholic belief and practice. No doubt, the agenda at Trent was ample, but it was much more restricted than the two terms and subsequent myths imply. The council was far from being as all-encompassing as was Vatican Council II. Under doctrine the council meant to treat only Protestant teachings that conflicted with Catholic. Thus Trent made no pronouncements about the Trinity, the Incarnation, and other Christian truths that Protestants also believed. The council essentially dealt with only two doctrinal issues, justification and the sacraments. In those regards it principally targeted Luther and gave much less attention to others like the Anabaptists and even Calvin, whom the council began to take account of only during the second period. During the last period, however, the council became painfully aware of the threat of Calvinism in France and especially of its iconoclastic outbursts. Thus at the very last moment the council in great haste passed a decree validating the veneration of sacred images.

Reform had a similarly precise focus. For the bishops at Trent, "reform of the clergy and Christian people"—or, as it was more commonly and concisely expressed, "the reform of the church"—meant in the first place reform of three offices in the church: the papacy, the episcopacy, and the pastorate. This last office comprised most specifically pastors of parishes, but it included a few others like certain chaplains charged with the "care of souls" in the strict canonical sense of the term. It was composed, therefore, of members of the local or, as we say today, diocesan clergy to whose positions were attached a benefice, that is, an endowed income. Benefices, in other words, were how the clergy supported themselves—how they "got paid." For clergy there was no such thing as a salary in our contemporary sense.

Only in a secondary way did Trent's reform include members of the male religious orders such as the Dominicans and Franciscans, who because of their vow of poverty could not hold a benefice, and who were directly under the authority not of bishops but their own elected superiors. Although the council in fact issued a decree on such orders, which included women's branches, they were not a primary focus. Trent was concerned with the male branches, especially insofar as they could operate independent of the bishops' authority through their papal privileges.

The church that was to be reformed, then, was the church often referred to today as the institutional or hierarchical church. Trent enacted regulations concerning "regulars," members of the religious orders, male and female, but principally to clarify their relationship to bishops. The council dealt of course with the laity and directed its efforts to "the reform of the Christian people," but it did so almost exclusively through directives for bishops and pastors. It intended to address "the reform of princes," who in those times could almost be considered part of the institutional church because of the important role they played in church procedures, as, for instance, in the appointment of bishops and even in councils themselves, but in the end it essentially had to abandon the idea.

As Jedin made clear, the driving motive behind the reform of the bishops and the pastors was pastoral effectiveness. Trent wanted to make them do their jobs, as those jobs were traditionally understood—to transform them from collectors of benefices to shepherds of souls.[23] This meant, first of all, compelling reluctant bishops and pastors to reside in their dioceses or parishes. Milan, the largest and richest diocese in Italy, had lacked a resident bishop for eighty years.

In the diocese of Grenoble on the eve of the Reformation only half of the pastors resided in their parishes, and in the diocese of Geneva, only 20 percent. Their duties were performed by "vicars," priests hired by them for the task. Similar figures prevailed in many places for bishops. Numbers like these can, however, sometimes be misleading. They obscure the fact that in many places the vast majority of pastors did live in their parishes. Moreover, some reported absences were for relatively short periods or for truly legitimate reasons.[24]

Even so, the problem was real and widespread. Seemingly without scruple, absentee bishops and pastors pocketed the revenue from the benefices and devoted their time and energy to other pursuits. The abuse was most glaring when individuals held multiple bishoprics or pastorates so as to collect the funds from them. In this regard, the best-known offender was Luther's nemesis, Albert of Brandenburg, who simultaneously held the archbishoprics of Mainz and Magdeburg and, equivalently, the bishopric of Halberstadt, of which he was the administrator. Jean de Lorraine, the uncle of Cardinal Charles de Guise, held three archbishoprics and nine bishoprics.

Trent's ideal, which in fact was simply an implementation of traditional canonical legislation and expectations, was straightforward: one diocese per bishop, who would reside in it, and one parish per pastor, who would reside in it. The council then supplied the bishops and pastors with job descriptions so that they would know what was expected of them as "shepherds of souls" once they arrived at their destinations. In its disciplinary or "reform" goals, Trent saw itself as promoting a more effective "care of souls." Contrary to its popular image, Trent was therefore a pastoral as well as a doctrinal council.

Almost every specific proposal "to reform the church" had financial implications. The benefice system was at the heart of the way the church operated, so that any reform that touched upon benefices touched upon somebody's pocketbook. Beyond benefices, however, lay other monetary issues. Funding had to be found for new institutions such as seminaries for the education of future priests. Penalties for bishops and pastors who neglected their duties were often fines. And so it went. Money played a fundamental role in the reforms that Trent tried to legislate, and it explains the resistance those reforms met both during and after the council.

The binary character of Trent's agenda, though sparked by Luther's twofold assault and formulated in the context of the different objectives of pope and emperor, was in fact traditional in councils, beginning with the first, the Council of Nicaea, in 325. When the emperor Constantine called the bishops of the Roman world together at Nicaea, he established a pattern that would persist through the ages. He treated the council as the ecclesiastical equivalent of the Roman Senate, which was a legislative and judicial body. The Council of Nicaea, therefore, and the councils that followed made laws and, after proper investigation, condemned heretics and other ecclesiastical criminals. It considered itself the final arbiter of disputes, from which there was no appeal, and it handed down its decrees as binding on the whole church, clergy and laity alike. The emperor took it upon himself to enforce the council's decrees.

In medieval terms, councils thus dealt with *fides et mores,* usually translated as "faith and morals" but more accurately as "doctrine and public behavior" (or "public practices," as in the administration of the sacraments).[25] Councils, as legislative and judicial bodies, dealt not with "faith" as an inner sentiment of the believer but with a dogma or teaching publicly professed by the church.

Although in practice the distinction between doctrine/dogma and theology did not always hold, it was basic. The former encompassed divinely revealed and publicly proclaimed truths, expressed in the first place in the traditional creeds, such as the Apostles' Creed, but it also included teachings that with a certain logic flowed from them. The latter consisted in reflection on the former and in explanations of it, as found, for instance, in treatises by the Fathers of the Church or, beginning in the High Middle Ages, in the writings of professional theologians such as Thomas Aquinas or Duns Scotus. Councils were professedly concerned with doctrine/dogma, not with theology, except of course when theology entailed some heresy or doctrinal error.

Councils dealt with "morals" not in the sense of ethical theories or principles but in the sense of observable public behavior, as befits laws and judicial sentences. The English word "mores" comes closer to the meaning of the Latin than does "morals." Councils were thus concerned with *actions* that benefited or harmed the individuals engaging in them, that benefited or harmed others, or that, for clerics, were consistent or inconsistent with the church's pastoral mission. They were concerned, finally, with actions that were consistent or inconsistent with the Christian faith. In practice and in theory, "mores" implied, therefore, a relationship more or less close to doctrine, but it nonetheless was for the most part the equivalent of "discipline."

Councils made use of a variety of forms with which to express themselves on doctrine and public behavior, but the most typical was the canon, usually a short ordinance proscribing or prescribing a certain behavior—"If anyone should *say* . . ." (not, "If anyone should *believe* . . ."). Or, "If anyone should *do* . . ." (not, "If anyone should *think* . . ."). The form was ancient and traditional, used by councils beginning with the first, Nicaea, in 325. The anathema with which canons generally concluded was a sentence of excommunication against anyone who contumaciously refused to comply.[26] Their stylistic ideal was a statement short and precise.

Trent adopted that ideal for all its statements, which were expected to be *nuda et simplex*.[27] Still, the final decrees sometimes run to considerable length. Moreover, couched as they often are in technical canonical and theological terminology, they are easily misunderstood and misinterpreted by those not skilled in catching the nuances such terminology entailed.

Trent thus fits into two already established patterns. First, its agenda consisted basically in *fides et mores*. Second, it made use of several forms to express itself, including ample use of the traditional canon. Despite popular conceptions of the council, Trent moved within those patterns with considerable caution. Although the vast majority of the bishops were strongly prejudiced against the Protestant Reformers, the council did not act in knee-jerk fashion. As the following pages will make clear, in its deliberations Trent expended considerable effort to arrive at equitable solutions to problems. Once the bishops recognized the centrality of the justification-by-faith issue, for instance, they took their time— seven months!—to formulate their response.

They were similarly cautious about reform issues, including two contentious ones that touched directly on people's lives—the celibacy of the clergy and vernacular liturgy. The council sidestepped the more pressing aspects of the former. Regarding the latter Trent said only that it was wrong to maintain that "the mass ought to be celebrated in the vernacular tongue only."[28] In other words, Latin was legitimate but not obligatory.

Surely one of the most ironical features of the Council of Trent is the absence of a decree on the authority of the papacy. The council did not even reiterate, as it did for Purgatory, the statement on papal primacy published a century earlier at the Council of Florence. Yet this was the one doctrine Protestants of every stripe, without exception, vociferously repudiated. All the prelates at Trent of course believed in papal primacy; otherwise they would not have been present. But they very much disagreed among themselves on the practical prerogatives that primacy entailed and especially on the precise relationship between the papacy and the episcopacy and, more specifically, on the relationship between the papacy and the council itself. It is true that in one of the last acts of the council the bishops stated that nothing the council enacted was to be interpreted as compromising the authority of the Apostolic See, but they did not specify further.[29] They could not specify further, as we shall see, without hopelessly tying up the council.

The attack of the Protestant Reformers on the papacy was just one piece of their radical redefinition of the church as it had been understood in the late Middle Ages. The council, in its intention to respond to all Protestant positions, should, it seems, have articulated its own definition. But it did not. Despite the ecclesial reality that bound the members of the council together, the bishops would have found it extremely difficult to articulate that bond in a way that dealt adequately with both the many Protestant positions and the diversity of opinions among themselves. Trent issued no decree as such "On the Church."

This lacuna does not mean that the prelates gathered at Trent did not share certain assumptions about the church that were so deep they did not need to reexamine them. Aside from their belief in an effective and divinely sanctioned form of papal primacy, they believed in the traditional episcopal structure of the church and the prerogatives and duties that came to the bishops simply because they were bishops. At the same time they believed that a council duly convoked and conducted had the authority not only to regulate church discipline but also to decide in a definitive way disputes about Christian dogmas. These were assumptions not shared by "Lutherans," that is, by Protestants. The reformers at Trent, finally, were intent on strengthening not papal but episcopal authority.[30]

Thus Trent's focus on bishops and pastors was a strong, though implicit, affirmation of the church as a hierarchical institution. That focus accounts, however, for two other omissions that from our twenty-first-century perspective are striking. Few aspects of Catholicism, indeed, of

Catholic "pastoral ministry," in the sixteenth century are more characteristic and significant than the intense missionary activity that began
with the Portuguese and Spanish conquests and explorations in the late
fifteenth century and continued with intense fervor and expenditure of
men and money into the seventeenth. On this phenomenon Trent ut-
tered not a word. It fell completely outside the council's purview of "reform of the church."

Confraternities or sodalities received passing mention in that
bishops had the right to conduct visitations of them and receive an annual account of their administration.[31] Not even intimated, however, is
that in many places in Europe these voluntary associations, made up
mostly of laity, and similar ones, such as the Third Order of the Dominicans, Franciscans, and other orders, provided many, perhaps most,
Catholics with their true spiritual homes and were more important in
their lives than the parish church. Protestant Reformers abolished them,
but Trent, curiously, took no notice of that fact. The council was interested in confraternities only insofar as they related to episcopal authority. In accordance with the canonical tradition, it fixated on ministry as
taking place in the parish church and, consequently, ignored the confraternities and similar institutions.

Besides these two phenomena the council had virtually nothing to
say about the new religious orders like the Jesuits and the Ursulines. It
observed the same silence for the several inquisitions that were functioning in full force—such as the Roman, Spanish, and Portuguese.
Like the foreign missions and confraternities, these institutions were
among the most characteristic and important in the culture of early
modern Catholicism—indeed, in the culture of the Counter Reformation! But they did not fall within the council's purview. Trent's preoccupation with the reform of the ecclesiastical offices of pope, bishop, and
pastor also meant that even issues like indulgences and the veneration of
the saints that were so "hot" out on the ideological field of battle could
not find a place on the agenda until the very last days, when the council
frantically rushed to complete its business.

The reform of the papacy was an abiding concern of the council that during the third period burst into a major and prolonged crisis. The concern included the traditional grievances about the luxurious lifestyle of the papal court and the loose morals of some of its members. On a deeper level it extended to curbing or eliminating the financial exactions that the popes laid on clergy and laity for ostensibly pious purposes. Resentment over such exactions in their different forms had simmered for generations. Luther posted his "Ninety-Five Theses" as a reaction to one of them, the "selling" of indulgences, and he capitalized on it in his "Appeal to the Nobility."

The sticking point at Trent, however, was the not unrelated practice of the papal court of giving dispensations from the canons that required bishops to reside in their dioceses and pastors in the parishes, and that stipulated one bishop per diocese, one pastor per parish. The dispensations fostered the widespread abuses of nonresidence and the holding of multiple benefices, at which reforming bishops at Trent took aim. If the heart of the Tridentine reform was to get bishops and pastors back home to do their job, papal practice was the loophole that threatened to make the council's legislation a dead letter. But to deal with the problem meant the council had to deal with the untouchable issue of "the authority of the Apostolic See." The conflict over this issue is a focal point in the drama of the Council of Trent.

Drama? The popular image of Trent is just the opposite of drama. Both admirers and detractors of the council have tended to imagine it as a monolithic and single-minded gathering, untroubled by rancor, confidently poised to take the steps necessary to put the Catholic house in order. The reality was anything but that. The council, extraordinarily difficult to convoke, was even more difficult to hold on course. During it, animosities and substantive differences surfaced that brought the council again and again to the brink of disaster. At the end the council was able to arrive at a considerable measure of resolution, but only after navigating hazardous waters and surviving hurricane-strength storms.

1

The Fifteenth-Century Prelude

In 1522–1523, less than two years after Luther's excommunication, the Imperial Diet, the *Reichstag,* met in Nuremberg. This large assembly of German princes and representatives of other political units of the Holy Roman Empire received from the new pope, Adrian VI, a document frankly confessing that the sins of the clergy were responsible for the current religious turmoil and promising to remedy the situation. On February 5, 1523, the Diet responded by demanding from Adrian a "free Christian council in German lands," which it considered the appropriate and traditional institution to settle the controversy over Luther and to undertake the often-promised, long-awaited reform.[1]

Underlying the Diet's demand were four assumptions that were of great import for the future: first, the papal bull *Exsurge Domine* condemning Luther's teaching and threatening excommunication was not the final word in the matter; second, only a council could be counted on for the impartiality required to judge Luther's case; third, that case was primarily a German concern and should be handled in Germany; fourth, reform of the church could not be conceived of apart from a council, a connection that was part of the legacy of the Council of Constance of the previous century but was also a traditional conviction. The demand thus fatefully linked Luther's cause and the reform of the church—twins conjoined at birth.

Even at this early date, the cry for a council had begun to resound fairly widely, principally in Germany but also in other parts of Europe. It soon swelled into a crescendo that grew ever more insistent with the passing of the years. No one took up the cry more consistently and passionately than the most powerful person in Europe, Emperor Charles V. His efforts for the convocation of a council intensified as the political and military situation in German-speaking lands became ever more ominous. Yet the council did not meet until twenty-two years after the Diet at Nuremberg called for it—a full generation. Why the delay?

Popes and Councils from Constance to Lateran V

The Council of Constance, which met from 1414 to 1418, precisely a century before the outbreak of the Reformation, inaugurated a new relationship between popes and councils.[2] This new relationship was an essential factor in delaying the convocation of Trent. In the three centuries before Constance, popes had called and presided over a number of synods and councils in which, despite disagreements, a generally smooth relationship prevailed between them and the bishops. That changed with Constance. The change made the popes wary. They learned to their dismay that a council could be used as a weapon against them.

Constance met to resolve the Great Western Schism, when two and then three men claimed to be pope. Among the three was John XXIII, now considered an antipope but at the time, and even into the twentieth century, widely considered legitimate. Under pressure from

Emperor-elect Sigismund, he convoked the council at Constance, which proceeded to depose him and another contender and to intimidate the third into resigning. The council then elected a new pope, Martin V (1417–1431), who received almost universal recognition as the legitimate successor of Saint Peter. As the council drew to a close, it issued the decree *Frequens* stipulating that henceforth the popes had to convoke a council at regular intervals in perpetuity—the first two at intervals of five or, if necessary, seven years, and thereafter every ten years.

In these actions the council acted on solid if not uncontested canonical grounds, as evidenced above all by the fact that its depositions of the contenders and its election of a new pope were at the time and subsequently accepted almost unanimously. A standard axiom of canon law stated that the pope could be judged by no one "unless he should deviate from the faith" *(Papa a nemine dijudicatur nisi deprehendatur a fide devius).* Canonists and theologians serenely discussed, therefore, the possibility that a pope might fall into heresy and that, if he did, he could be "judged," that is, deposed. They came to define heresy broadly so as to include grave scandal, for such scandal led the faithful into heresy or schism.[3]

But judged by whom? The traditional court of appeal in the church from the earliest years was a council, so it is not surprising that councils were the bodies to which canonists assigned the task. Thus, as the Schism dragged on and all efforts to persuade or threaten the contending popes to settle the matter by other means came to naught, the idea that a council was needed gained strength and was ever more widely proposed as the only possible remedy. This was the situation in which Conciliarism was born, a theory about the superior authority of councils in relationship to the papacy.

Unfortunately, since the term covers at least two understandings of that relationship, it has led to considerable confusion. The first, agreed to by mainline canonists at the time and even later, was that under certain dire circumstances a council might have to act against a pope. Reputable scholars argue that this was the interpretation operative at Constance, as expressed in its famous decree *Haec Sancta*. The second was more radical and, at least in the West, untraditional: not only are councils the supreme authority, but the popes are little more than the executors of their will. This understanding gained ground in many circles after the Schism was resolved, and it provoked, of course, strong papal reaction. There were, besides, many variations on both these interpretations.

Popes feared Conciliarism in all its forms. They recognized but also feared the role temporal rulers claimed in church affairs. Although John XXIII convoked Constance, Emperor Sigismund had taken the initiative and forced the pope to do so. In that initiative Sigismund had good historical precedent. He was simply making use of the traditional role of the emperor as Protector of the Church. His sixteenth-century successor, Charles V, took that role extremely seriously.

Contrary to what is sometimes implied, Constance, no matter what its relationship to Conciliarism, was not antipapal. It acted, rather, to save the papacy, which for the forty years of the Schism proved incapable of saving itself and seemed to be heading for self-destruction. The council was a last-ditch effort—and a successful one—to solve the scandalous problem after all else had failed. Even though Constance was successful in reestablishing the papacy, the Schism had inflicted almost irreparable damage on belief that the popes could be counted upon to handle properly their own affairs and the affairs of the church. The decree *Frequens* was a massive vote of no-confidence.

Besides resolving the Schism Constance set itself two other goals—the reform of the church "in head and members" and the eradication of heresy.[4] Even before the Schism, resentment had been building against "the head" because of three interrelated developments: the growing centralization of authority in the papal Curia at the expense of episcopal authority, the questionable financial implications of the procedures adopted by the Curia in the awarding of ecclesiastical offices, and, finally, the taxes and fees exacted from the higher clergy and others throughout Europe. Complaints against these developments never flagged. They continued all the way up to the Council of Trent. In its attempt to reform the head, Constance got down to specifics. On October 30, 1417, it published a list of reforms that it bound the new pope to undertake. The list took account of the major complaints and anticipated many of the abuses, including indulgences, that Luther denounced with such impact a hundred years later in his "Appeal to the Ruling Class." Among them:

1. The number, quality, and nationality of the lord cardinals.
2. Reservations of benefices to the Apostolic See. The reservations gave the popes power to make appointments to bishoprics and other offices, which entailed direct or indirect financial benefit to the papacy.
3. Annates, common services, and petty services. These are forms of taxation.
5. Cases that are, or are not, to be heard at the Roman Curia.
12. Not alienating to relatives and others goods of the Roman church and other churches.
13. The reasons and means by which a pope can be corrected or deposed.
14. The eradication of simony, the buying or selling of church offices.
15. Dispensations.
16. Revenues of the pope and the cardinals.
17. Indulgences.[5]

The council itself then issued decrees addressing a few of these problems.[6] These provisions made little headway after the council, but from this point forward reform of the cardinals surfaced again and again in official reform proposals as an object of major concern.[7] It would be a hot point of contention at the Council of Trent. Of greater practical impact, as things turned out, was Constance's ratification of the expression "reform in head and members." For the next century the expression served as a rallying cry for individuals and institutions nursing all manner of grievances. From 1417 until 1517, reform, understood in different ways by different parties, became one of Europe's most insistently recurring and inflammatory words.

The manner in which Constance handled "the extirpation of heresy," which specifically meant the condemnation of the teachings of John Wyclif and his two Bohemian followers, Jan Hus and Jerome of Prague, had important repercussions for Luther and thus for the convocation of Trent. Constance condemned, first, eighty-five and then another forty-five propositions attributed to John Wyclif, the long-dead English theologian. It then summoned Hus, very much alive, to answer for his teachings. Granted a safe conduct by the Emperor-elect Sigismund, Hus came to Constance only to be condemned there and, despite the safe conduct, handed over to the "secular arm" to be burned at the stake. A century later, Luther and his supporters cited the Hus case again and again as a reason for Luther, even when his safety was assured, to evade or outright reject summons to a trial.

Besides the propositions of Wyclif, Hus, and Jerome of Prague, the council also singled out for condemnation the teaching of Jacob of Mies (Strbro), an associate of Hus at Prague, who maintained that the laity had the right to receive Communion under the form of wine as well as bread. In its condemnation of Mies's position, the council put forth the teaching that "the whole body and blood of Christ are truly contained" under each of the forms.[8] Therefore, the Eucharistic cup could legitimately be withheld. This issue returned in urgent form at the Council of Trent.

Within three decades after the council, *Frequens* had become a dead letter. In accordance with it Martin V had dutifully, though with misgivings, convoked a council to meet in Pavia then Siena in 1423–1424, and then another to meet in Basel in 1431. He died, however, five months before Basel opened, leaving it in the hands of his successor, Eugene IV

(1431–1447). The new pope almost immediately ran into trouble with the council, whose necessity he did not see and whose potential for mischief-making he feared. It did not help matters that the council met hundreds of miles from Rome, a situation that increased the potential for misunderstanding.

Partly as a result of clumsy or ill-advised moves on Eugene's part, the council turned ever more radical and antipapal. The two parties were soon racing toward each other on a collision course, especially as the council took up "reform of the head." On March 26, 1436, it limited the number of cardinals the pope could appoint, invested them with pastoral obligations, and imposed upon them a modest lifestyle. It forbade the pope to name nephews as cardinals.[9] More devastating was the decree published a year earlier, on June 9, 1435, in which the council abolished throughout Christendom annates, an onerous form of papal tax on new incumbents in ecclesiastical offices that was for the popes a major source of income.[10] Eugene immediately denounced the measure and sent a solemn protest to all Christian rulers.

Meanwhile the Ottoman Turks continued to press against the great city of Constantinople (Istanbul), whose fall would not only mean the end of Christian rule there but also open the Balkans and Eastern Europe to Turkish armies. Reunion with "the Greeks" had been a papal priority ever since the Schism of 1054 between the two churches. When John VIII Paleologos, the emperor in Constantinople, showed himself interested in reunion, both Eugene and the council responded positively. The council offered several cities as possible sites for a council of reunion, but it excluded Florence and Modena because Eugene had proposed them. The Greeks favored the papal choices as cities of easier access for them, and, more important, because they realized that for the reunion to work (with its almost certain subsequent military aid to Constantinople), it had to be effected under the auspices of the bishop of Rome.

With that, Eugene's moment had at last arrived. He transferred the council from Basel to Ferrara and then to Florence, where the Greeks arrived in February 1439. He had struck a mortal blow to Basel. Although a considerable number of bishops at first remained there and were supported by the French monarchy as well as by other princes, they posed the danger of another schism. The prospect of a council of reunion, legitimately convoked by the pope, was as appealing as the prospect of another schism was horrifying. In January 1438, the still sizeable remnant in Basel suspended Eugene. The next year it declared him deposed and elected a new pope, Felix V, to succeed him. But as the council at Florence moved to a happy conclusion, Basel lost support and bit by bit sputtered to extinction. It was not, however, forgotten.

Long before its demise though, the council at Basel had in 1432 and 1434 declared that general councils were the supreme authority in the church. Then on May 16, 1439, it declared that doctrine a matter of faith, so that rejection of it was heresy. Whereas the action of the Council of Constance against the three papal contenders can be interpreted as an emergency measure in a time of supreme crisis, the decrees of Basel raised the superiority of councils over popes to the rank of a constitutional principle, valid at all times and in all circumstances. As to be expected, at Florence Eugene, in the bull *Moyses vir,* which was approved by the council on September 4, 1439, explicitly condemned the decree as "an abominable crime committed by certain wicked men dwelling in Basel so as to breach the unity of the church." Eugene used the bull, moreover, as a bill of indictment against Basel and as a long, self-justifying apologia for the way he had dealt with it.[11]

Although with *Moyses vir* Eugene carried the day at Florence, not everyone was convinced that his position was correct. The previous year, 1438, King Charles VII of France assembled a national council at Bourges, where he issued a decree, the Pragmatic Sanction, that essentially supported Basel on the supremacy of council over pope and on the necessity of holding general councils at regular intervals. The Sanction, which adumbrated Gallicanism and helped justify it, hung like a sword over the heads of the popes, especially when after the Hundred Years' War France emerged as the strongest and wealthiest political force in

Europe. After Charles the French kings continued to confirm the Sanction, insist upon it as a national policy, and refuse to recognize the legitimacy of the Council of Florence.

Meanwhile, in its quest for reunion the council at Florence focused on several long-standing differences between the Greeks and the Latins, but the sticking point of course was the authority of the papacy. Some Greeks were persuaded by arguments, some simply bowed to pressure, but they in any case agreed to a remarkably strong statement: the pope had "full power of tending, ruling, and governing the whole church."[12] This was a moment of supreme triumph for Eugene, a massive blow to the position that councils were superior to the pope, advanced at Basel. It marked the beginning of an era that Jedin defined as "the victory of the popes over the reform councils."[13]

The reunion with the Greeks ended in failure. Even in Florence many Greeks supported the reunion only tepidly, reluctantly, or perhaps with fingers crossed. When the delegation returned home, it met angry cries of shame and betrayal. The military aid against the Turks that the West promised and raised ended in disaster at Varna in 1444. Constantinople fell less than a decade later, in 1453.

That tragedy was in the future when Eugene returned to Rome from Florence with his prestige boosted by the success of the council. The success did not quell the papal fear of councils that Constance and Basel had stirred. The popes, quietly abetted by bishops who did not want to spend months away from home in large meetings without an urgent agenda, conveniently forgot *Frequens* and resorted to governing according to monarchical principles, qualified by regular consistories with the cardinals resident in Rome. In the consistories, a form of consultation with the cardinals assembled together, policies were discussed and major business enacted.

Juan de Torquemada, a Dominican theologian in the Curia, provided the popes with the theoretical grounding they needed to ignore or at least minimize the authority of councils and of the bishops who gathered at them. According to Torquemada in his treatise *Summa de Ec-*

clesia, the pope, Peter's successor, possessed all authority in the church. The pope parcels out to bishops whatever authority he deems fit, which he can withdraw at will. A council is essentially a bishops' meeting convoked and presided over by the pope, and its decrees have no validity until confirmed by him. Torquemada's ecclesiology, formulated during the pontificate of Nicholas V, Eugene's successor, took hold in the Curia from this point forward. At Trent it found strong and stubborn expression in the Italian prelates from the Papal States and, to a large extent, in those from the Kingdom of Naples in the almost ongoing crisis about the authority of the council in relationship to the pope.[14]

In a preemptive strike, Pope Pius II on January 18, 1460, issued the bull *Execrabilis* forbidding appeal to a council over the head of the pope. He also, to no avail, called upon the French bishops to work for the suppression of the Pragmatic Sanction of Bourges. Two decades later Pope Sixtus IV on July 15, 1483, in the bull *Qui monitis* also forbade appeals to a council, as did Pope Julius II on July 1, 1509, in *Suscepti regiminis.* The need to repeat the prohibition betrays the persistence of the problem.

The popes became particularly jealous of the right they claimed to be the sole agents in any reform of "the head," another issue that simply would not go away. In fact, with devout prelates, theologians, and laity throughout Europe that issue took on even greater urgency beginning with the pontificate of Sixtus IV (1471–1484), and outside the Curia most leaders in society assumed that a council was the only way to effect it. The popes might forget *Frequens,* but others did not.

With Sixtus the moral caliber of the papal court took a notable turn for the worse. He engaged in nepotism on an unprecedented scale, making six of his nephews cardinals, several of whom were patently unworthy. By conferring the cardinalate on thirty other men, another unprecedented number, he launched a secularization of that body that continued in almost unrelieved fashion for decades. To pay for his soaring expenses, he sold offices and privileges, while he enriched a swarm of relatives and arranged for some of them highly advantageous marriages. These were of course among the abuses that Constance had sought to correct. Now they seemed to be flaunted—and flagrantly.

Sixtus's successor, Innocent VIII (1484–1492), inherited his vast debts. To alleviate them he created unneeded positions in the Curia and Papal States and sold them to the highest bidder. The great social event of his pontificate was the elaborate celebration in the Vatican of his son Franceschetto's marriage to the daughter of Lorenzo de' Medici, the Magnificent, ruler of Florence. Innocent's was a shameful but, except for involvement in Italian politics, relatively uneventful pontificate.

The next pope, Alexander VI (1492–1503), stirred up resentment on a broad scale because of his shifting political alliances, his reckless promotion of his children, and his amorous affairs. As Cardinal Rodrigo de Borgia he fathered seven children and, most scandalous, he fathered two more while pope. No one was more outspoken in his denunciation of Alexander than the apocalyptic Dominican preacher in Florence Girolamo Savonarola. In his preaching against ecclesiastical corruption he explicitly named Alexander. When Alexander excommunicated him, he opened the way for Savonarola's political enemies in Florence to move against him, which led to his execution in the public square.

Savonarola represented an extreme, but other preachers, influenced by apocalyptic interpretations of history that promised a dramatic overturning of the present order of things, believed God promised them an "angelic pope," the very antithesis of the popes of the degenerate times in which they lived.[15] The end was nigh, or at least a strikingly new era was about to begin.[16] Even as this heated rhetoric prevailed in some reforming circles, preachers at the papal court itself, much more sober in their words, kept up the pressure for reform, which had to begin with "the head."[17] The pressure was so steady that under Pius II and two unlikely popes, Sixtus and Alexander, reform bulls were prepared but never promulgated.[18]

Alexander died on August 18, 1503. After the three-week pontificate of Pius III, a nephew of Pius II, the cardinals, upon receiving bribes and the promise of lavish benefices, unanimously elected in a conclave of a single day Alexander's mortal enemy, the intrepid Giuliano della Rovere, nephew of Sixtus IV. The new pope took the name Julius II (1503–1513). He was larger than life. Best remembered for his genius patronage of two genius artists, Raphael and Michelangelo, he evoked wildly diverging assessments from contemporaries.[19]

He owed his rise to his uncle's nepotism, yet he broke that now established pattern and did little to enrich or advance his family. Despite being elected with the help of bribes, early in his pontificate he issued a condemnation of simony in papal elections that imposed severe penalties on anyone implicated in the practice. He vigorously supported efforts to reform the religious orders. Although he spent great sums on military campaigns and art patronage, he was a frugal administrator. He inherited an empty treasury but left a full one. As a cardinal he sired three daughters, but as pope he in that regard behaved with propriety.

But Julius is also remembered as the warrior pope who brooked no opposition.[20] As head of the Papal States, he sought two principal goals: to regain for the papacy control over the States and to ensure their safety from outside incursions by expelling foreign armies from the Italian peninsula. He donned his armor, mounted his horse, and led the papal army to win back for the church especially the lands controlled by Cesare Borgia, son of Alexander VI. This enterprise as well as his subsequent ones entailed complicated diplomatic negotiations, shifting political alliances, and ongoing military campaigns. It won him foes from near and far, the most formidable of which was the king of France, Louis XII, against whose forces in northern Italy Julius had moved.[21]

His military campaign to drive the French out of Italy provoked the most severe crisis of his pontificate. In 1511 Louis, acting with the vacillating support of Emperor Maximilian I, persuaded a group of cardinals inimical to Julius to convoke a council at Pisa and to summon Julius there to answer their charges, especially his noncompliance with *Frequens*. This was precisely the kind of confrontation the popes had done everything to avoid since the debacle of Basel. Julius was particularly vulnerable in this regard because in the conclave before his election he had signed an agreement to call a general council within two years, and after he was elected he had again sworn to do so.

Julius with characteristic decisiveness met the challenge of Pisa head on. He convoked his own council to meet in Rome in the basilica of Saint John Lateran, his cathedral.[22] His hand had been forced. Despite his bravado, he confessed to his Master of Ceremonies, Paris de' Grassis, that he feared the council as badly as a schoolboy feared his teacher's rod.[23] In any case, this Lateran Council V (1512–1517) won out over Pisa even more easily than seventy-five years earlier Florence had won out over Basel. Julius ensured his control by holding it in Rome, where he could give it the closest surveillance. No surprise, the council's first act was to condemn the "pseudo-council" or "baby council" *(conciliabulum)* of Pisa and declare its decrees null and void.[24]

The prior general of the Augustinian order, Giles of Viterbo (Egidio da Viterbo), delivered the opening oration at the council, chosen for the task by Julius himself. He proclaimed that recent disastrous events were warnings from God to the pope to hold this council, which would initiate the long-awaited renewal of the church.[25] The first reform the council enacted and the only one while Julius was still alive was a solemn ratification of Julius's earlier condemnation of simony in papal elections.[26]

When Julius died in early 1513, Lateran V continued for another four years under his successor, Leo X (1513–1521). Lateran V, often dismissed in history books as poorly attended and of almost exclusively Italian membership, was in fact a sizeable gathering broadly representative of Latin Christendom. Well over 280 prelates were personally present at the council, of whom more than a third were from outside Italy.[27]

Lateran V dealt with a number of issues, including in 1513 an ineffective invitation to "the Bohemians" or Hussites to come to the council to recognize the errors that held them in thrall. Cardinal Tamas Bakocz, the council's legate to them, was empowered, however, to grant the Hussites the Eucharistic cup. The council also issued an exhortation to peace among Christian princes so that concerted military effort could be directed against the threat from the infidel Turks.[28] The threat was real, and devout Christians almost universally regarded Turkish victories as punishment for the sins of the church. Even after the outbreak of the Reformation, the popes of the era were often just as much concerned about the Turks as they were about the Protestants.

Two years later Pope Leo X, Giovanni de' Medici, had to face a more immediate military threat from the new king of France, Francis I, whose army penetrated so deeply into the Italian peninsula as to threaten Florence, over which the Medici pope himself ruled. Leo was forced into negotiations, which in 1515 resulted in the Concordat of Bologna between him and Francis. To ward off the king's forces, Leo made the immense concession in the Concordat of granting him and his successors nomination rights for all archbishops, bishops, and other leading prelates in France. This concession gave the king power to determine who would lead the French church, and it meant, as a consequence, that the Reformation would hold no political appeal for him.

In exchange the king spared Florence and the Papal States, confirmed the papacy's right to collect the revenue of the first year in office of every prelate, the hated annate, and renounced the Pragmatic Sanction of Bourges. On December 19, 1516, Lateran V ratified Leo's bull, *Pastor Aeternus,* in which the pope solemnly condemned the Sanction, declared it utterly inoperative, and imposed severe penalties on anyone supporting it. In the bull, moreover, he pronounced that when there is only one person claiming to be pope, he "has the full right and power to summon, transfer and dissolve councils."[29] With *Pastor Aeternus,* Leo hoped finally to lay to rest the specter of Basel and all claims of councils' superiority over undisputed popes. It was easier, however, to condemn such claims than to stamp them out. They would reappear in attenuated form at the Council of Trent.

Lateran V could not ignore reform. The issue was too much in the air, as preachers and others hammered away at it. While the council was in session in the early spring of 1513, for instance, two Camoldolese monks/hermits, Venetian patricians, came to Rome, where they composed a long and wide-ranging memorandum or treatise *(libellus)* on the reform of the church intended for Leo X. Their names were Paolo Giustiniani and Pietro Quirini. The document faithfully reflected the concerns of thoughtful and educated Christians of the decade just before the Reformation. Besides the long section on church reform, it contained separate sections on the need to convert the Jews and the Muslims and to work for the end of the schisms with the other Christian churches, such as the Maronites and the Greek Orthodox.[30]

The bishops as part of their reform efforts labored in vain to establish their own episcopal college in the Curia to promote and protect their interests and give themselves a permanent voice there. They resented and tried to limit incursions into their jurisdictional authority by cardinals, the religious orders, and the popes themselves. Although they persisted in their efforts to enact such measures, they finally had to bow to the resistance of Leo and the Curia cardinals.[31]

They did, however, manage to pass a long reform bull, *Supernae Dispositionis,* on May 4, 1514, which was principally concerned with the Curia. Toward the end, however, the bull extended to other matters, such as the suppression of blasphemy and sorcery.[32] The reform, professedly based on renewed implementation of long-standing provisions of canon law, insisted on proper qualifications of age, education, and character for anyone promoted to the episcopacy, on modest standards for food, habitation, and retinue for the cardinals, and on similar matters.

By now the ostentatious lifestyle of some of the cardinals had reached absurd standards. In the sixteenth century the average size of a cardinal's household *(famiglia)* was 100. Even after Trent, Carlo Borromeo, the most famous exemplar of a "reformed" cardinal-bishop, had a household of 150. An inventory of the wardrobe and other possessions of Cardinal Ippolito d'Este (1509–1572) ran 600 pages and listed, for instance, 79 pairs of gloves and over 50 red birettas.[33]

Supernae Dispositionis, riddled with escape clauses, failed to address the more urgent abuses to which Constance had long ago called attention. It dealt with papal financial exactions, dispensations granted by the popes from canon law, and "the number, quality, and nationality of the lords cardinal." By Leo's time the size of the papal court had swelled far beyond what it had been a century earlier. In an official list compiled in May 1514, the pope's major-domo listed a household staff of 683 persons—244 holding high office, 174 lower officials, and 244 servants. The list did not include the artists, Humanists, or military and diplomatic personages on the papal payroll.[34] In its provisions, *Supernae Dispositionis* not only failed by far to satisfy serious reformers but got sidelined in the uproar and tumult that exploded with Luther's posting of his Ninety-Five Theses the very year Lateran V concluded, 1517.[35]

How Bad Was It?

Reformers like Savonarola denounced their times as the worst of all. Although they cannot be taken at their word, abuses in the ecclesiastical system were widespread, extending far beyond Rome and the Curia. The most obvious of them was the absence of bishops from their dioceses, which seemed to betray that they had little interest in the spiritual welfare of their flocks. The same holds true for pastors of parishes. This situation put into jeopardy the church's pastoral mission, the only reason for its existence.

Although churches were full and religious practice high, reformers denounced the quality of the latter as arithmetic, formulaic, and based on the assumption that performance of certain ritualized acts obliged God to respond in favorable ways. Superstition and ignorance of the basic tenets of Christianity were, according to them, rampant, especially in the countryside, and principles of Christian morality everywhere flouted.

The gluttonous monk, lecherous friar, and gullible priest were commonplaces in the satire of the times. Boccacio's first story in the *Decam-*

eron centers on a characteristically gullible priest, the second on the conversion of a Jew who had concluded after a visit to Rome that with the papacy so corrupt the church had to be of divine inspiration, and the fourth on the complicity of monk and abbot in seducing a young woman. And so it went. In the "Prologue" to the *Canterbury Tales,* Chaucer lets the "Pardoner" draw a chilling portrait of himself as a priest who abuses his authority and seems proud of selling false relics for financial gain.

For seriously religious persons nothing perhaps was more disturbing than the commercialization of piety exemplified by the Pardoner. In Rome church offices were sold to the highest bidder, which was the ecclesiastical crime of simony in all but name. More widely observable was the traffic in indulgences, which, no matter what theological justification was offered, on the surface often looked like grace and forgiveness on sale at bargain prices. "Everything is for sale" is how many contemporaries viewed the Roman scene.

In colloquies such as "A Pilgrimage for Religion's Sake" and "The Funeral," Erasmus poked serious fun at relics, pilgrimages, wonder-working saints, apparitions of the Virgin Mary, and the petty but vicious rivalry among religious orders. In the "Praise of Folly" his depiction of the Scholastics' theological enterprise as vacuous and pastorally irrelevant hit home and threw oil onto the already blazing fires of theological controversy.

Relics, pilgrimages, wonder-working saints, and apparitions of the Virgin Mary did in fact play a large role in the piety of the time. So did images of Christ and the saints. To the list must be added the gaining of indulgences for oneself or for the dead. In these cases the sacramental principle of the spiritual being mediated through the material was operative, but the latter sometimes overwhelmed and suffocated the former. Reformers cried therefore for a more "spiritual religion." As the *Imitation of Christ,* the great fifteenth-century classic, urged in the opening chapter, "turn thy mind from visible things and rise to the invisible."

Viewed from these perspectives, the ecclesiastical and religious situation of Europe on the eve of the Reformation looks like a landscape of unrelieved desolation. In fact, as historians have conclusively shown over the past fifty years, the situation was complex to a degree that defies summary and that challenges the negative stereotypes that still prevail in the popular media. That the bishops at Trent were so intent on reforming themselves, that is, on making it as impossible as they could for themselves and their colleagues to evade their pastoral responsibilities, shows that even among them the situation was not so dire as previous generations believed. What is clear today is how different France was from Italy, England from Spain, Spain from both France and Italy, and Germany from the lot of them. Equally clear is that diversity prevailed among different socioeconomic classes in different parts of Europe. It may be possible to judge the religious fervor of the age as misguided but impossible to deny its vitality and intensity.[36]

Far removed from any movement of reform from "the head," self-generated reform of the clergy had been under way for some time, especially in the religious orders, virtually every one of which had its "Observantist" branch that professed to be following more faithfully than its counterparts in the order the lifestyle prescribed by their Rule. In the Spain of Ferdinand and Isabella, the stern Franciscan archbishop of Toledo, Francisco Jiménez (Ximénez) de Cisneros (1436–1517), imposed an Observantist reform first on the Franciscan friars and then on the women's branch, the Poor Clares.[37] In Spain as elsewhere such efforts were resisted, often successfully, but by 1517 the Observantist branch of the Franciscans and the correlative branch in other orders as well were in the ascendancy throughout Europe.

As archbishop, Cisneros successfully imposed a program of reform on the secular clergy that forced them to give up their concubines, preach regularly, and attend to their other pastoral duties. Most important, he made pastors reside in their parishes. This reform, as initiated by the Primate of all Spain and resolutely backed by Queen Isabella, who herself saw to the appointment of worthy prelates, helps explain why the Spanish bishops who met at Burgos in 1511 in preparation for Lateran V were such strong advocates for reform and why later the Spanish bishops played a leadership role as reformers at the Council of Trent. The reforms of Trent were to a considerable degree presaged in Spain.[38]

Cisneros published a small catechism for pastors to use in classes for children that he insisted they hold every Sunday. It is difficult to shake the misconception that before 1529, when Luther published both his "small" and his "large" catechism, instruction in the rudiments of the Christian faith was virtually nonexistent. In fact Cisneros's initiative in that regard was part of a new concern for instructing people in the "art of Christian living and dying" that gained momentum in the fifteenth century. Early in that century, for instance, Bishop Nicolò Albergati of Bologna organized a confraternity made up of teenage boys and adults to teach catechism.[39]

Cisneros founded the University of Alcalá (today the Complutense University of Madrid), which opened its gates in 1508. For it he procured distinguished scholars from leading universities in Paris, Bologna, and Salamanca. This enterprise indicates that universities, despite the criticism and satire often directed against them, remained respected and vibrant institutions. Although in them theologians and philosophers pursued their careers for the most part by poring over the same texts and debating the same questions as had their predecessors for generations, this routine does not mean they were not serious about their profession nor to a man unready to adopt new methods and address new issues.[40] Alcalá was, for instance, ahead of its time in its insistence on the study of Hebrew, Greek, and Latin as prerequisites for the study of theology and in its utilization of the new but fast developing discipline of philology in the study of sacred texts.

At the University of Salamanca, Francisco de Vitoria (Victoria, 1492–1546) broke new ground in legal theory and social ethics to the point of being considered the "father of international law," anticipating Grotius by more than a century. He sparked at Salamanca a new interest in Thomas Aquinas that reflected the renewed study of the Angelic Doctor that had for decades been gaining ground in Paris, Padua, and other places, including Rome, and that produced probably the greatest commentator on Aquinas in history, Tommaso De Vio, better known as Cajetan.[41]

At Alcalá Cisneros organized and funded at great expense the project that produced the six-volume Complutensian Polyglot, the first polyglot Bible ever published, in 1522.[42] It contained, among other things, the Hebrew, Greek, and Latin versions of the Old Testament and the original Greek and the Vulgate Latin of the New. The latter, printed in 1514, anticipated Erasmus's *Novum Instrumentum*, 1516, his critical edition of the Greek New Testament along with his new Latin translation. Both these publications were the fruit of the Humanist movement that began in Italy in the mid-fourteenth century with the poet Petrarch and that a century later led to the pioneering philological studies of the New Testament and other writings by Lorenzo Valla.[43]

The Humanist movement was responsible, therefore, for the recovery in reliable editions not only of the literary classics of Greece and Rome but also of the Bible and the Fathers of the Church. In that regard, Erasmus (1469–1536) was the culmination of the movement. In 1516, the same year he published the *Novum Instrumentum*, he published his nine-volume edition of the works of Saint Jerome, which was the first of his many editions of both the Greek and Latin Fathers. In these undertakings Erasmus was not acting as an antiquarian. He saw the Fathers as embodying in their style and message "the ancient and genuine" theology of the church, in contrast to the "modern" theologians, the Scholastics, whose method according to him was inept and pastorally irrelevant, even counterproductive.

Even more important, he saw the Bible, especially the New Testament, not only as the first and essential text for theological education but as the font from which all Christians should directly derive their religious devotion. He put his position eloquently in the concluding paragraph of his introduction to the *Novum Instrumentum*, in which he insisted that reading the New Testament would "bring you the living image of Christ's holy mind and the speaking, healing, dying, rising Christ himself, and thus render him so fully present that you would see less if you gazed upon him with your own eyes."

Erasmus, and the many others influenced by him, advocated therefore a reform of theological method and Christian piety that would be more directly inspired by the Bible and the Fathers. This reform was for him an integral part of a fourfold program he espoused in season and out—reform of theological method, reform of piety through interior appropriation of more biblically based sentiments, reform of ministry through return to simpler and pastorally more effective norms, and reform of formal schooling in accordance with the student-centered and ethically oriented educational philosophy of the Humanists.[44] This reform of interdependent parts had nothing directly to do with the traditional concept of "reform of the church," that is, reform pursued through imposition of discipline especially on the clergy in accordance with principles of canon law. In a larger sense, however, since the disciplinary reform of the era postulated devout and dedicated prelates, it was related to it.

Humanism was a complex, multifaceted movement based on the recovery of ancient literary texts, both pagan and Christian. It inherited an articulated philosophy of education from Cicero, Quintilian, and others that purported to produce not scholars secluded in their libraries and classrooms but men trained in the skills that would enable them to lead others in pursuit of the public weal. Quintilian succinctly enunciated the ideal, *vir bonus, dicendi peritus*—a good man, skilled in effective communication of worthy goals. In theory at least, the Humanist ideal was, therefore, strongly ethical in its orientation, and it was directed not so much to clerics as to laymen who would spend their lives "in the world."

Since classical rhetoric was the linchpin in the Humanists' program, it was almost inevitable that the movement would have an impact on preaching, the central Christian ministry. Contrary to what is sometimes implied, there was no dearth of sermons before the Reformation. Nor was there a dearth of criticism about them, principally for two reasons. First, although there were notable exceptions, preaching was generally done not by bishops and pastors, on whom the responsibility traditionally rested, but by members of the mendicant orders. Second, the preaching of the mendicants was either too highly intellectualized (the "university" or "thematic" sermons) or too highly moralistic, replete with miracle stories laced with threats of divine punishment for sin (the "penitential" sermons).

The fact remains that the mendicant friars (that is, the members of the Dominican, Franciscan, Augustinian, Carmelite, and Servite orders) were zealous preachers, as Luther, the Augustinian friar, exemplified. Their churches were centers of bustling pastoral activity, which because of their papally granted "privileges" they exercised almost independent of episcopal supervision. This was true to such an extent that bishops, sometimes resentful, sometimes grateful, used the mendicants' quasi-monopoly on pastoral ministry as an excuse for not residing in their dioceses.

The application of classical rhetoric to preaching, which began to have an impact in Italy by the late fifteenth century, was an attempt to respond to the prevailing sermon styles. By the early sixteenth century, it was on its way to dominating theory about how to preach, and its impact grew even stronger and more widely accepted as the century wore on. Although it took different forms in different settings, which included a notable difference between most Protestant and most Catholic forms, its principles took hold almost universally and prevailed unchallenged for the next four hundred years.[45] Frequent sermons, properly constructed and delivered, became an ever more insistently proclaimed ideal.

For Erasmus, as well as for the Italian Humanists who preceded him, education was a powerful instrument for the reform of church and society. Erasmus returned to this theme again and again in his writings, and in the fateful year 1516, when both his *Novum Instrumentum* and his edition of Jerome appeared, he also published "The Education of the Christian Prince" *(Institutio principis Christiani)*, dedicated to the young Prince Charles of Habsburg, the future Emperor Charles V. In it he articulated the principles according to which a prince should be educated and then laid out their implications for governing justly and mercifully. He, as well as other Humanists who wrote on education, assumed that the Roman virtue of dedication to the common good of society was consonant with the Gospel and a hallmark of the devout Christian.

The Humanists with Erasmus at their head mounted one of the most successful propaganda campaigns in all history to convince Europeans of the excellence of their style of education, of the indispensability of the communication skills it inculcated, and of the Christian character-formation it promised to deliver. The reality of the Humanists' schools surely did not always measure up to these ideals, but by the early sixteenth century the schools were becoming a pan-European phenomenon, destined to grow even more popular and ubiquitous within a few decades.[46] By the time the Council of Trent met, the conviction was widespread that "all the well-being of Christianity and of the whole world depends on the proper education of youth," that is, education in the Humanistic mode.[47] Pedro de Ribadeneira, a Jesuit, wrote those words, just at the time his order, the Society of Jesus, began establishing its network of Humanistic schools throughout the Catholic world.

Important though the new schooling would prove to be, it was far less pervasive than an older institution, the confraternity, which had for generations affected the religious outlook and practice of almost every strata of society. Confraternities were known by different names in different countries—fraternities or sodalities in English, *Brüderschaften* in German, *compagnie* or *confrérie* in French, *cofradía* in Spain, *compagnia* in Italy but *scuola* in Venice, and so forth. They were voluntary associations, self-governing and organized for purposes that were principally religious.

Confraternities were a more broadly based equivalent of the guilds organized for economic or professional goals, and, though there were earlier equivalents, they began to appear in Europe at about the same time as the guilds. They evinced an almost infinite variety in their patterns of piety, in the duties they undertook relative to their own members and to others, in their relationship to civil and ecclesiastical authorities, and in the socioeconomic composition of their membership. In general, however, members agreed to come together on a regular basis and obliged themselves to follow certain rules to promote their spiritual life.[48]

A particularly important confraternity called the Oratory of Divine Love, founded in Genoa in 1497 with branches later in other important Italian cities, had procedures and protocols not untypically reminiscent of a religious order.[49] The branch in Rome included Gaetano da Thiene, an official in the papal Curia later canonized, and Giampietro Carafa, later Pope Paul IV. These two men in 1524 founded the Theatine Order, which indicates how seriously the members took the religious observances inculcated by the Oratory.

No matter what the socioeconomic status of their membership, almost all confraternities engaged in forms of social assistance to their members, and some undertook the support of hospitals, foundling homes, and similar institutions. Confraternities did not exclude a certain measure of conviviality through sponsorship of festivals of various kinds, which in some confraternities got out of hand. In his "Appeal to the Nobility," Luther castigated the societies for being little more than eating and drinking clubs.

Confraternities were to be found in virtually every city and larger town across Europe and sometimes in rural villages. Major cities had a large number. In Lyons at the end of the fifteenth century, for instance, there were at least 30, whereas in Rouen, a city of about 40,000, there were a whopping 131. For the most part the members were adult males, but women were included in some. Most notably in Florence but also in other cities, youth confraternities flourished. The Third Orders affiliated with the mendicant orders like the Dominicans and the Franciscans were in many regards similar to the confraternities and were an integral part of this picture of organized lay piety, and their membership was extensive.

Although some confraternities had priest-members, more were exclusively lay. They might hire a priest as chaplain for the celebration of Mass and administration of the sacraments, but the members led their meetings, prayer services, and other acts of devotion. For large numbers of Christians, therefore, confraternities were much more important for their practice of the faith than the parish church, even though some confraternities were parish-based. By the mid-sixteenth century they were so numerous and such well established realities that, viewed from one angle, they at times seemed almost to define the religious landscape of a given city or neighborhood; viewed from another, they looked like civic or municipal institutions, religiously motivated—making a distinction virtually meaningless at the time. From whichever angle, however, they were not branch offices of either the parish or the town hall but self-determining entities working in some self-defined way for the spiritual benefit of their members and, in some instances, for the benefit of others.

What was the quality of the Christianity the members practiced and professed? As always, that is an almost impossible question to answer. In certain instances, their pious practices, which might include public acts of bodily penance such as self-flagellation, can seem morbid, routinized, and motivated by the quid-pro-quo understanding of grace widespread at the time. In certain instances their meetings may have been little more than occasions for a party. In more instances, however, the evidence points to the members' having a grasp of basic doctrines and of the obligations and interior sentiments they implied for the believer.[50]

The Devotio Moderna, a movement that originated in the Low Countries at the end of the fourteenth century and that spread in literate circles into much of Western Europe, is another instance of response to spiritual yearning. *The Imitation of Christ,* a call to an inner-directed life and one of the classics of Christian spirituality, is simply the best-known product of the Devotio and characteristic of its piety. The *Imitation* was read by clergy and laity alike. The absenteeism of pastors and the sometimes slack or inept performance of their vicars do not, therefore, necessarily mean that the spiritual needs of the ordinary lay person were not being met.

We return to the basic question: how bad was it? Assessments differ depending upon what evidence is examined and, perhaps more important, upon what criteria are applied to evaluate it. The age had its share of ecclesiastical rogues and benefice-chasers but also of devout and dedicated churchmen. Ignorance and superstition abounded, but so did efforts to remedy them. Bishops might be absentee careerists, but even in their dioceses Christianity at the grass roots could be engaged and lively thanks to the religious orders and the confraternities.

Was the glass, then, half empty or half full—or two-thirds empty, or two-thirds full? It is perhaps safest to dodge questions like these and resort to the flabby generalization that these were neither the best nor the worst of times. We surely cannot take at face value reformers' sometimes perfervid denunciations of their age as utterly depraved. Nonetheless, the image of a papacy seemingly more concerned with securing ample income for itself than with providing pastorally responsible bishops was widespread. That image was grounded in the reality of the situation and made credible by flagrant violations of the most fundamental ideals and principles of canon law.

On three further points, moreover, sturdy generalizations can be made. First, the Reformation could have happened only in a society passionately concerned about religion. Second, the Reformation could almost certainly not have succeeded, or succeeded as it did, had it not been for an extraordinarily important shift in political leadership that took place in Europe between 1509 and 1520. Third, that shift, along with papal fear of councils, explains the long delay in the convocation of the Council of Trent.

2

The Struggle to Convoke the Council

In late 1517 an Augustinian friar, essentially unknown outside the small city of Wittenberg, where he was preaching and teaching, set off a movement that convulsed Europe. By any rational reckoning this should not have happened. Luther had neither money nor political status. He almost immediately managed, moreover, to provoke the enmity of some of the most powerful institutions and personages in Europe. Yet he not only survived but became the founder of the Reformation and, more broadly, the iconic hero in Western culture for all those who, at risk of life and limb, challenge "the establishment," whatever that establishment might be.

Luther's success was surely due in large part to his religious message. His doctrine of justification by faith alone, easily misunderstood though it was, struck a deep chord. People responded to a teaching that promised a more personal relationship with God and was based directly on the text of Scripture. The practical conclusions Luther drew from his doctrine especially regarding church hierarchy and religious practice struck possibly an even deeper chord. His message sounded like the answer, finally, to the many calls for reform of the church that for so long had gone unheeded. It led to a radical dismantling of traditional ecclesiastical structures, a phenomenon that produced jubilation in some quarters but rage and cries of sacrilege in others.

Nothing in Luther's teaching had more radical implications in the minds of his Catholic opponents than his utter repudiation of the papacy. Ranking just below that was his rejection of four or, more likely, five of the traditional seven sacraments. But for rank-and-file Christians, Luther's Reformation was most unavoidable and obtrusive for three other reasons—his repudiation of clerical celibacy, his translation of the Mass into the vernacular, and the physical attack a few of his followers launched against sacred images.

Radical and socially subversive though these teachings appeared to contemporaries, another, perhaps more subtle principle less consistently taken into account by his opponents was just as important. When Luther repudiated "reason" as a basis for theological argument, he hurled a challenge at the program for that argument that had held sway in the universities since the thirteenth century, that is, the program of Scholastic theology. In rejecting one style of theological discourse, he became the creator of another. He became, in the words of Gerhard Ebeling, a "linguistic innovator."[1]

Great dichotomies marked Luther's language, such as the unbridgeable chasm between Law and Gospel and between faith and works. Whereas the Scholastics tried through definitions and distinctions, through ever greater refinement of concepts, to arrive at resolutions among seemingly incompatible realities, Luther preferred paradox. He explicitly framed his theses for his "Heidelberg Disputation" of 1518 as a set of "theological paradoxes." In justification the Christian emerges, for Luther, at one and the same time as righteous and sinner—*simul justus et peccator.* For the Scholastics such a position made no sense whatsoever, as if he were saying something could be black and white at the same time.

Luther's discourse was relational, occasional, and psychological, theirs logical, systematic, and metaphysical.[2] Underlying the two styles were values and thought-patterns that were as profound as they were diverse. They were also, however, often implicit, not clearly recognized or reckoned with. They were the two proverbial ships passing in the night, which is a crucial factor in assessing the effectiveness of the Council of Trent's response to Luther.

A Pope, Two Kings, and an Emperor: 1523–1534

Despite the power of his personality and the appeal of his message, Luther could not have survived, and the movement he sparked not have had the impact it did, had it not been for that special configuration of political forces that came into being in the fateful second decade of the sixteenth century. That configuration also had a determining impact on both the prehistory of the Council of Trent and its course once it met. It is difficult to imagine a historical situation with such high stakes in which religion and politics were more inextricably intertwined.

In 1509 the young Henry VIII of the House of Tudor came to the throne of England, a kingdom now recovered from the devastations and disruptions of the War of the Roses and eager to take its rightful role in international politics. In France in 1515, the young Francis I of the House of Valois ascended the throne of the most powerful country in Europe, and that year he successfully invaded Italy to win as his prize the rich Duchy of Milan, traditionally claimed by the Holy Roman Emperor. That triumph allowed him, as mentioned, to sign with Pope Leo X the Concordat of Bologna, which delivered into his hands the nomination of French bishops.

The next year Charles of Habsburg at the age of sixteen inherited from his maternal grandparents, Ferdinand and Isabella, the throne of Spain, which included the Kingdom of Naples and all the Spanish dominions overseas. Three years later, in 1519, he was elected Holy Roman Emperor, defeating through bribery his chief rival, Francis. The election consolidated Charles's claims, under various titles, to lands that today roughly comprise Germany, Holland, Belgium, Austria, Switzerland, the Czech Republic, Hungary, Slovakia, parts of northern Italy, and eastern France.

With the imperial election, therefore, Charles, whose aunt was the queen of England, Catherine of Aragon, emerged as unquestionably the strongest man in Europe. When Luther appeared before him in 1521 at the Diet of Worms to plead his cause just a few months after his excommunication by Leo X had been promulgated, Charles after a brief hearing rejected Luther's petition and declared him, as a heretic, an outlaw of the empire. That verdict should have ended Luther's career and, if Luther failed to retract, led to his execution. No ruler in Europe, it would seem, was in a better position than Charles to bring Luther to justice.

But, as has often been observed, Charles's very power was his weakness. It aroused fear and resistance from just about everybody not utterly devoted to the Habsburg cause. His own German nobles, who in many cases were autonomous rulers of their territories, powerful in their own right, were avidly protective of their traditional prerogatives and apprehensive that Charles had the resources to ignore, curtail, or eliminate them. They resented him and saw in the religious turmoil sparked by Luther's success a chance to reduce him to size. Within a short while many identified themselves with Luther's reform. One such, Frederick the Wise of Saxony, was able by virtue of his special prerogatives as an Elector of the empire to provide Luther with protection in defiance of Charles. Even nobles who remained Catholic, which of course included bishops, were reluctant to support measures that strengthened Charles's hand.

The French king, who by his campaign in Italy had challenged imperial claims to Milan by successfully taking it as his own, felt surrounded by Habsburgs—Charles to the south in Spain, Charles along his eastern borders, and Charles's aunt across the channel in England. He was bent, therefore, on weakening his great rival, even if it meant giving aid and comfort to the Lutheran party in Germany. In 1521 he opened military hostilities against Charles, the first of four such ventures over the next twenty years in which he consistently suffered defeat but rebounded to go on the offensive again. In this first campaign he lost Milan to Charles, but he mounted a second in 1524 and won it back, only to lose it again the next year.

Charles on his eastern frontier faced, moreover, a newly aggressive Turkish offensive led by Sultan Suleiman the Magnificent, another of those long-lived and remarkable rulers of the era. The fall of Constantinople in 1453 had opened to the Turks the gates to Europe. Hardly had Suleiman come to the throne in 1520 when he led his troops in a successful campaign against the Christian strongholds of Belgrade, Rhodes, and most of Hungary, so that by 1529 he arrived at the gates of Vienna itself. Only with difficulty did Charles rally the German nobles to take up arms to lift the siege and drive back the infidel.

Charles needed the help of his German nobles against Francis and against Suleiman. As more and more of them took up Luther's cause, he had to pay them heed. In 1531 a few princes and cities formed the Schmalkaldic League, a military junta for self-defense against Charles. The league quickly gained members, which included certain "free cities," and began to expel bishops from their dioceses, confiscate church lands, and in general obstruct Charles's plans. It was an important force in promoting the Reformation, as the effective leadership gradually passed from theologians to the heads of the league. Meanwhile the league besought Charles, with sometimes questionable sincerity, to see to the convocation of "a free Christian council in German lands," an echo of the petition of the Diet of Nuremberg in 1523. But the slogan now concealed a list of non-negotiables as well as an understanding of the function of a council that for Catholics radically redefined it.

Charles, who early emerged as the unswerving standard-bearer for the Catholic cause, was convinced that a council provided the best hope

FIGURE 2 *Pope Paul III and His Nephews* (Titian, 1545). The painting depicts the aged pope the year the Council of Trent opened. "Nephews" is the euphemism for his two grandsons: Cardinal Alessandro Farnese, his namesake, and Alessandro's brother, Ottavio, who later, after the murder of their father, Pierluigi Farnese, became Duke of Parma. (Museo e Gallerie Nazionali di Capodimonte, Naples. Courtesy of Getty Images.)

for peace and reconciliation. For the next twenty years he did his utmost to see the council become a reality.[3] He pursued this goal out of a sincere piety and a conviction that, although Luther was a heretic, the issues he raised, especially those concerning church reform, deserved a fair hearing. He saw the council as a way of conciliating the Lutheran nobility and avoiding civil war—or, as the years passed, of at least showing that he had done his best to avoid it. If a council achieved such goals, however, the result would be a consolidation of Charles's power within the empire, which was an aspect of his campaign for a council not lost on his enemies.

It was certainly not lost on Francis I. He saw clearly the relief that a successful council would bring to Charles. Although he often gave the contrary impression, he may not have been opposed in principle to a council. But a council "in German lands" sounded like a council marching to the emperor's drum.[4] The king had, moreover, another reason to be extremely wary. The Parlement of Paris, the University of Paris, and much of the French episcopacy rejected the Concordat of Bologna as illegitimately delivering to the king control over the church, an offense against the French church's traditional "liberties." They appealed for a council to redress their grievances. Francis saw a council, therefore, as possibly jeopardizing the control that the Concordat guaranteed him. "The Most Christian King," to give Francis his official title, saw the council as a danger, therefore, to his domestic interests as well as to his foreign.[5]

The political advantage Charles would gain from a successful council was not lost on Pope Clement VII. In 1523 Clement succeeded the austere and dour Dutchman Adrian VI, a one-time professor and rector of the University of Louvain and former tutor to the young Charles of Habsburg. Some months after Adrian's election, Cajetan, by this point a cardinal, rejoiced that "the head" was now already reformed.[6] But Adrian, though well intentioned, was rigid and gauche, and he managed to alienate even those in Rome sympathetic to the reforms he tried to initiate.[7] Aware to some extent of the gravity of the German situation, as his legate to the Diet at Nuremberg in early 1523 made clear, he seems not to have grasped its complexity. His in any case was a short pontificate of scarcely a year that had no impact on the great religious and political crisis that daily became more severe.[8]

The new pope, Clement VII, Giulio de' Medici, elected after a conclave of fifty days, was the illegitimate son of Giuliano de' Medici, who before Giulio was born was assassinated on Easter Sunday, 1478, in the cathedral in Florence. Giulio was, accordingly, raised in the household of his uncle, Lorenzo the Magnificent, and thus benefited from the same excellent education received by Lorenzo's son, Clement's predecessor as pope but one, Leo X. One of Leo's first acts as pope had been to brush aside the canonical impediment of his cousin's illegitimacy to make him a cardinal and archbishop of Florence. Leo also heaped upon him ecclesiastical benefices in a number bountiful even for the Renaissance papacy.

Historians of almost all stripes judge Clement harshly.[9] As pope he struck his contemporaries as indecisive and vacillating, and in fact sharp reversals of political policy marked his pontificate. Like his cousin Leo, he was sincerely but conventionally devout. Also like Leo, but in an even more volatile military situation, he let political concerns dominate his decisions, which meant trying to make sure above all that the Papal States and his native Florence were secure.

He feared Charles V. The emperor, through his Spanish crown ruler of the Kingdom of Naples just south of Rome, had after his victory over Francis in 1522 established himself in the north in the Duchy of Milan, ominously close to both the Papal States and Florence. The prospect of Charles to the south and Charles to the north was a threat almost too much to bear. Although Charles had promoted his candidacy for the papacy, Clement made the bold move of siding with Francis against him. He was barely elected in 1524 before he concluded a treaty with the French king.

But when at the Battle of Pavia in 1525 the emperor defeated Francis a second time and took him prisoner, Clement attempted a reconciliation. Once Francis had been set at liberty, however, Clement reversed course and, along with several other powers, formed with Francis the League of Cognac against the emperor. Henry VIII joined the league the next year. The war that followed, fought principally in Italy, led by 1529 to another defeat for Francis. Worse was Clement's fate. In 1527 imperial troops in Italy marched victoriously south and by the spring were at the gates of Rome. On May 6 they broke into the city.[10] Charles did not sanction the terrible sack that ensued, during which Clement barely escaped capture, but he afterward tried to take advantage of it to bring pressure on the pope.

Despite the emperor's efforts, Clement was able to resist him to the end on the question of the council.[11] For a century now, popes had realized that even under the best of circumstances a council held mortal dangers for them. These were hardly the best of circumstances. Not only did Charles at this moment seem strong enough to dominate the agenda of the council, but Clement felt himself personally vulnerable in the highest degree. He had been born out of wedlock, suspicions spread that he had been elected through bribery, and his policies had managed to alienate just about everyone, most especially the emperor. The council might try to depose him or, surely, call him to account for his conduct.

After the sack of Rome Charles's moment seemed finally to have arrived. On November 5, 1529, Charles and Clement met in Bologna and for four months lived there under the same roof in the Palazzo Publico. As a result of their conversations Charles believed he had wrung from Clement an agreement to convoke a council, but, as astute observers noted at the time, Clement's agreement was highly qualified. In the few years of life left to the pope, he continued to set down conditions, make promises, and engage in other delaying tactics. As Jedin said of him, "He did not dare refuse a council, but he had no intention of bringing it about."[12] Charles, for all his power, was in the last analysis powerless over Clement's deft evasions.

Charles's distrust of the pope grew even stronger when he learned that Clement had arranged for his niece, Catherine de' Medici, age fourteen, to marry Henry, the second son of King Francis. The emperor demanded that Clement use the occasion to obtain from Francis his consent to a council. Of course nothing of the sort happened. In 1533 Clement traveled to Marseille for the wedding, presided at the ceremony, made sure the marriage was consummated, and, to the dismay of the emperor, named four new French cardinals. The young bride would as an adult and queen regent of France play an important role regarding the Council of Trent in its final phase.

During these same years, Clement faced another momentous decision. Henry VIII had long petitioned for a declaration that his marriage to Catherine of Aragon was invalid, and he was more than intimating schism if the declaration should not be granted. Francis I made common cause with Henry. Clement dithered as long as possible, in a case that was in fact complicated from a canonical viewpoint but that also had ominous relevance for his relationship with Charles, determined to protect his aunt's honor, and even more ominous relevance for his relationship with Henry. When, however, the archbishop of Canterbury, Thomas Cranmer, took matters into his own hands and declared Henry's marriage to Catherine null and the marriage to Anne Boleyn legal, Clement was forced to act. On March 24, 1534, he issued his final decision declaring Henry's marriage with Catherine valid.

Clement died five months later. Meanwhile, Henry VIII responded by procuring from Parliament the Act of Supremacy, which made it high treason to refuse to acknowledge the king as supreme head of the English church. The executions the next year of John Fisher, the bishop of Rochester, and Thomas More, a former chancellor of the realm, signaled that a critical, perhaps irreparable parting of the ways had occurred. The papal bull that year excommunicating the king made the break official.

These developments put Henry firmly in the anticouncil and anti-Habsburg camp, and they solidified his cooperation with Francis I. In that year, 1535, Henry and Francis agreed to cooperate with the Schmalkaldic League against Charles, a move in which Henry's principal motive was to prevent the new pope, Paul III, from calling a council. A council might review Henry's marital situation, condemn the execution of Fisher and More, and rally Europe against the English king.

Paul III and Charles V: Uneasy Companions on the Road to Trent

Fifty days to elect Clement VII. Two days to elect his successor. Why such a contrast? Cardinals from contending camps converged in their dismay over Clement's seemingly shilly-shallying policies, which many blamed for the sack of Rome. More important, the mood had shifted. Concern, even panic, over what the future might hold was widespread. The sack, a portent of worse things to come? The Turks, seemingly unstoppable on the eastern frontier, controlled the eastern Mediterranean and raided southern Italian cities almost at will. The Schmalkaldic League threatened war in Germany. Luther was still at large. His teachings had spread far and wide throughout northern Europe—and, the unthinkable, had penetrated even into Italy! England was in schism. In this perilous time the French king seemed to be playing a duplicitous game.

Something had to change. In Alessandro Farnese, who at sixty-seven was the oldest participant in the conclave, the others saw a man they thought was up to the task. Farnese had been a cardinal since 1492, for forty-two years. He knew the ropes and knew how to make them work. Widely respected for his diplomatic skills, his firmness of purpose, his intelligence, and his good judgment, he had not hidden his disagreements with Clement's political policies or Clement's disregard of his advice. In the rivalry between Charles and Francis, he believed the Holy See needed to maintain a policy of absolute neutrality. He had long and publically proclaimed the necessity of a council. He seemed to be the man of the hour.

Shortly after his election as Paul III, he announced three goals for his pontificate.[13] The first was to effect peace among Christian princes, by which he meant in the first place between Charles and Francis. The second was to convoke a council to deal with the religious problems, and the third to organize and promote a crusade to push back the Turks. These goals were interrelated, with the success of one being to some extent dependent upon the success of the other two. Years later, in 1542, in his bull convoking the council at Trent, he reiterated those same three goals.

In his younger days as a cardinal, Alessandro Farnese had behaved like many of his peers and begot three sons and a daughter. In 1512, however, he broke with his mistress, was ordained a priest six years later, and then undertook in his diocese of Parma an implementation of the reform decrees of the Fifth Lateran Council. From that point forward he became part of the small reform party in the Curia. His concern was genuine but hedged with qualifications.

Clouding his vision was passion for the welfare of his family, especially for his children and grandchildren. This passion, sometimes blind, was not simply a scandal that dismayed reformers. It led him as pope into political maneuvers that badly hindered him from accomplishing his three goals by involving him in intrigues and sometimes devious political maneuvers that damaged especially his relationship with Charles V. He tipped his hand almost immediately after his election when he nominated two teenage grandchildren as cardinals—Guido Ascanio Sforza (age sixteen) and Alessandro Farnese, his namesake (age fourteen). Then in 1538 he nominated a cousin, Niccolo Gaetani di Sermoneta (age twelve), and much later, in 1545, Alessandro's younger brother Ranuccio (age fifteen). He in other ways prodigiously provided for his family.

During his pontificate of fifteen years, he created seventy-one cardinals, an unprecedented number. Many of his nominees were men of probity, some much more than that. They included Reginald Pole, a cousin of Henry VIII; Giampietro Carafa, future pope and, as mentioned, a founder of the new, reforming religious order, the Theatines;

FIGURE 3 *Charles V at the Battle of Mühlberg* (Titian, 1548). Titian painted this portrait of the emperor at the time of his great military victory over the coalition of Lutheran princes in the empire known as the Schmalkaldic League. (Museo del Prado, Madrid. Courtesy of Getty Images.)

and Gasparo Contarini, a learned and devout Venetian aristocrat. By his nominations Paul did not drive out of the college all ambition or corruption, but he did much to temper the secularization that had begun with Sixtus IV. This was an important step forward.

In 1536, two years after his election, Paul established a small commission *(consilium)* headed by Contarini and with Pole and Carafa as members to draw up a memorandum on "the reform of the church" in anticipation of a council. A year later the commission issued a secret report, in which the second paragraph contained these blunt lines:

> the origin of these evils was due to the fact that some popes, your predecessors . . . [engaged for themselves] teachers not that they might learn from them what they should do but that they might find through the application and cleverness of these teachers a justification for what it pleased them to do . . . [teachers] who taught that the pope is lord of all benefices and that therefore since a lord may sell by right what is his own, it necessarily follows that the pope cannot be guilty of simony. Thus the will of the pope, of whatever kind it might be, is the rule governing his activities and deeds: whence it may be shown without doubt that whatever is pleasing to him is also permitted. From this source as from a Trojan horse so many abuses and such grave diseases have rushed upon the church of God that we now see her afflicted almost to the despair of salvation.[14]

The report was leaked and used by the Lutherans as proof positive of the corruption of the papacy. Lutheran exploitation was surely a factor persuading Paul not to move, or to move with extreme caution, on its specific provisions, most of which dealt with dispensations from canon law in exchange for a consideration and with similar procedures that at least looked like simony and that had contributed so mightily to setting off the fury against the papacy.

The sad fact was that fees ("compositions") for "graces" granted through the papal office known as the Datary were deeply resented throughout Europe and a source of grave scandal, yet they brought in so much money that their abolition or radical reform was for the popes unthinkable. The Datary alone, through fees and taxes for the granting of dispensations, indults, privileges, and benefices, brought in well over 100,000 ducats a year, about half of the Curia's total income. The Datary was, however, only one among the many glaring instances of such "grievances" against the Holy See. "Reform of the head" threatened to subvert major sources of revenue of the financial system in which the papacy operated.

Paul took action, however, in other areas that had immense impact on the future. In 1542 he established the Roman Inquisition, soon to be known as the Holy Office (today, the Congregation for the Doctrine of the Faith). For its first decade the Inquisition moved tentatively, but when Giampietro Carafa, one of its original members, became pope in 1555, it moved into high gear. Even more important was the official approval Paul III granted several new religious orders, the best known of which is the Jesuits—officially, the Society of Jesus. He also approved the Barnabites, Somaschans, and the Ursulines, an important women's order. The Ursulines were the first in a notable surge of similar orders of women who engaged in active ministry that became a hallmark of early modern Catholicism.

But the council was the burning question. The obstacles to it were greater than ever. Wise heads believed that the chances of its accomplishing a reconciliation now, a generation after the posting of the Ninety-Five Theses, were virtually nil. The Lutheran "movement" had crystallized in Germany into a recognizable social reality on its way to becoming an institution, clearly set off from the Catholic church by a creedal statement, the Augsburg Confession of 1530. This nascent institution was now led by powerful nobles who, sincere though they may have been in their new faith, had confiscated church property for themselves or for others that they had no intention of relinquishing. At the grass roots the clergy had taken wives and begot children, which attached them to the reform with the strongest possible human bonds. There was for them no turning back.

The animosity between Charles and Francis was greater, not less, than before. Henry VIII's break with the papacy seemed final. Even more radical Reformers, whom contemporaries called Anabaptists and who looked to them like anarchists, had sprung up. The list could go on. Less obvious but just as serious was now the widespread belief that the council would never happen. Skepticism about papal promises in that regard infected virtually everybody, perhaps especially the Catholic episcopate. Clement's tergiversation had done deep damage. As Paul's early efforts to convoke a council failed one after the other, skepticism degenerated into cynicism, which accounts for the fact that in December 1545, when the Council of Trent actually opened, only a handful of bishops showed up for it.

At the time of Paul's election, therefore, the prospect that Charles, exasperated, would give in to the clamor for a national council in Germany—"free Christian council in German lands"—which would probably mean the complete triumph of Lutheranism, hung ominously in the air. Also in France voices had been raised for a national council, and they would continue to demand such action for the next two decades. The French could well do without a council that they feared Charles had in his pocket.

In the meantime, between the end of Lateran V and the opening of Trent, several local councils had been held. The archbishop of Lyons convoked a provincial council in 1527 for three purposes: (1) to raise money for the ransom of the king's sons held hostage by the emperor as a condition for the king's own release; (2) to stamp out the Lutheran heresy; and (3) to reform the behavior *(mores)* of the clergy.[15] The council's stipulations against Lutheranism suggest that the members had little or no knowledge of it, and they do little besides affirm the legitimacy of the church's discipline on fasting and of its belief in the efficacy of prayers for the dead. The council forbade the publishing, selling, buying, and reading of Lutheran books. In establishing procedures and norms to make sure that only worthy candidates received holy orders, the Council of Lyons manifested a concern common to the other local councils that became a leitmotif at Trent.

The agenda of the provincial Council of Bourges the next year had the identical threefold agenda, but regarding Lutheranism did nothing more than prohibit traffic in Lutheran writings.[16] The council forbade the preaching of indulgences without the permission of the local bishop and prescribed that rectors of churches preach to their flocks every Sunday. In 1536 Archbishop Hermann von Wied convoked a provincial council at Cologne whose decrees consist almost entirely in proposing ideals and regulations for the reform of clerics.[17] The fact that the archbishop, formerly a fierce enemy of the Lutherans, was now on his way to joining them helps explain why the synod contained not a word against them.

By far the most important of these gatherings was the Council of Sens convened in Paris on February 3, 1528, with the twofold aim of combating heresy and "reforming the church."[18] Its decrees were published on October 9. They took aim at Luther as their principal target but also condemned Melanchthon, Karlstadt, François Lambert, and Oecolampadius. Formulated and edited by the well-known theologian from the Paris Faculty of Theology Josse Clichtove, they began with an attack on Luther's teaching on justification and, more specifically, on the relationship between faith and works.[19] Luther's teaching on justification, especially because of its emphasis on human depravity and the impotence of the will, was, the council maintained, a modern form of Manichaeism. This analysis was typical of Catholic understanding of Luther at the time. But Luther, the council also maintained, was guilty of propagating as well the heresies of Arius, Vigilantius, Peter Waldo, and Marsilius of Padua.

Although the Council of Sens equated Luther's teaching with ancient heresies, it deserves credit for hitting on the justification issue as the crucial doctrinal point, which none of these other councils did. It also deserves credit for balancing what it said about Luther's teaching with an insistence that Pelagius erred in the opposite direction. The church, the council implied, steers a midway course, teaching that three things are required for salvation: faith, good works, and grace. Of these three grace is the first and most important—"primo tamen et principaliter."[20]

The council then took up specific issues that the "reborn errors" raised. It dealt with them by making use of Scripture, church councils, church tradition, the consensus of the ancients, and the constant practice of the church. It thus implicitly but unmistakably rejected Luther's "Scripture-alone" principle as the basis for establishing Christian dogma. It sorted out the "reborn heresies" into sixteen headings, the index for which reveals what informed contemporaries believed were the issues at stake in the religious controversies:

1. On the unity and infallibility of the church.
2. That the church is not invisible.
3. On the authority of councils.
4. That it is the church's prerogative to determine which books belong in the canon of Scripture.
5. Some things are to be firmly believed that are not contained expressly in Scripture.
6. On human constitutions [and decrees].
7. On fasts prescribed by the church.
8. On the celibacy of priests.
9. On vows, especially monastic.
10. That there are seven sacraments of the church.
11. On the sacrifice of the Mass.
12. On satisfaction, Purgatory, and praying for the dead.
13. On the veneration of the saints.
14. On the veneration of sacred images.
15. On free will.
16. On faith and works.[21]

The list anticipated to a remarkable degree issues the Council of Trent subsequently took up. That is true even though Trent in some cases, as mentioned, decided not to decide. The decrees of Sens were known and respected far beyond northern France, as evidenced by the fact that at Trent Italian and Spanish bishops invoked them when it served their purposes.[22] In treating these sixteen issues Sens gave no quarter and defended Catholic practice without a suggestion that at least on some of them a concession might be made or a change might be called for.

Such a polemical or at least apologetic stance was standard among Catholics at the time, but there were some who tried to find ways to bridge at least a few of the differences. Among them was Cajetan, one of the most esteemed Catholic theologians of his time, the former master general of the Dominican order, and perhaps the most respected commentator on Aquinas of all times. He is most widely known, however, for his encounter with Luther in 1518 at Augsburg.

In 1530, he drew up for Clement VII a remarkable memo in which he suggested allowing the laity to partake of the Eucharistic cup and, more radical, allowing priests in Germany to marry. He believed, as did other cardinals, that the church should not require fasting or reception of the sacraments under pain of sin. He even went so far as to propose that for reunion no formal retraction should be required of Lutheran theologians, only that they profess to believe what the universal church has always believed, and of Lutheran princes only a private affirmation of belief, no public ceremony.[23]

Dire though the situation was, therefore, when Paul III almost immediately set out in earnest to convoke a council, hope of healing the religious divisions had not altogether evanesced.[24] Through nuncios Paul began negotiations with the leading figures throughout Europe. As a result he reached the decision to hold the council in Mantua, which, though in Italy, was a fief of the empire (and therefore technically "in German lands"), close enough to Rome (though not in the Papal States). Schmalkalden objected to the place as well as to the fact that the council was not "free," that is, the pope would preside either in person or through legates. Francis, fearful that it would be dominated by the emperor, set down conditions but eventually gave his assent. Henry VIII, now excommunicate, was out of the picture. Bishops expressed skepticism.

Despite the problems, on June 2, 1536, less than two years after his election, Paul III published the bull *Ad Dominici Gregis Curam* summoning a General Council to meet at Mantua on May 23, 1537.[25] All bishops and abbots were to appear in person. The emperor and other "princes"—the kings of France, Portugal, Scotland, and Spain, for instance, as well as the Duke of Bavaria, and others of similar rank—were to do the same, or, if they were legitimately impeded, send a representative. Thus all the leaders of Christendom, lay and clerical, were to be present. The long-awaited meeting now seemed assured.

It was not to be. As was perhaps to be expected, Schmalkalden rejected the invitation on the grounds mentioned above. Francis threw up obstacles, which resulted in not a single French bishop's receiving the bull of convocation. Then he opened another military campaign against Charles. The fatal blow came, however, from the Duke of Mantua, who insisted that the pope provide a guard of five to six thousand men for the city—a demand interpreted as the equivalent of a refusal to host the council. Not only would the cost to the papacy have been unsustainable over a lengthy meeting, but such a force of armed men would give every impression of a council held in bondage by a papal army.

Paul scrambled for an alternative city. This meant postponing the opening, a move that gave skeptics welcome grist for their mill and increased their number. The pope eventually prevailed upon the Republic of Venice to provide Vicenza, which, although not in papal territory, could by no stretch of the imagination be considered "in German lands." No one was happy except the many who opposed a council in the first place. Problems multiplied. Finally, in the spring of 1539 Paul had to suspend the council indefinitely. The upshot was that, through no fault of his own, he lost credibility and was judged to be playing the two-faced game of Clement VII.

It was, moreover, becoming ever clearer—to Paul, to Charles, and to many others besides—that the Lutherans almost certainly would not come to a council convoked by the pope and held under his auspices. At this point Paul planned to attend the council in person. This meant that if a council were held—and Paul, though frustrated at the moment, was determined to make it happen—the Lutherans would be condemned in their absence, which would inevitably mean their armed resistance to the emperor's implementation of the council's decrees. The dreaded civil war!

Charles, with aggressive enemies on his eastern and western borders, did not want to spend his resources fighting a third enemy in his own backyard. The Lutherans, aware of Charles's resources, anticipated that if he marshaled his forces against them, they could hardly prevail. Some, moreover, wanted to ease the tension and amicably settle the religious question. Paul, committed to a council, was, however, more than ready to forgo it if a solution less threatening to the papacy and its practices could be found. It was against this background that the idea of a religious colloquy between Catholics and Lutherans was born, gained momentum, and finally won the approval of these three parties.

After fits and starts, the usual barrage of recriminations back and forth, and seemingly endless negotiation, the most significant part of the colloquy took place at Regensburg (Ratisbon) in early 1541. The emperor's presence showed his resolve to see the colloquy end in an understanding. With Melanchthon and Martin Bucer among the interlocutors for the Lutherans and Cardinal Gasparo Contarini as chief spokesman for the Catholics, the colloquy, at least from that perspective, augured well. They were among the best informed from their respective sides and exercised within them a moderating influence. Contarini, moreover, many years earlier had had a deep religious experience that convinced him of the overriding power of grace, which in turn made him appreciative of Luther's teaching. Luther himself, an excommunicate and outlaw of the empire, could not attend.

At the beginning things went so well that the colloquy reached an agreement on the crucial issue of justification, as by faith working through charity. But then discussions broke down irreparably in debates about the church, the sacraments, and transubstantiation. By June it was clear to all that this desperate attempt to bridge the differences had failed. The agreement over justification was accepted by neither Rome nor Wittenberg.[26]

Even though a council would surely provoke a crisis, Paul III was now more convinced than ever that it was the only option, for to do nothing seemed even worse. He was also further convinced that reconciliation with the Protestants was impossible and that the council, therefore, was for the benefit of Catholics. On June 15 he communicated to the emperor through Contarini that he was going to convene the council immediately.

Once again negotiations opened on the council's location. Not France nor Spain because the Germans would not go. Not Germany because the French would not go. Not the Papal States because the Protestants would not go. The plea for it to be held "in German lands" continued to prevail. The range of possibilities was extremely small. Paul and Charles were able to agree to Trent, the emperor's first choice. On the Italian side of the Alps (and therefore, though not ideal, acceptable to Paul), Trent was under Habsburg hegemony and therefore could be considered "in German lands." Francis objected that Trent delivered the council into the emperor's hands.

Over the date of May 22, 1542, Paul III in the bull *Initii Nostri Huius Pontificatus* convoked "a holy, ecumenical, and general council to be opened the first day of November of the present year 1542 . . . in the city of Trent, for all nations a commodious, free, and convenient place." He again set forth the three interlocking goals of his pontificate: peace among Christian princes, the resolution of the religious division, and, with those two accomplished, a holy war against "the Turk, our godless and ruthless enemy." He devoted much of the bull to reviewing his efforts up to that point to accomplish those goals.

The bull was published on June 29, the feast of Saints Peter and Paul. Less than two weeks later Francis declared war against Charles. The declaration immediately destroyed any possibility of holding a council in which the two major powers would sit together in the same room. Charles, furious now at Paul for his policy of neutrality in the face of what the emperor saw as the king's many crimes, which included colluding with Schmalkalden and even with the sultan, declared flatly that for the duration of the war it would be impossible for bishops and others from the empire to be sent to the council.

Paul, like his predecessor and many others, had always been wary of Charles. His refusal now to aid Charles with men and money was not the first strain on their relationship, and it certainly would not be the last. In their quest for a council Paul and Charles had forged an uneasy and fragile alliance. In this instance, even without the emperor's cooperation, Paul continued with plans for the council. He appointed legates, among whom was the young but already skilled Giovanni Morone, and dispatched them to Trent.

But obstacles sprang up on all sides. Paul himself seemed to waver in his resolve for a council, especially for a council meeting at Trent, so far from Rome and in the Habsburg domains. During the months that dragged on, Paul and Charles at one point arranged to meet for five days at the small town of Busseto near Parma to settle their differences. Since rulership of the Duchy of Milan was an up-front point of contention between Charles and Francis, the pope suggested a solution: in exchange for a large sum of money, Charles would bestow the duchy on Ottavio Farnese, one of the pope's grandsons. The proposal, ill advised in the extreme, strengthened Charles's suspicions that in the long run family advancement guided Paul III's policies. Nothing came of the proposal but distrust.

The war continued. On September 29, 1543, ten months after the date originally set for the opening, Paul III published the bull *Etsi Cunctis* once again suspending the council. The few bishops who had appeared at Trent left for home. They would be loathe ever again to take seriously a summons to a council. Everything seemed lost, especially as the relationship between Charles and Paul degenerated further due to many causes, not least of which were the dynastic machinations with

Francophile implications of another papal grandson, the young, talented, and ambitious Cardinal Alessandro Farnese.[27]

Then, in the summer of 1544, Charles scored such important victories over Francis that his army threatened Paris itself. The French king sued for peace, and in September in a secret clause in the settlement between the two monarchs, the Peace of Crépy, he agreed to a council being held at Trent, Cambrai, or Metz and committed himself to sending bishops and theologians. With the war over and with Francis's agreement to cooperate on the council, the principal obstacle had been removed. Paul moved into action and, with the concurrence of the two monarchs, announced in November that the council would meet at Trent on March 15, *Laetare* Sunday, the fourth Sunday of Lent, four months hence.

The date was unrealistic. Rulers throughout Christendom had to be informed. Bishops, theologians, and others then had to make preparations for a long trip and for a long period away from home. They had to be convinced that this time the council would happen. Paul himself was in no rush. Only on February 22, 1545, three weeks before the day designated for the opening, did he announce his legates for the council. Pleading his advanced age (he was close to eighty), he would not attend the council in person. The legates, acting in the pope's name and with his authority, were empowered to preside over the council, with exclusive right to propose items for the agenda.[28] Paul gave them a secret bull, also dated February 22, specifically granting them authority to transfer the council to another city and even to dissolve it if necessary, a provision whose use two years later provoked one of the great crises of the council.[29]

Two of the three legates set out for the journey north—Cardinals Marcello Cervini and Giovanni Maria Del Monte, the president of the council and the head of the legation. When they made their ceremonial entrance into Trent on March 13, no prelate other than Tommaso Sanfelice, the bishop of La Cava de' Tirreni, a small diocese south of Rome, had arrived there to take part in the council. Even the third legate, Cardinal Reginald Pole, had not shown up. On the great day itself, March 15, the heavens opened with a torrential rain that poured down from morning until night. Cervini and Del Monte did not stir from their lodgings—"ut domum exire nedum legati," as Cervini's secretary (later secretary of the council), Angelo Massarelli, noted in his diary.[30]

The Council Opens

Skeptics once again had their day. For at least the fourth time the long-awaited and many-times-promised council failed to materialize on a day solemnly announced to the whole world. Although at the beginning of March Paul had ordered the bishops of the Curia and the superiors general of the five mendicant orders to be on their way, those gentlemen took their time. Charles himself requested only seven prelates out of the entire Spanish hierarchy to prepare to make the journey. From the well over one hundred bishops in the Kingdom of Naples, the Spanish viceroy selected only five. Bishops from eastern Europe pleaded that they could not come because of the Turkish peril. And so it went. In such a situation it is not surprising that by the first week in April only a half-dozen bishops had appeared.

Even Cardinal Pole had not yet set out for Trent. This cousin of Henry VIII opposed the king's marriage to Anne Boleyn, for which Henry retaliated by executing Pole's mother, the Countess of Salisbury, and other relatives. Pole feared that thugs hired by Henry might try to assassinate him as he made his way northward to Trent.[31] Later that month, however, taking whatever precautions he could, he undertook the journey. He made it to Trent only on May 4, almost two months after the date assigned for the official opening.

By then more bishops had straggled in. Charles V's envoy to the council, Diego Hurtado de Mendoza, had also arrived. For the solemn liturgy on Pentecost Sunday, May 23, seventeen bishops and five superiors general of the mendicant orders took part. These numbers were pitifully small. For that reason as well as for complex negotiations between

Charles and Paul, the legates were forced time and again to postpone the opening.

A political development of great importance was taking place in the relationship between the two men. The emperor, flush with his victory over Francis and convinced that the Schmalkaldic League had weakened, decided to go to war against it, and he persuaded the pope to be his ally, sending men and money. Two factors moved Charles to this decision. First, he could not tolerate forever the threat of this inimical armed force within the very bounds of his empire, and, second, he was now persuaded that on their own Lutheran leaders would never agree to go to Trent as long as the league gave them cover. With a victory over the league, Charles could force them to go. If they were still able somehow to resist, he could force them afterward to accept the council's decisions. This was "the emperor's great plan," as Jedin calls it.

Charles and Paul were now partners in an enterprise other than the council, even though the two were directly related. The pope's contribution to the emperor's plan was not small. It included the promise of 12,000 soldiers for a period of four months, plus a subsidy of 200,000 ducats along with extensive rights to ecclesiastical revenues in Spain.[32] The two rulers distrusted each other, but at this point they were able to lay their misgivings aside as they waited for spring, when the emperor would be able to put his forces onto the field of battle.

At Trent bishops and theologians continued to arrive, some of whom were men of considerable ability. From Spain they included two Dominican theologians—Bartolomeo Carranza, later archbishop of Toledo and primate of all Spain, and Domingo de Soto, a highly respected theologian and former confessor to the emperor. The exiled bishop of Upsala, Olaus Magnus, enjoyed a deserved reputation for learning. Girolamo Seripando, the prior general of the Augustinians, was a theological luminary who would play an especially important role in the discussions on justification, as well as being one of the few major figures to participate in all three periods of the council.[33] Although in late summer more bishops arrived, the numbers remained small.

Meanwhile the legates, hard pressed from all sides and more discouraged perhaps than anyone else, had exhausted their credibility with promises of an opening that never happened. Rumors spread, solidly founded, that the pope wanted to transfer the council to another city, possibly even to Rome. The emperor in the meantime insisted that, once opened, the council deal at least for a while exclusively with reform and not touch doctrinal questions. Amid these tensions the legates and the others assembled for the council found in the bishop of Trent, Cardinal Cristoforo Madruzzo, a host who did his utmost to provide for their comfort and well-being and who entertained them lavishly in his magnificent residence, the Castello del Buonconsiglio.

Then, finally, on November 13 word arrived by courier from Rome that the council would open on December 13, *Gaudete* Sunday, the third Sunday of Advent, 1545. And thus it came to pass. At 9:30 that morning the procession made its way through the streets of Trent from the church of the Most Holy Trinity to the Romanesque cathedral of Saint Vigilius, where the spacious, raised chancel or sanctuary had been converted into space for the council to meet.

Present as full-fledged council participants were the four cardinals (the three legates plus Madruzzo); four archbishops (from Aix, Palermo, Upsala, and Armagh); twenty-one bishops (all from Italy except for four Spaniards, one Frenchman, one Englishman, and one German), and five superiors general of the mendicant orders.[34] The showing was absurdly small and disproportionately Mediterranean.

Francis, after seeming ready to send a sizeable delegation, reneged, so that only one French archbishop and one bishop opened the council.[35] Charles did better. German bishops pleaded that they could not leave for Trent because of the precarious situation in their dioceses, which meant that only the procurator of the archbishop of Mainz showed up. But with four prelates from Spain, five from the Kingdom of Naples (including Sicily), and Cardinal Madruzzo, who was always listed in official documents as *Germanus,* the imperial party was relatively strong. Paul as well as the other Italian princes were, in proportion to the large number of bishops in their realms, ineffectual or reluctant when it came to getting them to the council.

Present in the chancel at the opening ceremony, however, and augmenting the council as voting members, were three Benedictine abbots and the five superiors general of the mendicant orders.[36] Present in the church itself were forty-two theologians, all but four of whom were from the mendicant orders, plus several diplomats accredited to the council, and a number of local notables, including women.

After Del Monte celebrated the Mass of the Holy Spirit, he began the formalities that officially opened the Council of Trent. When the formalities were finished and Del Monte had imparted the final blessing, the choir intoned the *Te Deum*. Five hours had elapsed since the procession set out for the cathedral. When the *Te Deum* ended, the prelates, beginning with Madruzzo and the legates, spontaneously turned and embraced one another, many with tears in their eyes—"con le lacrime agli occhi," noted Massarelli. They had just participated in an event they had long despaired of ever seeing happen.[37]

3

The First Period, 1545–1547

[handwritten notes]
Dealt c̄ .
1) "Justification" Luther's by "faith alone"
   & original sin
2) residence / # of parishes / benefices
3) Sacraments 7 vs Luther's 2 { Bapt / Euch
4)

On December 18, five days after the solemn opening, the prelates gathered in the great hall of the Giroldo palace, which is where the plenary working sessions of the council, the "General Congregations," were to be held.[1] These General Congregations, which usually met in both the morning and the afternoon of a given day, were the venue for discussion and debate on the issues facing the council.

They must be distinguished from the "Sessions," which were one-day, formal, principally ceremonial occasions that were always held in the cathedral. The opening ceremony on December 13 was, thus, Session 1 of the Council of Trent. The subsequent Sessions, besides a Mass, an oration or sermon, and other, more properly religious ceremonies, essentially consisted in reading the decrees that had been debated and finalized in the previous General Congregations. The reading was followed by the final vote approving them. Over the course of the three periods of the council, there were only twenty-five Sessions (listed in Appendix A) but hundreds of General Congregations. In addition to these two types of plenary meetings, there were smaller working groups that prepared and edited drafts of documents and performed other tasks as necessity arose.

That first General Congregation, on December 18, did not go particularly well. The two French prelates—the archbishop of Aix and the bishop of Agde—proposed suspending further action until "the Most Christian King" sent envoys, prelates, and theologians.[2] The proposal got nowhere but raised suspicions that this was a ploy by Francis I to obstruct the council. An even more serious problem emerged. It became clear that neither the legates nor anybody else had prepared an agenda for the council or tried to compose a set of procedures. During the long ten months in Trent while the legates and the others awaited word about the opening of the council, they, for whatever reason, had taken virtually no steps to ensure a brisk start to the council.

The General Congregations of December 22 and 29 fared little better except that in the latter the critical question of who had the right to vote was, after heated discussion, settled: bishops of course had the right; and, yes, the superiors general of the mendicant orders; yes for the abbots but in a restricted way; no for envoys and theologians. The proctors or vicars of absentee bishops could express their opinion but not have a true vote.[3] Much time was also consumed in questions of precedence in seating, in order of speaking, and in other matters of protocol, which throughout the council continued to cause problems.

Meanwhile, with a Session announced for January 7, the General Congregation of January 4 had to prepare for it. During that meeting Giovanni Maria Del Monte, the president, informed the council about some points contained in a letter from Cardinal Alessandro Farnese, the person through whom his grandfather normally communicated with the legates. The letter stipulated that the council was to begin by addressing the doctrinal issues but in such a way that only the errors of the Reformers and not the Reformers themselves be condemned. The first part of the stipulation about beginning with doctrine slipped by at that moment, as if the council were acquiescing. The latter part the council implicitly adopted so that it became standard procedure, different from previous councils at which offenders such as Arius and Hus were condemned by name.[4]

The only item the legates presented for the agenda of the upcoming Session three days hence was an innocuous decree, drawn up probably by Del Monte, on "the manner of living" during the council, which exhorted everyone to prayer, fasting, courtesy in argument, and so forth. Surprisingly, the decree sparked a sharp debate, not about the contents, with which it was difficult to disagree, but about how the council described itself in the opening words, "This holy Council of Trent, lawfully assembled in the Holy Spirit . . ." Braccio Martelli, the bishop of Fiesole, destined to be a thorn in the legates' side, insisted that the phrase "representing the universal church" be inserted, in conformity with the practice of previous councils.[5] The legates feared that the expression, which in fact was used only at Constance and Basel, might imply that the council had power to act against the pope, as did those earlier councils. They took the bishop's intervention as an ominous sign.

As the discussion evolved, Del Monte let slip that the pope had to be consulted on such a change. His comment immediately raised the emotional heat in the room. It unwittingly broached the explosive question of the authority—that is, the freedom and autonomy—of the council vis-à-vis Paul III. After verbal fireworks, arguments in favor of leaving the wording as it was finally seemed to prevail, but in the formal vote on the document at the Session on January 7, nine prelates signified on their ballots approval only on condition that the contested words be inserted.

Those nine votes constituted slightly less than a third of the voting members of the council, not a sufficient number to require changing the wording or re-opening the discussion, but large enough to signify dissension in the ranks. The votes, along with other factors, gave rise in the minds of some of those present to suspicions of Lutheran-friendly sentiments in their midst. It signaled, also, that Pisa, Constance, and Basel had not been forgotten and that the question of the relationship between pope and council would dog Trent from its opening until its close. It was destined to be a major issue-under-the-issues.

The vote was a wake-up call for the legates—the assembly would not meekly follow their lead. Although Paul III had given them exclusive right of proposal in the council, that did not mean, they now saw, that they could altogether control the council's direction. The incident also brought home to them that they had to tread warily if they wanted to avoid opening discussion on the hot but fundamental question of the council's freedom to act. Despite their efforts and the efforts of their successors as legates, the question simply would not go away. It at times surged to the surface to threaten the council's very viability.

The legates operated on a short leash from Rome. In just a little over a week, for instance, between January 5 and 14, they sent five reports to Paul III, yet the pope complained that he was not kept well enough informed. He wanted "details about everything"—"minutamente il tutto."[6] Nervous about the direction the council might take, he saw the legates as executors of his directives, and to them he, in fact if not in theory, conceded little discretionary power. The legates, moreover, were not the only persons at the council writing to Rome. Others took it upon themselves to inform the pope about what was going on, and they did not hesitate to communicate to him their unfavorable assessment of the legates' conduct.

Paul had meanwhile established in the Curia a deputation of cardinals to advise him on the council. The commission reviewed the legates' reports and also the drafts of the council's decrees. The pope took no important step without seeking the commission's advice. He similarly in consistory consulted with the whole assembly of the cardinals of the Curia before taking any important decision regarding the council. As the council wore on bishops and envoys came to resent these procedures and complained that the pope was holding a minicouncil in Rome to monitor and control the one in Trent.

At this point the council seemed stalled, and the legates puzzled about how to get it moving. By the time of the General Congregation on January 13, a whole month had gone by, and nothing substantial had been accomplished. On that day, however, Del Monte finally asked the members of the council to give thought to the order in which they would address their two tasks—doctrine and reform. At the next General Congregation, five days later, the debate opened, with a number of interventions favoring dealing with reform before doctrine, an option the legates knew Paul III would not tolerate. In fact, just ten days earlier, as mentioned, Del Monte had communicated to the council Farnese's stipulation that doctrine was to be the first item of business, to be completed before addressing reform.

Madruzzo spoke first. As the bishop of Trent, imperial territory, he not surprisingly followed the path favored by Charles V—the council must begin with reform. His argument was standard: abuses caused the problem, and therefore reform of the abuses must be the first step in resolving it: "If the cause is removed, the abuse is more easily removed."[7] Other bishops seconded him, using that same argument, long traditional among Catholics. The session ended without resolution. "Different opinions were expressed by different persons"—"Varia varii dixerunt," say the official Acts of the council, a summary applicable to most of the council's discussions.[8] Irony was not lacking in Madruzzo's advocacy of reform. He was the bishop of Trent and the administrator (really therefore bishop) of Brixen, an abuse surely to be targeted in any discussion of reform.

The subject had to be taken up again at the next General Congregation, on January 22, which opened with a long intervention by Madruzzo defending his position. During the proceedings, Agostino Bonuccio, the learned and fair-minded superior general of the Servite Order and one of the few voting members of the council who knew the writings of the Reformers first-hand, helped tip the debate.[9] He countered Madruzzo's moralistic argument with the correct observation that in the Reformers' opinion bad teaching had caused the bad practice. Therefore doctrine should have precedence. When the influential and highly respected Cardinal Pedro Pacheco, the bishop of Jaén, spoke in favor of treating the two on parallel tracks, the issue reached its critical point.

The council began to recognize that the two subjects were closely related. By the end of the Congregation, it determined almost unanimously to treat dogma and reform in tandem.[10] Every decision on dogma would be accompanied by one on reform. This was the solution the legates had advocated and supported, and it became the pattern the council followed throughout its course. The legates were pleased.

Paul III was not. Through Cardinal Farnese he expressed his disapproval of the council's taking up reform, afraid that this would inevitably touch upon the practices of the Curia.[11] His displeasure was so severe that it gave rise in Rome to rumors he would recall the legates and replace them with others. It fell to Cervini to reply. The parallel pattern, he insisted, was the best the legates could manage. He argued that for the legates to insist upon another course would be disastrous and hinted that, if the pope himself began the reform of the Curia, he would forestall council action in that regard. This was by no means the last time Cervini made that point in his communications to Rome.

In no one were the abuses decried by reformers more glaringly exemplified than in the person who stood at the pope's right hand and communicated his directives to the council, Alessandro Farnese. Shortly after naming him a cardinal at age fourteen, Paul named him vice-chancellor of the Roman Church, one of the most important ecclesiastical offices in the church after the papacy itself. At about the same time he conferred upon him two of the wealthiest benefices in Christendom—the archbishoprics of Avignon and Monreale. That was only the beginning. Alessandro in the course of his long career held thirteen bishoprics, though not all at the same time. The income he derived from these and his many other benefices was enormous. It is small wonder that the House of Farnese wanted to hold discussion of reform at bay.

Until the legates received assurance that the pope accepted, however reluctantly, the parallel tracts, they could not put up for discussion a decree authorizing it, scheduled though it was for a solemn vote at Session 3 on February 4. They had to resort, therefore, to evasions to justify to the council why no formal action was being taken on the matter. The council members were, of course, astute enough to realize what was going on, which sowed between them and the legates further seeds of suspicion.

When February 4 rolled around, the only action the council took was publicly to subscribe to the Nicene-Constantinopolitan Creed. Cervini adduced the precedent of ancient councils as justification for the measure. In the Middle Ages, moreover, Lateran Council IV, in 1215, had opened with a creed, and the Council of Florence, in the bulls of union with both the Armenians and the Copts, included one.[12] In the mid-sixteenth century, with accusations of heresy flying through the air, having the council fathers profess their orthodoxy was not an unreasonable measure. Still, for Trent to do nothing more than that in a solemn Session after six weeks of meetings seemed almost a mockery of what was expected on such an occasion, as those present were aware.

The council had little to show for itself, but that was about to change. Moreover, the situation was not as bleak as it seemed. The legates, for instance, finally won Paul III's reluctant approval of parallel decrees. The agreement was a major step forward. During these early weeks, also, the council established that it was not going to be a rubber stamp, and it had begun to gain a sense of itself as a body. By discussing seemingly superficial matters of protocol, it had laid remote but important foundations for procedural mechanisms that were thorough and fair and that opened effective communication between bishops and theologians.

Neither before nor during the council was a comprehensive set of procedures drawn up, approved, and committed to writing. By February, however, two absolutely fundamental procedural principles were firmly in place—the legates' right to set the agenda; and the pattern of issuing in each instance parallel tracts of doctrine and reform. But by a process of trial and error in these early months mechanisms rapidly developed for handling the business of the council. By April basic patterns were in place that, with sometimes considerable ad hoc improvisation, prevailed to the end of the council.[13]

In matters of doctrine the following became standard steps:

1. On a given issue, one or more persons, often theologians, scrutinized the Reformers' writings to develop a series of questions derived from them or to extract questionable or heretical statements. These questions or statements were numbered and called articles and were then delivered to the theologians and the bishops.

2. Theologians accredited to the council took the floor in turn and presented their views on the articles. There was thus no "debate" as an ongoing give-and-take but only in the attenuated sense of a serial presentation of similar or dissimilar views on a topic: "Each theologian gives his opinion, either defending or opposing the heretics' positions."[14] These meetings, which might go on for many days or weeks, were called Congregations of Theologians or, later, the Congregation of Minor Theologians to distinguish them from Major Theologians, that is, bishops with degrees in theology. They lasted for several hours and met twice a day, morning and afternoon. Although bishops were not strictly required to attend, they knew these Congregations were for their benefit. Most therefore considered attendance a duty and availed themselves of the opportunity, especially as these Congregations assumed the status of an official procedure of the council. The bishops listened in silence.

3. The bishops themselves then in similarly serial fashion offered their opinions on the articles during the General Congregations. They had at their disposal summaries of the theologians' opinions, put together by Massarelli, the council's secretary.

4. When the bishops finished speaking, usually after a number of such General Congregations, a deputation of bishops, aided by theologians, formulated a draft decree.

5. The bishops then in General Congregations discussed and amended the draft, which sometimes had to be redrafted more than once.

6. The final version was approved in a formal Session, open to the public.

This process, though long and tedious, was thorough and built consensus. The goal was to achieve a unanimous or nearly unanimous approval of the decree in its final form.

The theologians played therefore an indispensable role at Trent and were fully integrated into the council's functioning. They came to the council at the behest of their sovereigns, their bishops, or their religious orders, which means the pope had no say in choosing them except for those he sent in his own name. During the second period, for instance, the pope named two theologians, the emperor seven, Queen Mary of Hungary (the emperor's sister) eight, the bishops fifteen, the religious orders twenty-two. The overwhelming majority of those named were from the mendicant orders. Before coming to Trent relatively few had direct knowledge of the writings of the Reformers, and far, far fewer could read German. Although the theologians had been trained in dispassionate analysis of texts, they almost without exception read the Reformers with unsympathetic eyes.[15]

For reform issues the process, as it developed, was simpler, swifter, less formalized, more varied, and often modified, sometimes drastically. The theologians played no formal part in it. The legates sometimes reserved the draft to themselves, an unpopular procedure with many members of the council. At other times a deputation of bishops with degrees in canon law, known as the Congregation of Canonists, drew up a draft decree, which was then discussed by the bishops in General Congregations. After the initial go-around the draft was remanded back to the legates or canonists for reformulation. When a majority of bishops were satisfied, it was submitted to final and formal vote in a public Session. Here, too, virtual unanimity was the goal.

Deputations or committees of various kinds, therefore, played an important role at Trent. Some, as mentioned, formulated drafts of decrees, while others undertook different tasks as occasion warranted. The members were chosen in different ways—sometimes by secret vote of the bishops, more often by nomination by the legates, who then asked for approval from the assembly. Sometimes, however, the legates did not ask—an understandably unpopular procedure. During the last period of the council, Cardinal Giovanni Morone, the president of the legates, on occasion convened in his quarters a number of prelates of his own choice to hammer out issues of special difficulty before they arrived at the floor of the council, a procedure that saved time in the General Congregations but that as "private meetings" also did not please everybody.

As mentioned, major players in the council were the envoys of the various heads of state whose bishops took part in the council. Upon their arrival in Trent they made a solemn, ceremonial entrance into the city. When they appeared in the council chambers for the first time to present their credentials, they addressed the council, an important opportunity for them to inform the prelates of their sovereign's priorities for the council. Then they assumed their seats of honor, which sometimes sparked serious controversy over the order of precedence that the seating indicated. If they were laymen, they did not have a vote on the documents nor could they without special permission address the council except on that first occasion. The exalted status they enjoyed is clearly indicated in the official records of the council, where they are always listed before the archbishops and bishops, just after the legates and cardinals.[16]

They were far from being passive observers. They sometimes with insistence confronted the legates with the wishes or demands of their sovereigns, with whom they kept in close contact, and they often served as the rallying point for the bishops from their sovereign's domains. They sometimes received previews of reform documents before the bishops saw them, and were asked their opinion on them. During this first period, Charles V was ably represented by Diego Hurtado de Mendoza and Francisco de Toledo, both laymen. The former brought with him his splendid library, a resource badly needed at Trent. The latter was so important in both this and the second period that some critics spoke of Trent as "The Council of Toledo."

In the three legates, finally, the council had competent leaders. Both Del Monte and Cervini were subsequently elected pope, and in 1549 Pole missed being elected by only a slender margin. Different in personality and perspectives, the three men were able to work together without major incident, which would not be true for the legates at the third period of the council. Yes, they were the pope's men through and through, especially Del Monte and Cervini, imposed on the council by Paul and not elected by it. They generally proved themselves adroit in steering a middle course between Paul's insistent directives and the equally insistent will of the council fathers. To have bowed to one or the other of those two forces would have meant disaster for the council. If the legates let the council have its way against something Paul adamantly opposed, Paul would not hesitate to dissolve it. If the legates too ostensibly gave in to Paul, the council ran the danger of rebelling and exacerbating the problems rather than resolving them. This situation was far from ideal, but nothing about the Council of Trent was ideal. It rested precariously on a bed of fragile and shifting compromises.

Paul III made Del Monte a legate, indeed, president of the council, because he was a skilled canonist and had considerable experience in practical affairs—governor of Rome, for instance, and governor of Bologna and the Romagna. Just as important, Paul knew that, should the matter come up, Del Monte would defend the principle of papal superiority over a council. He also knew that he would not allow questions of reform to venture into forbidden waters.

Del Monte suffered recurring bouts of illness, especially gout, which meant he periodically had to delegate the presidency to another legate, but he never lost his leadership role. Sometimes blunt and impulsive, he also could lessen tensions by humor and quick wit. In keeping with his canonical background, he took as his special remit the deliberations dealing with reform. Important though he was for this first period, he was even more important for the second, which, as Pope Julius III, he convoked himself.[17] He is perhaps best defined as a careerist, a "company man," concerned to do the right thing but within narrowly circumscribed parameters.

To Marcello Cervini, who owed his rise to Farnese patronage, Paul III had before the council confided several important diplomatic missions and made him a mentor in diplomacy to the young Alessandro. Of the three legates, Paul seemed to trust him the most. Charles V trusted him least. Cervini, loyal to the Farnese, did not hide his displeasure at prelates at the council who opposed the papal program. But he was a conscientious churchman who became ever more won over to the cause of reform, while firmly believing it best done by the papacy rather than by the council. When upon his election as pope he discovered that two nephews, aged fifteen and thirteen, were in Rome expecting to benefit from his election, he, in striking contrast to Paul III, refused to grant them an audience and ordered them to leave the city.

Cervini had no formal training in theology, but he developed a keen interest in the Fathers of the Church and sponsored the publication of some of their writings. At Trent he was therefore sensitive to the doctrinal issues and, in accordance with his Humanist training, urged fidelity to the *fontes*, that is, to the writings from the ancient church considered normative. From Trent he sent hither and yon for texts needed to throw light on the issues. At the council it therefore fell to him to guide the doctrinal agenda, just as to Del Monte the reform.[18] He died in 1555 only three weeks after being elected as Pope Marcellus II.

In the Anglophone world Reginald Pole is the best known of the three legates, not for his role at Trent but for his role later as papal legate to Mary Tudor's England and as archbishop of Canterbury during her brief reign.[19] Ostensibly for reasons of health, he left Trent in June 1546, barely six months after the council began. Although his absence was supposed to be temporary, he never returned. Even during those first months at Trent, he operated in the shadow of Del Monte and Cervini.

Why did Paul III choose him as a legate, a decision almost designed to infuriate Henry VIII? We can only speculate. Although Pole had lived in Italy for a number of years and felt at home there, he gave an international balance to the legation. His published "letter" to Henry VIII on the unity of the church in 1535–1536 was taken as a robust defense of papal primacy. At about the same time Paul showed his confidence in him by appointing him to the Commission on the Reform of the Church that issued the *Consilium,* quoted earlier, with its blunt words about papal abuses.

Pole's membership in the circle of devout persons made up of Contarini, Morone, the poet Vittoria Colonna, and others (sometimes called the *spirituali*) had through study of Saint Paul led him to an understanding of justification not unlike Luther's. Although keenly interested therefore in the issue, he left Trent just as the discussion began. He managed to fend off every effort to have him return. He remained, however, a respected figure in the Roman ecclesiastical scene. Three years later, in the conclave upon the death of Paul III, Pole lost the election to the papacy to his former colleague as legate, Del Monte.[20]

Scripture, Traditions, and Preaching the Gospel

With Session 3 behind them, the legates planned to take up Original Sin, a doctrine inseparable from justification and therefore leading right into the heart of the issues central to the Reformers. But in the end they decided that, especially because of controversy over which books belonged in the canon of Scripture, the council needed first to address that problem so as to establish the basis on which it could legitimately make its doctrinal points. The legates almost certainly did not anticipate how long and difficult the discussion would be, especially as it quickly moved beyond the narrow question of the canon. The council spent the next two months elaborating two relatively short decrees: the first "On the Sacred Books and Apostolic Traditions," and the second "On the Vulgate Edition and on the [Proper] Way of Interpreting Sacred Scripture."

Luther and other Reformers had in one form or another questioned or rejected the canonical status of the so-called Apocrypha (or deuterocanonical books), the books received by the early church from the Greek Old Testament, the Septuagint, that were not part of the Hebrew Bible. The Apocrypha included books such as Tobit, Judith, and First and Second Maccabees. Luther's giving preferential ranking even to certain books he recognized as canonical, especially to the Epistle to the Romans, and his dismissal of the Epistle of James as "an epistle of straw" contributed to the urgency of the topic. Moreover, his insistence on "Scripture alone" as the basis for Christian faith and his rejection in that regard of all "human" traditions added a further, crucial element to any discussion dealing with the role of Scripture in doctrinal and theological argument.

There was, however, a broader background. The textual and philological aspects of the Humanist movement had made Europeans aware of discrepancies between the biblical text in its original languages—Hebrew and Greek—and the received Latin translation, the Vulgate. This research had in turn spawned new Latin translations. Erasmus's translation of the New Testament has already been mentioned, but other scholars were also hard at work. Sancti Pagnini, an Italian Dominican, was, for instance, a pioneer in his Latin translation of the Hebrew Old Testament and the Greek New, published in 1528. It carried a letter of approbation from Pope Clement VII and was used by both Catholics and Protestants.[21]

The printing press, born almost simultaneously with the beginning of critical philology in the middle of the fifteenth century, made widely available not only these new Latin but also vernacular translations. The same was true for Scriptural commentaries and paraphrases, which had also proliferated in the early decades of the century. The prelates at Trent considered some of these texts suspect or clearly heterodox, and some prelates were in principle opposed to vernacular Bibles.

At the General Congregation of February 12 discussion opened on the canon. A clear consensus emerged to reaffirm the "wide canon," that is, including the Apocrypha, which had been ratified at the Council of Florence a century earlier.[22] The council at Trent felt, in fact, that it was not free to contravene such an important enactment of a previous council. But questions arose as soon as it became clear that the Reformers were not the only ones to question the status of the Apocrypha and, indeed, that the controversy over them went back to the patristic era, with Jerome rejecting them as part of the canon and Augustine defending them. Under these circumstances, should the council, if it accepted the Apocrypha as canonical, undertake a defense of its position? Or should it at least take note of the problem and make some comment about a special status for the Apocrypha within the canon?

Bonuccio made a crucial intervention: the council should not try to resolve questions long disputed among reputable theologians, certainly not among the Fathers of the Church such as Jerome and Augustine. Such questions should remain open. That is the course the council should follow in this instance, and that is the understanding we have of the canon approved by Florence. Bonuccio's intervention helped turn the tide. The council agreed simply to affirm the Florentine canon but with the understanding that it was not taking a stand on the disputed question. Up until Session 4, on April 8, the matter occasionally came up again for discussion, but essentially the council did not move beyond where it was on this day.[23]

That absolutely crucial qualification of the decree may have been clear to the prelates at the council, but the text they produced gave no hint of it. In the context of the controversies of the sixteenth century, in fact, the decree reads like an unqualified affirmation of the wide canon. No wonder, then, that Catholics appropriated and clung to that canon as a mark of their identity, to be defended in its integrity against all comers. This decision constituted the first instance of subsequent misunderstandings of what the council intended that became standard interpretations, impossible to dislodge even from the minds of scholars who should know better. In this case at least, the council itself must be held responsible for the misunderstanding.

With the canon settled in principle, the council moved to the even thornier question of traditions and their role in determining Christian faith and practice. Before opening the question to a General Congregation, the legates on February 20 convened the theologians to thrash out the parameters of the problem, the first instance of such a meeting, which thereafter became standard procedure. February 20, 1546, marked, therefore, the birth of the Congregation of Theologians. The bishops, present for the meeting, listened but did not intervene. The theologians' deliberations surely raised the level of the discussions in the subsequent General Congregations and made the bishops, as well as the legates, aware of the complexity of the problem. Beyond that it is impossible to say what impact they had.

There were, as the discussion in the General Congregations made clear, many different kinds of traditions. Doctrinal traditions. Disciplinary traditions. Ecclesiastical traditions. Apostolic traditions. Traditions with an obvious basis in Scripture. Traditions with seemingly little or no such basis. Fasting on Friday? Infant baptism? The sign of the cross? The observance of Sunday? Auricular confession? Christ's descent into hell, which was an article of the Creed but not easily or at all found in the New Testament? Communion under both forms, bread and wine, an early apostolic tradition no longer observed? Are the decisions of previous councils traditions? What about the writings of the Fathers?

These questions and more burst onto the floor of the council at the General Congregation of February 26. Many questions, few answers, much confusion, considerable disagreement. Were not all truths necessary for salvation found in Scripture, asked the bishop of Chioggia?[24] Should not the council list the traditions it accepts as the basis for its decisions, asked the bishop of Sinigaglia?[25] Was not the council wasting its time on a matter of little importance, asked the bishop of Astorga, to the surprise of virtually everybody?[26] The confusion and differences of opinion made one thing clear: a precise definition of the traditions under consideration was absolutely necessary.

In view of Luther's Scripture-alone principle, the most fundamental question facing the council in this regard was whether or to what extent there were truths or practices essential to Christian belief and life not found in the New Testament. By Scripture alone Luther in the first instance meant to exclude "philosophy" or "reason," that is, Aristotle's Ethics, which taught that goodness was possible without faith and grace. But in Luther and especially in later polemics the principle soon extended to traditions and ceremonies. For the council the problem was complicated by the fact that the Fathers of the Church and even medieval theologians like Aquinas seemed in their up-front statements to hold a Scripture-alone principle, even though in reality their positions were generally more qualified.[27]

After the discussion of February 26, confused though it was, the deputation responsible for drafting the first decree (doctrinal), scheduled for approval at the next Session, set about its task. In the meantime the council turned to the parallel (reform) decree, that is, a decree on abuses regarding Scripture and ways to promote correct understanding of it. What was the council to say about different versions of the Bible, both Latin and vernacular, about commentaries, about the responsibilities of publishers, booksellers, and bishops in this regard, about the reading of the Bible by ordinary Christians? In German-speaking lands Luther's brilliant translation of the New Testament from the Greek (1522) had run through a hundred printings in just one decade.

Because of the practical implications of these questions, the bishops showed a keener interest in them than in the seemingly more academic problems they had until then been dealing with. Opinions differed sharply about vernacular Bibles—they were the font of all heresies, or they were the essential nourishment for the godly life. The debate became so heated on this issue, especially in a sharp exchange on March 17 between Cardinal Pacheco and Cardinal Madruzzo, though they were the two "imperial" cardinals, that the legates hoped, in vain, to avoid its being raised again.[28] But Pacheco, adamantly opposed to vernacular Bibles, would not let the issue rest.

For the council the problem had political ramifications and therefore extended beyond the desirability or the dangers of vernacular translations. In France and Spain (as well as England) such translations had long been forbidden. If the council advocated them, the episcopacy and probably the crown would countermand the decree. If it forbade them, Germany, Italy, Poland, and other places where they were allowed would react just as negatively but for the opposite reason.

Latin was the international language of theological discourse, Catholic and Protestant, and the official language of the council. Thus the question of the Latin Bible was unavoidable, especially in light of the criticisms leveled at the Vulgate for the past century, ever since Lorenzo Valla's *Adnotationes in Novum Testamentum* comparing the Greek original with the Vulgate. The bishops and theologians at Trent, many of them Humanistically trained, knew very well that the Vulgate needed revision, but were its problems so serious as to prevent its use by the council in its deliberations and by the church at large? If they were, what was the alternative text? Should the council in any case recommend that the Vulgate be revised? If so, by whom?

Discussion on how to deal with printers and booksellers proceeded with less rancor and fewer complications because the council had precedents. Not only had local councils such as Bourges and Sens taken measures against Lutheran books, but even before the Reformation broke out Lateran V had published a decree prohibiting the printing of books dealing with religious issues without the prior permission of the local bishop.[29]

Finally, on March 22 the council fathers received the drafts of the two decrees, "On the Sacred Books and Apostolic Traditions" and "On the Vulgate Edition and the [Proper] Mode of Interpreting Sacred Scripture." These texts were subjected to further criticism in the General Congregations from this point forward until Session 4, on April 8, but the drafting deputations had managed to produce documents that substantially survived the rhetorical and theological fireworks that exploded in the council chamber, especially over the relationship of Scripture to apostolic traditions and over the publication of the Bible in the vernacular.

Regarding the former issue, for instance, Jacopo Nacchianti, the bishop of Chioggio, created an uproar by declaring, "To put Scripture and traditions on the same level is impious."[30] Regarding the latter, Pacheco and Madruzzo had another go at it on April 1. Del Monte forestalled a rejoinder by Pacheco by ringing the bell and bringing the Congregation to a close.[31] On that same day Pietro Bertano, the bishop of Fano, one of the sharpest minds at the council and a key member of the drafting deputation, had put the delegation's declaration of the Vulgate as "authentic" into a broad context:

> We do not consider it an abuse that there are various and different translations of the Bible because this was tolerated in ancient times and should be tolerated today. . . . We wish the Vulgate edition to be accepted as the one authentic version. . . . We do not reject other versions, since we do not want to restrict Christian liberty. Moreover, we do not want even to reject the translations by the heretics, in conformity with the example of antiquity. For it is evident that Aquila, Symmachus, and Theodotion were indeed heretics, and still their translations were not rejected by the ancient church.[32]

That day the council members began voting on the two documents, a process that continued through the next two Congregations.[33] In the

Congregation of April 3, less than a week before the Session, agreement was quickly reached on two points: first, that anonymously printed Bibles should be prohibited, and second, that one edition should be declared authentic, that is, reliable for use in preaching and teaching, and all others, including Protestant ones, were to be passed over in silence, a species of compromise that became typical of the council.[34]

To the relief of the legates, the council was ready for Session 4, on April 8, even though aspects of the reform decree had to be carried over. In comparison with the opening Session, December 13, the number of archbishops had doubled from four to eight and the number of bishops had done almost the same. Prelates had therefore continued to arrive, but the representation was still embarrassingly small.

The Session, which included a long sermon or oration by Bonuccio, the Servite, seemed to go off well. In the course of it, Bonuccio warned the prelates against trying to stamp out every possible aberration and especially against shouting "heresy" and "to the flames" at anybody with whom they disagreed. He spoke of faith that "embraces, beyond assent to the wisdom of the gospel, a certain hope and confidence [fiducia] in the goodness of God and his church that forgives our sins. In this very confidence [fiducia], which Christ looked for in those he healed, is situated and grounded the true and perfect character of Christian faith."[35] It would be difficult to distinguish this definition of faith from Luther's.

An ugly incident followed. Domingo de Soto, the distinguished Spanish theologian, found grave fault with how Bonuccio spoke of faith and of an invisible church, but he also probably felt that the admonition against finding heresy in every corner was directed against himself. If so, the admonition incited rather than restrained him. In conversations after the sermon he accused Bonuccio of promoting heretical ideas. The situation rapidly reached crisis level when Bonuccio overheard him and demanded a public apology. Only after the legates made the two men confront each other in two separate meetings was a measure of civility achieved.[36]

But the principal event in the Session was the ratification of the two decrees.[37] The first decree is three paragraphs long. The most important passage occurs in the first:

> Our Lord Jesus Christ, the Son of God, first proclaimed with his own lips this gospel . . . then he bade it be preached to every creature through his apostles as the source of the whole truth of salvation and rule of conduct. The council clearly perceives that this truth and rule are contained in written books and in unwritten traditions that were received by the apostles from the mouth of Christ himself or else have come down to us, handed on as it were from the apostles themselves at the inspiration of the holy Spirit . . . the council accepts and venerates with a like feeling of piety and reverence [both the Old and New Testaments] . . . as well as traditions concerning both faith and conduct . . . which have been preserved in unbroken sequence in the catholic church.

The next paragraph is a simple listing of the books of the canon, and the third is an anathema of anyone who "in conscious judgment" rejects any of the books of the Bible or the traditions.

Several aspects of the decree need comment. First, as mentioned, the affirmation of the wide canon is problematic because it obscures the council's intent regarding the Apocrypha. Second, although Trent clearly postulated two media through which the message received from Christ and the apostles is transmitted, most (but surely not all) scholars agree that the council did not intend to determine just what the relationship was between those two channels of communication (not "sources," as they have sometimes erroneously been called)—it did not intend, for example, to suppress the view expressed by some of the council fathers about the "sufficiency" of Scripture for salvation.[38]

Third, despite how the decree is often described in theological literature, Trent spoke not of Tradition, that is, of some global category of transmission, but only of traditions, in the plural. Although at this point the council deliberately did not name any, it surely meant quite specific doctrines and practices (infant baptism being an obvious example). Fourth, the council is precise about the traditions of which it is speaking: they are apostolic (originating in Christ or the apostles); put negatively, the council is not speaking of "human" or "ecclesiastical" traditions. Moreover, it is speaking of those apostolic traditions that have been operative in the church "in unbroken sequence" (they have not fallen into desuetude at any point).

Finally, this insistence on unbroken continuity with the apostles will emerge in the council as a leitmotif, a standard justification of its positions vis-à-vis Protestant positions. A response to the Protestant accusation that the church in its teaching departed from the gospel, Trent's insistence on continuity contributed to the Catholic historiographical tradition emerging at this time, in which continuity sometimes was so emphasized as to leave precious little room for change. The emphasis persists as a recognizable Catholic trait even to the present.

The second decree requires less comment. Although in designating the Vulgate as "authentic" (reliable) the drafting committee did not intend to suppress other Latin versions, the decree was subsequently interpreted in that way. It condemned those who in interpreting Scripture turned it into superstition, magic, detraction, flattery, which is an echo of the decree of Lateran V. It said nothing about translations of the Bible into the vernacular.[39] It strictly prohibited, however, anonymous books dealing with matters of faith and prescribed that authors writing on sacred subjects have their books examined and approved by the local bishop, even if the writers were members of religious orders otherwise exempt from episcopal jurisdiction. It insisted that the Vulgate not be printed again until thoroughly corrected—*emendatissime.*

With those decrees now ratified, the legates felt satisfied that after two difficult months they had finally brought the council through to a resolution, not perfect, perhaps, but the best that could be managed under the circumstances. To their dismay they soon discovered that their satisfaction was not shared in Rome, as was made bluntly clear to them in communications, all dated April 17, from four different persons. In general, the people in the Curia, including Paul III, complained that the council had accomplished little—"molto poco," said the pope.[40] In particular, they were puzzled and annoyed that the Vulgate got off so easily, and they did not hesitate to remind the legates that the problems with that text were much deeper than printers' errors. The crudest and most insulting criticism came from one of the legate's own cousins, Giambattista Cervini, "We thought you'd give us a bouncing baby boy, but you produced a crippled little girl."[41]

Dispirited, the legates soldiered on in their thankless task. On April 13 they presented the council with the draft of a reform decree concerning Scripture that it had not had time to deal with and still meet the April 8 deadline for Session 4.[42] The document, a holdover, in effect a Part Two of the reform decree of Session 4, now served as the template for the decree to be approved at the next Session. Early on the council had realized that if it were to effect a reform of pastoral practice, it had to do more than root out evils. It had to take some positive steps, which is precisely what it now attempted to do.

In essence the decree proposed two measures. It ordered, first, that lectureships in Scripture be established in dioceses and religious houses for the instruction of the clergy, especially with a view to improving preaching. The measure was essentially about remedial education, an effort to address the problem of clerical ignorance. By according a privileged role to Scripture it also endorsed a fundamental principle of the Humanists' program, for which Erasmus was the best-known spokesman. The decree wanted to make sure "that the heavenly treasure of the sacred books . . . [not] lie inert and inoperative." The emphasis on the Bible as the touchstone for clergy education found favor with the bishops at the council but was received with reserve by the theologians, who had been trained in Scholasticism and favored that more systematic program.[43]

Second, to ensure that the message of the gospel was proclaimed, the decree mandated that bishops and pastors preach to their flocks on Sundays and Holy Days, a first manifestation of what would become a major preoccupation of the council, providing items for a job description for bishops that would make them into pastors according to the pattern of bishops of the patristic era such as Ambrose and Augustine.

Although these proposals seem on the surface modest and uncontroversial, they brought bounding to the floor of the council several problems of deep consequence that would trouble it for the rest of its history. Requiring bishops and pastors to preach regularly implied that they were present in their diocese or parish, but, as Pacheco reminded the council, his former diocese of Pamplona had not seen a resident bishop for eighty years. Pacheco could with good conscience call the problem to the council's attention because for the six years he was himself bishop of Pamplona, 1539–1545, he had conscientiously resided in the diocese and discharged his episcopal duties.

It was at this moment, therefore, that the absolutely crucial issue of residence made its first appearance at Trent, where bishops of the imperial party like Pacheco now pressed for early discussion of it. Though the legates were able to set it aside for the moment, they saw that it had to come to the floor. As events turned out, episcopal residence ended up as the lightning-rod issue of the council and the defining element in its pastoral reform.

The original draft dealt also at some length with bishops' responsibility for supervising the preaching in their dioceses and thus brought into the open one of the bishops' greatest grievances. The mendicant orders enjoyed in some localities almost a monopoly on preaching. Bishops' resentment of them was fierce and long-standing. The bishops complained that the friars, loaded with papal privileges exempting them from episcopal control, preached what they wanted, where they wanted, when they wanted, flaunting their exemptions in the bishops' faces. The bishops' fury had erupted so violently at Lateran V thirty years earlier as to make the orders fear the council would suppress them. Only Pope Leo X's intervention saved the day for them.[44]

At Trent the bishops were in the main more moderate, but bitter words were exchanged as they tried to impose on the mendicants their right of supervision. Martelli, the outspoken and fiercely independent bishop of Fiesole, lashed out against the mendicants in a long speech on May 10 that was so intemperate that it disrupted the session and brought Cervini and Pole to the defense of the friars.[45] What specifically upset Del Monte was Martelli's denunciation of the orders' privileges, which the legate saw as an implicit attack on the authority of the papacy. He also objected to Martelli's designating bishops as "vicars of Christ," which since the thirteenth century had been a title reserved to the pope.

The more immediate problem for the bishops, however, was how the lectureships were to be funded, especially by the poorer dioceses. The council devised and approved several measures and incorporated them into the decree, but, more important, it for the first time came face-to-face with a brutal fact. Reform had financial implications, sometimes radical. From this point forward those implications affected virtually every reform measure the council undertook. Directly or indirectly somebody had to pay for reform. Not surprisingly, therefore, in the reform decrees of the Council of Trent, taken in the aggregate, finances play a remarkably large role.

For well over a month the council dealt with this decree and only toward the end of May turned to Original Sin. Three weeks before that happened, Francisco de Toledo, Charles V's envoy to the council, paid separate visits to each of the legates to express the emperor's wish that the council complete its work on reform before taking up any doctrinal issues. The legates, knowing that the pope would never acquiesce to such a program, were able to deflect the move, and the emperor did not press it. The incident shows, however, that even with the council now close to five months in course the old differences between pope and emperor about the council's priorities and its order of business had not disappeared.

In its final form the decree mandated lectureships on Scripture for every diocese and religious house and indicated various ways they could be financed. It mandated that such lectureships be established in the houses of study of the mendicants but did not indicate that they displace the Scholastic system traditional in them. It placed supervision of the lectureships firmly in the hands of the local bishop. It did the same for preaching, although it allowed the mendicants freedom to preach in their own churches without being directly authorized by the bishop if they were certified by their own superiors and presented the certification to the bishop. It reminded bishops that they had the authority to restrain and punish those who preached outlandish or heretical ideas.

Most important, the decree mandated that "all bishops, archbishops, primates, and all others who preside over churches are personally [per se ipsos] bound, unless legitimately impeded, to preach the holy gospel of Jesus Christ." Indeed, it defined such preaching as the bishops' "principal" or "special" duty—praecipuum episcoporum munus.[46] The decree marked the first appearance of this idea, to which the council would recur later and upon which it placed great weight.

The decree's larger significance lies, first of all, in its insistence on the authority of the bishop. It was the first step in making Trent into a radically bishop-centered council, intent on enhancing the bishop's role as chief pastor of his diocese. Moreover, with this decree as its beginning the council would in its course bit by bit mandate a number of duties detailing how the bishop was to spend his time once he took up residence. Through a long, sometimes painful, and occasionally inconsistent trajectory, it aimed at promoting an episcopacy dedicated to its traditional pastoral responsibilities, in which preaching held pride of place. This ideal had found expression before the council in literature emanating especially from Humanistic circles, but an ideal it was. It flew in the face of widespread, deeply imbedded social realities, hardily resistant to change.

Original Sin and Justification

In the early months of 1546 the legates still had no clear plan for the agenda on doctrine. In close consultation with Rome they for a while considered proposing a discussion of the binding authority of the decrees of previous councils and similar matters as a basis beyond Scripture and traditions for establishing the church's teaching, but they finally rejected that option. They came to realize how complicated and contentious it would be and how it would open the door to the dangerous subject of the relative authority of popes and councils. They finally decided to move right to the heart of the controverted doctrines, which meant Original Sin and justification. Determined to have a decree ready on the former subject in time for Session 5 on June 17, they on May 24 and 25 convened the theologians for preliminary discussions.

Saint Paul's teaching in the Epistle to the Romans (5:12–21) and First Corinthians (15:22) that through Adam's "Fall" sin and death came into the world was the starting point for the doctrine. According to the teaching developed especially by Saint Augustine in his controversy with the Pelagians, Adam's sin was transmitted by generation from parents to children and affected all members of the human race. Although Christ redeemed the world from that sin, concupiscence remained even in the baptized.

Up to that point Catholics and Lutherans were in agreement. Before the council, however, Catholic controversialists had attacked Luther's teaching, as they understood it, principally on three points: his identification of concupiscence with Original Sin, which meant that Original Sin remained even in the baptized; his insistence that concupiscence was itself a sin in the full sense of the word rather than an inclination to sin; and his consequent insistence on the total corruption of human nature and the utter impotence of the human will regarding salvation. At issue, to put it in its simplest terms, were two things: what the effects of Original Sin were in the individual and what the effects of the remedies for it were that Christ provided. The vast majority of Catholic theologians were loath to admit that the Fall had totally corrupted human nature or that baptism did not render the person truly and intrinsically pleasing to God.

The matter was of course complicated, in the first place because

Luther was not a systematic writer. The Augsburg Confession, the statement of belief authored principally by Philipp Melanchthnon that Lutheran leaders presented in 1530 to Charles V, succinctly expressed their position: "It is also taught among us that we cannot obtain forgiveness of sin and righteousness before God by our own merits, works, or satisfactions, but that we receive forgiveness of sin and become righteous before God by grace, for Christ's sake, through faith, when we believe that Christ suffered for us and that for his sake our sin is forgiven and righteousness and eternal life are given to us. For God will regard and reckon this faith as righteousness, as Paul says in Romans 3 and 4."[47]

The Confession was a conciliatory document, quite different in tone from many of Luther's writings. Note, for instance, that it speaks of justification through faith but not "through faith alone." It was widely circulated, sometimes in slightly different versions, and known at Trent. Not all Catholic theologians, especially members of the Augustinian Order, were convinced "the Lutherans" were altogether wrong in their teaching on both Original Sin and justification, and at Trent the Augustinians' prior general, Girolamo Seripando, was among them. A few others believed that in this instance the differences were more a matter of words than substance. Most felt that the most urgent matter was the accusation that the church taught and subscribed to Pelagianism, the you-can-save-yourself-if-you-just-try-hard-enough version of Christianity.

In their long letter to Farnese on May 28, the legates, fully cognizant of the situation, informed him of the wide range of positions the theologians held and told him that their policy, therefore, was to focus the debate on the most essential points of the church's belief.[48] The most authoritative statements of official teaching on the matter up to that point had been in several provincial councils in antiquity, whose texts were available at Trent—the Second Council of Milevum (417), the Fifteenth (possibly, Sixteenth) Council of Carthage (418), and the Second Council of Orange (529).

Against this background the legates on May 24 submitted to the theologians for their consideration a series of questions under three headings, which came down to the following. First, who contracts this Sin and in what way? From Scripture and traditions what can be said against those who deny the doctrine? Here the legates of course meant the Pelagians. Second, how is this Sin different from other sins, and how can that difference be described? Third, how are we freed from it, and do any traces remain? If so, what are their effects?[49]

Over the course of two days the theologians presented their views, after which in a series of General Congregations the bishops did the same. These were not easy discussions. Opinions were expressed that at least on the surface seemed incompatible. The legates meanwhile commissioned a small deputation to draw up a draft document and submitted it to the theologians, who on June 10 and 11 in the presence of the whole council once again offered their opinions and recommendations.

The draft consisted in four canons. The theologians of course had many suggestions for improvement, but they especially called for more precision. The next draft tried to respond to that call but found it difficult to do so without making use of Scholastic terminology. It now included a clause saying that the council bypassed the question of the Immaculate Conception of Mary (whether Mary was conceived without Original Sin), which was still controverted among Catholics.

The legates received another request from Charles V to delay publication of the decree until after he had undertaken his war against Schmalkalden and achieved victory. They again politely but firmly refused to accede to the emperor's wishes and went ahead with Session 5 on June 17 for the approval of the decree on lectures and preaching and the decree on Original Sin, which now contained six canons.[50] Prefaced to the latter decree was an important statement about the basis on which the council grounded its teaching that goes beyond "Scripture and traditions": "Following the witness of the sacred Scriptures, of the holy Fathers, and of the most authoritative councils, as well as the agreement and judgment of the church, it [the council] determines, confesses, and declares as follows regarding Original Sin."

The first three canons simply restate the condemnations by the councils of the patristic era of positions attributed to the Pelagians: that Adam was not changed for the worse by his sin, that Adam's sin harmed him alone, and that the sin is removed by some human or merely natural powers. The fourth was directed against the Anabaptists, who denied the validity of infant baptism, and the sixth stated that the council did not intend to include Mary in the decree, thus leaving the question open.

Only the fifth canon dealt directly with the teaching at issue. It condemned the view that the guilt of sin remains in the baptized even though it is not attributed to them. It affirmed, further, that "God hates nothing in the reborn [in baptism]" and, indeed, loves them as "innocent, stainless, pure, blameless and beloved children of God." It affirmed that concupiscence is not called sin in the full and proper meaning of the word but, rather, is "a result of sin and inclines to sin."

Taken as a whole, the six canons fulfilled the legates' desire to present a lean and altogether basic statement. They show only the slightest traces of Scholastic terminology. The fifth served as a grounding for the next item on the doctrinal agenda, justification. Not everybody was thoroughly satisfied, especially with the description of concupiscence. Seripando, for instance, finally voted in favor of the decree, but the bishops of La Cava and Pesaro did not. The legates had reason to be gratified. The council was moving ahead.

Present at the Session on June 17 were roughly sixty archbishops and bishops, about the same number as at the previous Session. The legates of course hoped that the number of bishops at the council would increase, but they knew that if the increase came from Spain, France, and Germany, pressure for more radical reform would also proportionately increase. The prospect made them apprehensive.

In January Francis I had set in motion a plan to send a large delegation of prelates, but by March he had abandoned it. Although his reasons for reverting to his earlier policy were, as always, complex, the news of the military alliance of the pope and the emperor against Schmalkalden confirmed his fears that the council was working in the emperor's favor. In late June the king dispatched three envoys to the council but no prelates to supplement the two (sometimes three) already there.[51]

This decision meant the French episcopate was virtually absent from the council, but so was the German. Charles V needed the German bishops at home to support his policy. He was, however, well served by bishops from his other domains, especially from Spain. Cardinals Pacheco and Madruzzo were the recognized leaders of these "imperial" bishops. Representing Charles were, as mentioned, his two envoys, Mendoza and Toledo, who according to standard protocol took precedence in all ceremonies over the envoys of Francis.

On June 21 Cardinal Cervini proposed that the council now take up two further questions: justification (doctrine) and residence (reform). The council agreed but only after objections to treating such important matters before more bishops arrived. In his presentation Cervini stressed the far greater complexity of the justification issue than anything the council had as yet faced.[52] The council had already approved holding the next Session on July 29, little more than a month hence. Prelates who at the time believed the date optimistic were more prescient than they could possibly have imagined. That Session took place not on July 29, 1546, but only after an interval of six difficult months, on January 13, 1547.

The legates were aware of the importance of what the council now undertook. In their report to Rome on June 21, they said, "The significance of the council regarding dogma lies chiefly in the article on justification." They stressed, moreover, that residence was the principal issue for reform, which would easily move through the council once it was clear the Holy See did what it could on its part. They reassured the pope that once decrees on those two subjects were formulated and approved, which would be accomplished by the end of July, the council could quickly be brought to conclusion.[53]

After Cervini opened the General Congregation on June 21, Cardinal Pole made one of his rare interventions. He had been ill and absent for most of the discussion on Original Sin, and on June 28, just a week after this intervention, he left the council for good, missing virtually the whole of the protracted discussion of justification. On June 21 he tried to set the tone for addressing the matter, exhorting those present to increase their prayers that God through the Holy Spirit show them the truth. He urged them to read widely on the matter with an open mind. Included in their reading must be books of "our adversaries," which were to be studied with the same unbiased desire to arrive at the truth as when reading any other book. The bishops should not conclude that "Luther said it. Therefore it is false." Heresy always contains some element of the truth. The council should hold to a middle course, lest in refuting an error it fall into the opposite extreme.[54]

The legates put the theologians to work. To focus the theologians' interventions they provided them with six questions, whose origins we do not know: (1) What is meant by justification? (2) What are its causes —what is God's part, what is ours? (3) What is meant by being saved by faith [as found in the Epistle to the Romans, 1:17, 3:22–26, etc.]? (4) Do "works" (human actions) and the sacraments play roles in justification, and, if so, what are they? (5) Can we describe the process of justification? (6) How from Scripture, apostolic traditions, previous councils, and the Fathers can the true doctrine be discovered and supported?[55]

For six days, beginning on June 22, the theologians in turn expressed their views to the council. Only sketchy accounts of what they said survive, but we can probably assume that their interventions, uncoordinated, left some bishops as confused as enlightened. At the end, however, the prelates surely agreed with Cervini's warning that the task ahead of them was the most complex they had faced.

After the theologians the bishops took the floor, some speaking for two or more hours at a time. Some were well versed in the subject. Their approach, like that of the theologians, was generally framed by Scholastic categories, and, despite Pole's words, they often seemed unwilling to concede any merit whatsoever to Luther's position. There were, however, important exceptions. Seripando was convinced, for instance, that the decree had to dispense with Scholastic distinctions and categories and that it had to take religious experience into account.[56] Such experience was, after all, the starting point for Luther's teaching.

On July 6 the bishop of La Cava, Tommaso Sanfelice, made bold to speak of the "slave will" and of justification "by faith alone," expressions identified with Luther.[57] After another intervention on July 17 he overheard Dionisio de Zanettini, the Franciscan bishop of Chironissa and Melopotamos, say he was "either a knave or a fool." That was the spark that set off one of the most famous incidents in the whole council. When a moment later Sanfelice confronted him face-to-face, Zanettini repeated the insult. With that Sanfelice, furious, grabbed him by his beard and shook him violently, at which Zanettini shouted for all to hear, "I have said that the bishop of La Cava is either a knave or a fool, and I shall prove it."

Colleagues pulled the two men apart, and a semblance of order was restored. The legates of course could not ignore what had happened. They tried to find an equitable solution. It was clear that, despite the offense, Sanfelice was gravely at fault. They confined him to a convent, but released him about a week later when Zanettini made a plea on his behalf. As things turned out, however, the incident marked the end of Sanfelice's participation in the council—not because of what he said about justification but because of how he had behaved.[58]

On July 23, a week after the Sanfelice incident, discussion of the six questions finally ended. It had lasted for fourteen General Congregations. By that time the legates had ready the first, lengthy draft of the decree, drawn up by a committee of four bishops elected by secret ballot, to which the legates added a few theologians. Cervini oversaw this process and the progress of the decree through the council. Less than a week remained before the Session scheduled for July 29. During that week the document never made it to the floor. The council was distracted from the business at hand and ridden with anxiety over the consequences of decisions taken far distant from the Giroldo palace.

Earlier in the month Paul III and Charles V had completed final negotiations for the war against Schmalkalden, and the pope's two grandsons, Ottavio and Cardinal Alessandro, set out to conduct the papal army to the German battlefields. In Germany itself hostilities had already opened, and rumors spread in Trent that Lutheran troops were ready to capture Innsbruck or seize the Brenner Pass, both of which were ominously close to Trent. On July 26, Ottavio Farnese arrived in the neighborhood with 12,000 infantry and 800 cavalry. Cardinal Madruzzo hosted a banquet for Farnese's officers, which almost all members of the council attended. Even under these circumstances Del Monte tried to force a vote on the as-yet-undiscussed draft so that the Session could be held on time. The council refused, and the Session was prorogued indefinitely.

These developments, which panicked some council members, provided the two legates with a plausible reason for translating the council southward. Del Monte's blunt and awkward handling of the situation brought him at the General Congregation on July 30 into open conflict with the imperial cardinals, Pacheco and Madruzzo. At one point Pacheco shouted at Del Monte, "You treat us as if we were your lackeys!" The bitter exchanges in the council chamber scandalized those present. The incident only strengthened the "imperialists'" conviction that the legates were manipulating the council. It at the same time strengthened the legates' repulsion at the control they thought Charles was trying to exert and increased their determination to move the council. They brought Paul III to their way of thinking.

Through the next three months the question of translating the council, or suspending it, grievously troubled the relationship between Paul and Charles and continued to unsettle the atmosphere in Trent. In the end, however, the legates' plan was foiled. The emperor would not hear of it, and eventually Paul III, who had vacillated, insisted the council stay where it was and continue its work. The city did not in fact seem to be in any real danger, at least not at the moment.

A longer-lasting and unfortunate outcome of the incident was a polarization of the council into an "imperialist" faction (bishops principally from Spain and the Kingdom of Naples) and a "curialist" faction (bishops principally from the Roman Curia and the Papal States). The former distrusted the legates, felt that the opposing faction was not serious about reform, and believed that remaining at Trent was a principle that could not be compromised.

In the meantime bishops found the situation an excuse to seek at least temporary refuge elsewhere. Just as serious, the two legates, sick unto death of Trent and feeling themselves frustrated at every turn, seemed for a while to carry out their duties in almost perfunctory fashion. They had not, however, given up hope of moving the council. The council itself, deprived of the strong leadership the legates had earlier provided and reduced in membership, languished. The mood was sour. The cost of living high.

Even so, on August 11 the bishops finally took up the draft on justification, which from the outset was heavily criticized. We know from Seripando's notes, for instance, that he disagreed with it on every critical point. It soon became clear that it had to be replaced. Only at the General Congregation on September 23, however, did the legates deliver to the council a new draft, authored principally by Seripando, upon whom Cervini had more and more come to rely for theological guidance. Although this draft underwent considerable revision in the months that followed and was in fact replaced by other drafts, it remained the foundation on which all subsequent changes rested.

It introduced, moreover, an important change in form. The canons were preceded by fifteen "chapters." Rejection of false teaching is the burden of the canons. The chapters, one or more paragraphs long, are essentially pastoral instructions or teachings on the positions the council adopted. They are the positive, reverse-image of the canons. This format, new for a council, became standard for most Tridentine doctrinal decrees from this point forward. In the official parlance of the council such paragraphs were called *doctrinae* to distinguish them from the canons, but, despite how they were designated, they were considered to carry less doctrinal authority than the canons.

The September draft was recast, principally by Seripando, and delivered to the council on November 5. In fourteen General Congregations lasting until December 1, it too was criticized, emended, and re-worked. Toward the end of November Seripando felt constrained to deliver a long intervention whose real purpose was to vindicate before the assembly his orthodoxy.[59] Feelings were running high, due as much to the seemingly endless process as to the complexity of the subject itself. That the process was protracted was due in part to the determination of the imperial bishops, led by Cardinals Pacheco and Madruzzo and by the two envoys, Toledo and Mendoza, to prevent the publication of the decree, or, at least, to delay publication as long as possible. But not to be underestimated was the concern of those present, especially Cervini, to make sure that every aspect of the teaching and every ramification received the attention it deserved. The protracted process meant that the decree was examined, revised, scrutinized, and worked over like no other document in the council.

Finally, by the beginning of the new year, the text was ready. Paul III signified willingness to go ahead with its publication regardless of the emperor's wishes. Charles, with the war against Schmalkalden going well, decided not formally to oppose publication. The council, eager to move ahead, agreed to January 13 for the next Session, even though this meant rushing through discussion of the crucial issue of residence. When at the end of December Del Monte moved that issue forward, he asked only two questions: what should be the penalties for nonresidence, and who is to enforce them. The questions bypassed the explosive issue of papal dispensations. It also treated the matter as effectively legal, as embodying nothing more than a church regulation.

With Pacheco leading the charge, bishops especially from the emperor's domains let loose with scathing criticism of the draft, which was essentially the work of Del Monte.[60] The document dodged, they maintained, the real problems. Although it levied financial penalties against absentee bishops, it contained the fatal escape clause, "unless legitimately impeded." It hit the bishops where it hurt most, their pocketbooks, but it fell far short of what was needed both for them and for the pastors.[61]

Del Monte insisted on presenting it at the Session on January 13. To his chagrin, it barely squeaked by, receiving a large number of negative or highly qualified votes. Although he announced that the decree could not be considered approved, he was in effect later overruled by the council itself. The setback on January 13 made it clear to the legates that the council had to return later to the reform of the episcopate and pastorate. Regarding residence the issue that most needed to be addressed was the problem of multiple benefices, bypassed in the present decree without mention.

In striking contrast to the reform decree, the decree on justification passed unanimously.[62] Much credit for this outcome must be given to Cervini for sensitively shepherding it through the tortuous route it traveled. The decree is long, with sixteen chapters followed by thirty-three canons. In a standard English translation the full text runs to about eleven pages of small print. In some regards it betrays the Scholastic culture of its major architects, but it is couched, as Seripando and many others insisted, in largely biblical language.

Although impossible to summarize in a way that adequately takes account of its sophistication, the decree is based on a few basic principles. The first is that justification is God's work—nothing humans do strictly on their own, not even their "good works," counts in God's eyes in passing from sin to forgiveness, righteousness, and renewal of spirit. This principle, already stated in canon 3 in the decree on Original Sin, was a further repudiation of the Pelagianism of which Luther and his followers accused Catholics. According to the decree, the beginning, middle, and end of any movement toward grace was itself an effect of grace, which preceded, accompanied, furthered, and accomplished the movement.

The first three canons express this principle forcefully:

1. If anyone says that a person can be justified before God by his own works, done either by the resources of human nature or by the teaching of the Law, apart from divine grace through Jesus Christ, let him be anathema.

2. If anyone says that divine grace through Jesus Christ is given

solely to enable a person to live justly and to merit eternal life more easily, as if each could be done through free will without grace, even though with a struggle and with difficulty, let him be anathema.

3. If anyone says that, without preceding inspiration of the Holy Spirit and without his help, a person can believe, hope, and repent as he ought so that the grace of justification may be granted to him, let him be anathema.

The second principle was that, though justification is not the result of human striving, the human agent contributes something to it, always on condition that that something is preceded and accompanied by grace. The individual "freely consents" to the movement of grace, but the freedom of the consent is operative under the influence of grace. Scholastic theologians since the High Middle Ages offered explanations about how this curious, one-sided partnership worked, and they continued to do so after the council in disputes that often turned ugly. But the council determined, as a matter of principle, to do nothing more than declare the two faces of the teaching and to forgo attempts at explanation, especially if the explanation entailed siding with Franciscan theologians over Dominican, Augustinian over Franciscan, and so forth. Chapter 5 of the decree put the matter succinctly:

Although God touches a person's heart through the light of the Holy Spirit, neither does that person do absolutely nothing in receiving that movement of grace, for he can also reject it, nor is he able by his own free will and without God's grace to move toward justice in God's sight. Hence, when Scripture says, "Return to me and I will return to you," we are being reminded of our freedom; when we answer, "Restore us to yourself, O Lord, that we may be restored," we are admitting that we are forestalled by the grace of God.[63]

This second principle rested, therefore, upon another: in the Fall the will was weakened and inclined to sin, but it was not rendered altogether evil or utterly impotent. This principle, intimated in the decree on Original Sin, was here given explicit articulation. It provided a basis or at least a context for the further principle that in justification the soul of the individual was truly changed for the better. Justification, in other words, was not simply attributed to the person, which was the Lutheran position as the council understood it, but actually effected an inner transformation through "the grace and charity that is poured forth into their hearts by the Holy Spirit" (canon 11). It established a new relationship of friendship with God.

The transformation effected by grace meant that the individual, now united with Christ as branch to vine, was able, always under the influence of grace, truly to merit his or her salvation and further sanctification. If the person should through grave sin forfeit the grace of justification, the sacrament of penance provided the remedy for the situation. Finally, while in adults justification certainly began with faith, it was accomplished not by faith alone but by faith conjoined with hope and charity, which made the cooperation of the individual with grace efficacious to salvation.

The decree was without doubt a major accomplishment of the council. Although within decades bitter disputes among Catholics as to how to understand the relationship between grace and freedom broke out, climaxing in the protracted Jesuit-Jansenist controversy of the seventeenth and eighteenth centuries, the decree provided an official touchstone to which Catholics could have recourse.

Luther died the year before the decree was ratified. How well did it meet his challenge? In its canons did the council condemn Lutheran positions or distortions of them? Are Luther and Trent in any measure reconcilable? Theologians, especially since the early twentieth century, have debated these questions and come up with different responses. Surely, the Joint Declaration on the Doctrine of Justification agreed to by the Lutheran World Federation and the Catholic Church in 1999, which laid out areas of agreement and disagreement four hundred years after Trent, is a landmark in attempts to answer such questions.[64]

The fundamental problem in reconciling the two positions is that they are manifestations of different intellectual cultures, the one more academic and analytical, the other more personal and existential. The same words have different connotations and perhaps even denotations, and the emotional framework is more different still. The interpreter's task, therefore, is to get beyond the words to the systems of which they are an expression. Luther's justification-by-faith-alone was his eureka experience that, as he saw it, liberated him from the jaws of spiritual death. He clung to it, therefore, for dear life. Trent's decree was the intellectuals' emotionally cool response to Luther's spiritual anguish.[65]

Residence and Sacraments

A week after the unsatisfactory vote on the decree on residence on January 13, the legates, at the suggestion of Pacheco, established a committee of canonists to come up with something better.[66] This committee, meeting now for the first time, was, as mentioned, the counterpart to the Congregation of Theologians. It was to handle reform just as the theologians handled doctrine. It prepared drafts of documents, but its members did not publicly present their opinions to the bishops as did the theologians.

The Congregation of Canonists did not in fact become as standard in the council's operating procedures as did its theological counterpart. The legates, who tended to give free rein to bishops and theologians in doctrinal matters, tightly controlled the drafting of the reform decrees and used the canonists only to the degree they felt they needed them. Nonetheless, canonists in one way or another played major roles in the formulation of the reform decrees, an enterprise that badly needed their expertise and skill because of the complicated legal and fiscal questions that reform often entailed.

In the General Congregation of February 3 debate opened on a draft of eleven reform canons. An implicit principle guiding the draft was that office and benefice were inseparable—you get the money only if you do the job.[67] But of course you cannot do the job if you are holding two bishoprics. Simple though this principle was and traditional in canon law, it badly needed articulation and reinforcement. On this very point, however, the text contained escape clauses.

When the first phase of discussion on the draft concluded on February 7, Del Monte made a crucial intervention in which he, echoing the decree itself, for the first time in a plenary meeting of the council clearly enunciated that the objective of the council's reform decrees was the more effective "care of souls."[68] Those decrees were thus pastoral in intent. In the final version of the document the expression "care of souls" or "salvation of souls" occurs five times.

In this instance, as in every instance involving residence, the question of papal authority simmered beneath the surface and at times broke into the open, with tense results. When on February 24 Martelli, the bishop of Fiesole, obliquely raised it, Sebastiano Pighino, the bishop of Alife, created an uproar in the General Congregation by accusing Martelli of speaking ill of the Holy See. Tempers rose, with one bishop exclaiming, "There's no longer any freedom in this council." Order was restored, at least temporarily, when Robert Wauchope, the archbishop of Armagh, recently returned from Rome, said that the pope had expressly told him that he wanted every member of the council freely to speak his mind on both doctrine and reform. No one was to be reprimanded, even if he spoke heresy, as long as he was willing to submit to the judgment of the council.[69]

Paul III eased tensions in another way when in early January he had forwarded to the legates a bull, *Nostri Non Solum,* saying that in the future no dispensations would be given to bishops for holding several dioceses simultaneously. In February he decided to issue a decree forbidding the same for cardinals. Although just how and with what vigor these measures would be implemented was not clear, they encouraged the reform-minded at the council and raised their hopes that the pope was ready to do more than pay lip-service to problems.

At Trent the reform decree, easily ratified by the council at Session

7 on March 3, 1547, consisted of fifteen chapters, which are difficult for readers today because of the complicated canonical situations they had to take into account. The strength of the decree lay in its insistence on stringent measures to ensure that competent persons assume offices entailing "the care of souls," its requirement that persons holding multiple bishoprics resign all but one, and its stipulation that bishops visit every church in their jurisdiction every year to satisfy themselves that the care of souls and needed repairs in the physical fabric of the church were being properly carried out.[70] The council returned to these matters again within a few months and then again, with a vengeance, many years later during its third period. That very fact indicates problems with the decree. Nonetheless, the decree already contained the nucleus of the Tridentine reform of pastoral offices.

After the initial discussions on residence, from February 8 to 22 the council took up the sacraments, the other major doctrinal issue facing it besides justification, to which, in fact, the sacraments were closely related. Luther wrote extensively on this subject, but fundamental was his treatise "On the Babylonian Captivity of the Church" (1520). While Catholics had many problems with Luther's teaching, three were crucial. First, he insisted that there were only two sacraments, baptism and the Eucharist, rather than the seven traditional since the middle of the twelfth century. He allowed for penance but denied that it had any sacramental character that Catholics could recognize. Second, he seemed to deny intrinsic efficacy to the sacraments, as if they were merely privileged incitements to greater faith. He thus seemed, finally, to minimize the role the sacraments play in justification and the pursuit of holiness.

In January Cervini had already put together a small committee made up of Seripando and a few theologians, including Diego Laínez and Alfonso Salmerón, members of the recently founded Society of Jesus, who were appointed to the council by Paul III himself and therefore as papal theologians enjoyed precedence in speaking before the others and were always listed first among the theologians in any official documents. Other than that they operated like all the others.

The committee examined the writings of the Reformers, especially Luther, and extracted from them thirty-five propositions that conflicted, or seemed to conflict, with Catholic teaching. The legates submitted these propositions ("articles") to the Congregation of Theologians, which met nine times between January 20 and 29 in the presence, as usual, of the bishops.[71]

Differences of opinion among the theologians emerged but not nearly so sharply as in previous Congregations. Since the High Middle Ages theologians had devoted considerable attention to the sacraments, which meant they felt secure in addressing them. Although the different schools of medieval theology did not agree about many particulars related especially to metaphysics, they agreed on the essential dogmatic issues.[72]

The Council of Florence in its reconciliation with the Armenian church published, on November 22, 1439, a decree that contained a long section on the sacraments, which affirmed the sevenfold number and pronounced on each in turn.[73] The theologians and the bishops believed they were not free to diverge from such a solemn teaching of a previous council and therefore that they had a blueprint in hand. In principle the council wanted to avoid using Scholastic terminology and, more basically, shaping their decisions in the highly intellectualized Scholastic framework. In dealing with the sacraments, however, it was almost impossible to avoid doing so because the medieval Scholastics were the ones who had fully elaborated the theology of the sacraments, and their successors were the theologians of the council.

The result of the Congregations of Theologians was a classification of the propositions into four categories, beginning with the propositions the theologians unanimously condemned. The prelates received the list as the basis for the debate in the General Congregations, which opened on February 8. During the February debates a few bishops demanded that the Reformers—and their writings—be condemned by name. The legates and the majority were opposed, and the council in this regard continued as it had from the beginning.[74]

On March 1, the bishops debated a list of canons Cervini presented to them, which was divided into three sections: thirteen dealing with the sacraments in general, fourteen with baptism, and three with confirmation. The remaining five sacraments, about which the bishops had already heard the theologians' opinions, were to be dealt with later, after these had passed muster on March 3 at Session 7, which was just two days away.[75] The legates were obviously doing their best now to move the council at a much brisker pace.

Except for an introductory paragraph, the decree consisted exclusively in canons—no preliminary chapters as in the decree on justification. The absence of chapters was Cervini's doing. He was convinced that the council could forgo chapters on the sacraments because the decree on justification provided sufficient context for them. Four years later, however, during the second period of the council, the legate Marcello Crescenzio reversed this decision and insisted on chapters.

The thirteen canons on the sacraments in general laid out the basic framework that characterized the council's treatment of each of them from this point forward. They are, therefore, fundamental. The first condemned three propositions: that Christ did not institute all the sacraments; that there are more or fewer than seven, which are baptism, confirmation, Eucharist, penance, extreme unction (today called anointing of the sick), holy orders, and matrimony; and that some of these seven are not truly sacraments.

The remaining canons of course also made crucial points: the sacraments are not equal in dignity; they are necessary for salvation, though not every one of them is necessary for every individual; they have an intrinsic effect on the soul of the recipient and are more than a mere nourishment of faith (they are thus "*efficacious* signs"); they must be conferred by the proper minister and be performed using the proper rites.[76]

The canons on baptism were as much directed against the Anabaptists as anyone else. They therefore affirmed the legitimacy of infant baptism and condemned the view that one must wait until adulthood to receive the sacrament. Canon 4 affirmed the traditional teaching that baptism administered by heretics was valid as long as they did so in the name of the Trinity and with the intention of doing what the church does.[77] The three canons on confirmation are notable for how little they say.[78]

Session 7 on March 3 moved ahead without incident. The decree on the sacraments passed unanimously. Although the reform decree received qualified votes, an indication that bishops intent on a more radical reform were not satisfied, it passed easily. For perhaps the first time in the council a generally optimistic mood prevailed. The big issues of justification and residence had been dealt with. Although work on the sacraments had just begun, what remained promised to move ahead as quickly and smoothly as had the past month. In his sermon at the Mass of the Holy Spirit that day the preacher projected this sense of satisfaction and accomplishment.

The end of the council, if not quite in sight, seemed to be just beyond the horizon, probably not attainable by Session 8, set now for April 21, but surely as early as May or June. On March 3 no one was prepared for what unfolded during the next ten days. No one could have foreseen the momentous consequences of the decision taken at that time.

Bologna

In the General Congregation on March 7 the forty-six prelates who were present took up the canons on the Eucharist. They continued the discussion two days later, and it went so well that it seemed only one more Congregation would be required to wrap up this first go-around on the document. After the last intervention that day Del Monte rose to inform the bishops of a development that required a decision on their part.[79] He reminded those present that the legates had made clear they would inform the council of any dangers threatening it or the health of its members. He then told them that in the few days that had elapsed since the Session almost a dozen prelates had left the council and more had asked permission to do so. A sickness had broken out in the city that had caused the death of Enrico Loffredo, the bishop of Capaccio, only twenty-six years old. Del Monte went on. The legates in their concern consulted the council's official physician, Girolamo Fracastoro, and Del Monte's personal physician, Balduino de' Balduini. The doctors concurred that the sickness was a contagious and deadly disease that could be the forerunner of a plague. Del Monte read the doctors' report. In it Fracastoro, a highly respected physician who for his day held advanced theories about contagious diseases, added that he himself did not intend to remain in Trent.[80]

Under these circumstances, Del Monte said, he and his colleague Cervini felt they had to lay the matter before the council, by whose decision they would abide on condition that it did not entail the dissolution of the council. He did not explicitly state that what they had in mind was to translate the council to another city, but nobody missed the point.

From the doctors' report it is clear that the disease was typhus and that it had claimed victims in Trent. What was not clear was how many victims. Did it really look as if the disease was developing into an epidemic? This was the question that agitated the council. The next day, March 10, the legates produced a set of witnesses who testified that the disease was widespread, whereas the opponents of the move, led by Pacheco, tried to show that convincing evidence in that regard was lacking. Pacheco, who had personally spent hours trying to ascertain just how many people had the disease, was in fact closer to the truth. He demanded that, in any case, the pope and the emperor be consulted before a decision of such magnitude was taken, and on his own he sent off a courier to Charles V.[81]

If the council were to move, to what city? Everybody was aware that a body as large (and controversial) as the council could not simply pull up stakes and expect to be welcomed wherever it chose to land. Negotiations, probably lengthy and of uncertain outcome, would be required. That was true except for the cities of the Papal States, and among them Bologna was the most obvious. It was considerably closer to Trent than Rome, which meant that the members of the council could reach it in a relatively short time. It was large enough easily to accommodate the council, had excellent library resources, incomparably better than Trent's, and was altogether more comfortable. No surprise, therefore, that Del Monte proposed Bologna as the best option. Things were moving fast.

In the sixteenth century the very mention of plague was enough to create panic, as it did now among some of the bishops. Even beyond escaping the danger of contracting the disease, many welcomed the thought of finally getting out of Trent and settling in a more amenable location. But translating the council out of Trent, which was "in German lands," to another city, especially a city in the Papal States, threatened explosive political consequences.

In the early months of 1547 the political landscape of Europe had shifted in important ways. Henry VIII died on January 28, and Francis I two months later. If Charles V defeated Schmalkalden, which now seemed likely, he would be able to force the Lutherans to attend the council and thus bring to completion his "great plan." He was, moreover, holding the Turks at bay. Everything seemed to be working in Charles's favor at this point.

His relationship with Paul III, however, had gone from bad to worse. Their military alliance had expired in January, and Paul refused to renew it. The emperor was desperately in need of money. In spite of every effort on his part, the pope refused to contribute anything further, and he even recalled his troops. Paul of course wanted to see the Lutherans defeated but was haunted by the fear of an emperor who, victorious, could do what he would. Charles for his part could not understand why at this crucial point the pope would not come to the aid of the Catholic cause in Germany. In these circumstances translation of the council to Bologna promised to be more explosive a move than ever. It held the potential of permanently and fatally rupturing the relationship between the two rulers.

On March 11, forty-eight hours after raising the issue, the legates posed to the council the fatal question. Bishops categorically opposing the translation were in the minority but fierce in their conviction that a translation was wrong. Nonetheless, two-thirds of the bishops cast their votes in favor of moving the council to Bologna. Fourteen cast their votes against it; with one exception, they were from Spain or other Habsburg domains. The lone Italian among the fourteen was Martelli, the feisty bishop of Fiesole. Among the bishops favoring the move the overwhelming majority were Italians, especially those financially dependent upon the Curia.

Only then did the legates produce the bull of February 22, 1545, authorizing them to remove the council to a city of their choice if the situation warranted it and to forbid anybody who remained behind to try to continue the council. Up to that point virtually no one at the council knew of the bull's existence.[82] The revelation stunned the assembled bishops.

Del Monte then officially declared that a decision to move the council to Bologna had been legitimately reached and that Trent was no longer the site of the council. He forbade any protests against the decision and ordered all present to proceed to Bologna, where they were to arrive no later than April 21, the date earlier set for the next Session. Some bishops, anticipating the outcome of the vote, had their horses waiting outside the council chamber. With their bags already packed, they made for the door, mounted their steeds, and on them galloped outside the city within minutes of the close of the meeting.

Later that day the legates wrote to the pope to inform him of what had transpired, and the next day, March 12, they themselves set off for Bologna. Most bishops had already cleared out. The fourteen who opposed the move, however, stayed behind and refused to budge. The momentous decision had been taken without consultation of pope, emperor, or even the officials of the city of Bologna. The legates had reason to be uneasy, for they were not sure even what the pope's reaction would be.

How are we to assess what happened? Doubtless there was cause for concern. If an epidemic developed, the bishops and the others would have been trapped inside Trent and forced to remain there because neighboring cities would seal their gates to protect themselves. Besides being a plague-infested city, Trent under the circumstances could not be provisioned with food and other materials. The fact that Fracastoro himself refused to stay underscores the potential for disaster. To have awaited authorization from the pope or the emperor or both, with the wrangling that would certainly have ensued, was utterly unrealistic.

Yet at this point only a handful of people in the whole city had contracted the disease. Why not wait at least a few days to see if the contagion was indeed spreading? As it turned out, Trent did not suffer an epidemic. With questionable haste the legates brought the matter to a vote. An expeditious resolution was required, surely, but as expeditious as this? They argued that the other obvious measure, adjourning the council for a specified period to see if an epidemic developed, would be the equivalent of dissolving it. But was that true? Although the legates were doubtlessly sincere in their protestations that they would abide by the council's decision, they made clear by word and gesture that in their opinion transferring the council to another city was the only solution.

As early as the previous summer Del Monte and Cervini had tried to take the council out of Trent. Now, with Charles's almost certain victory over Schmalkalden, they had even more reason to fear pressure from him on the direction of the council. For both of them, moreover, Trent had become a crucible in which they experienced little besides pain and frustration. Leaving Trent meant, somehow, leaving the confinement of the prison the city had come to represent for them.

The terrifying specter of plague delivered into their hands the just cause for which they had been looking. In their handling of the question of translation, they cannot be altogether absolved from the sin of manipulation. They played a dangerous game whose outcome bore heavy consequences. Their success in obtaining the vote they wanted meant that, instead of the speedy end of the council for which they had worked so hard, the Council of Trent would not finally be brought to conclusion for another sixteen years. Jedin saw, besides, a much more grievous consequence: "If there had been no translation of the Council of Trent to Bologna, the German schism might have had a different issue."[83]

4

The Middle Years, 1547–1562

Were it not located in the Papal States, Bologna would have been an ideal city for the council. Although often oppressively hot in the summer, it had a milder climate than Trent. Then as now it was noted for its good food. A large city by sixteenth-century standards, it had a population of about 50,000, roughly the same as Florence and Rome. Lodging was plentiful. The Palazzo Campeggi (today Bevilacqua), where the General Congregations were held, was a spacious and beautiful Renaissance building from the late fifteenth century. The church of San Petronio, located right at city-center, was perfect for the Sessions, at which large crowds were expected.

Bologna boasted one of the oldest and most prestigious universities in Europe, rivaled only by Paris. Unlike Paris, renowned especially for its theology faculty, Bologna was known for its faculty of law, both civil and canon, which attracted students from all of Europe. The university did not have a theological faculty until 1364. That faculty, altogether different in structure from its Parisian counterpart and of lesser repute, consisted essentially in a consortium of the *studia,* or "houses of study," of the many important convents of the mendicant orders in the city.[1] The influx into the council of experts from these institutions made the size of the Congregations of Theologians at Bologna considerably larger than at any other time in the history of the council. On April 29, 1547, Massarelli counted more than eighty present that day.[2]

These institutions also boasted extensive libraries with just the kind of collections the council needed for its work. The Dominican convent was especially important because talented young members of the order from all over Europe were sent there to complete their studies. These and other students were admitted as auditors to the Congregations of Theologians until their numbers grew so great—over 300 on April 2, 1547—that the practice was stopped.[3]

"The Council of Bologna," 1547–1549

Charles received the news of the transfer to Bologna at Nördlingen on March 15, 1547, just a few days after it happened. Furious, he held the legates, especially Cervini, responsible. He hoped Paul III would repudiate what they had done and hold true to his promise of a council "in German lands." Just as the legates felt the council's freedom threatened in Trent, Charles felt it threatened in a city of the Papal States. To acknowledge Bologna would be to betray his promise to the German Protestants and offend even many German Catholics.

The two legates arrived in Bologna five days later, on March 20. Meanwhile in Rome news of the translation caused misgivings, and Paul was notably perturbed when he received word from Charles in effect demanding return to Trent. On March 27, however, the legates received reassurance that the pope not only approved the translation but in consistory had told the gathered cardinals that no more was to be hoped for from Trent. The Germans had been awaited there for two years and had never shown up.

That same day, a happy one therefore for the legates, Cervini celebrated Mass in San Petronio to mark the council's coming to the city. Del Monte, suffering from one of his recurrent attacks of gout, could not attend, but present were the governor of the city, other civic officials in great number, and a large congregation, which constituted an embarrassing contrast with the meager contingent of prelates from Trent—two archbishops and ten bishops.[4] A month later the Session on April 21, though solemnly celebrated in San Petronio, was forced to publish a decree admitting that because so few bishops had shown up the matter scheduled for promulgation had to be deferred until the next Session, set for June 2.[5]

Through his ambassador at the imperial court, the pope sent word to the emperor of his approval of the translation. He reminded the emperor that many councils had been held in Rome itself, and he threw oil on the fire by asking him to tell the prelates remaining at Trent to move to Bologna. When on April 14 the ambassador presented Charles with this reply, the emperor flew into a rage. "Get out! Get out!" he shouted.[6]

On April 24, however, Charles won his decisive victory over the army of the Schmalkaldic League at the Battle of Mühlberg. Despite his anger at the pope and his distrust, he wanted at all costs to avoid a complete break in their relationship. The day after the battle his confessor, Pedro de Soto, wrote an impassioned letter to Cardinal Farnese begging the pope at this crucial moment for the Catholic cause to return the council to Trent. Protestants, he said, would simply laugh at any decisions taken in a city of the Papal States, and even Catholics would not take them seriously. Moreover, the legates were wrong in their insistence that the most controversial issues had already been dealt with. On the contrary, those most important for religious practice had not even been touched upon—the Eucharistic cup for the laity, the laws on fasting, veneration of the saints, Purgatory, priestly celibacy, and monastic vows.[7] The list underscores how very different were the perspectives of the imperial court not only from those of Paul III but from those of the council itself.

An impasse had been reached. It would continue to play itself out in different forms until the death of Paul III. The emperor's victory over Schmalkalden only increased the pope's fear of Charles, now seemingly all-powerful. Paul was not eager to strengthen his hand further. On April 25 he ordered to Bologna all bishops resident in Rome. By that time the Theologians' Congregation was already functioning and dealing with the five remaining sacraments.[8] Then on May 9 the General Congregation took up where it had left off in Trent, that is, with discussion of seven canons on the Eucharist. At this point only twenty-five prelates were present, still outnumbered by the theologians.[9]

For the doctrine of the Eucharist there were two major issues—the Real Presence of Christ under the form of bread and wine, denied by Zwingli and others, and transubstantiation, the doctrine that the substance of the bread and wine was changed into the substance of Christ's body and blood, a doctrine denied by Luther. Added to these were three closely related issues. The first was the granting or withholding of the Eucharistic cup to the laity, which entailed the belief defined at the Council of Constance that both the body and the blood of Christ were present under each of the two forms, the bread and wine. Even into the twelfth century the practice of receiving under both forms had continued in some areas. But from that point forward it became ever less common and finally disappeared. By the sixteenth century the single form had become universal but also a subject of contention since its advocacy early in the previous century by "the Bohemians," that is, the followers of Jacob of Mies and Jan Hus.

The second issue was the widespread Catholic practice of worship of the Eucharist in settings outside the ritual of the Mass (as most vividly exemplified in processions and other rites associated with the feast of Corpus Christi), denounced by Luther and others as an abuse. The third was the belief that the Mass was a true sacrifice, a doctrine vigorously denounced by Luther for two reasons in particular: first, as "sacrifice of the cross" it detracted from the unique and sufficient sacrifice on Calvary, and, second, it turned the ritual into a "work," with an ascending movement from the priest to God. Rather than such a "sacrifice of the cross," the Mass was for Luther "the Lord's Supper," with a descending movement of mercy from Christ to the people hearing in faith. Because the council at this point treated the Eucharist as a sacrament in and of itself, outside the context of the Mass, it did not address the sacrificial character until later.

Each of these issues, of course, had implications that raised further questions and thus provided a field day for the theologians. Before the council left Trent, the bishops had listened to them through thirteen Theologians' Congregations, so they were well informed when the debates resumed in May at Bologna. By the end of the month the council, now numbering about forty prelates, had in hand eight canons ready for promulgation, but on May 30 a letter arrived from Rome by express courier requesting a postponement of promulgation until August.[10]

The next day, after a long and stormy discussion, the council decided to hold the Session as planned but not publish any decree "of substance" (decretum substantiale). The reasons adduced, as Massarelli recorded them in his diary, were several. First and foremost was the hope of winning the emperor over from his refusal to recognize Bologna and to allow his bishops to leave Trent. Second, the canons on reform were not ready. Finally, neither the new king of France nor the emperor had sent a single bishop, and it seemed prudent to await developments and hope for an amelioration of that situation before promulgating any further decrees.[11]

The decree of prorogation published in the Session on June 2 explained the council's failure to publish anything more because of its desire "to continue to treat with kindness those who have not come."[12] It set the date for the next Session, September 15. That Session, never celebrated, was the last the Bologna assembly ever scheduled, a telling symptom of the tentativeness of the situation. The end result was that these canons on the Eucharist, like all the other decrees later decided upon at Bologna but never promulgated, were to a large extent exercises in futility.[13]

On June 6 the council turned to the sacrament of penance. As usual it was Seripando, Cervini's favored theologian, who extracted passages from Lutheran writings related to it.[14] He was surely among the best qualified for the task. The procedure had the advantage of providing sharp focus for debate but the considerable disadvantage of lifting statements out of context, which often entailed distortion of meaning. The proof-texts that resulted from the procedure were intrinsic to the method of argumentation used by Scholastic theologians since the thirteenth century and, hence, were accepted by the council unquestioned.

Luther's inability to find in this sacrament the peace of soul he sought was a catalyst for his key insight of justification by faith alone. We are accepted by God as justified not by our striving—certainly not by our striving to confess to a priest each and every misdeed and to summon up in our souls sufficient contrition for them—but by our trust in his promise of forgiveness and grace. Luther's reflections on the sacrament thus cut to the very heart of his message.

He stoutly maintained that the gospel prescribed confession of sins but not as the Catholic church understood and practiced it. In Scripture, for instance, there was no warrant for the enumeration of sins as the church required. Moreover, the Catholic form of absolution indicated that the priest absolved penitents from their sins, but, Luther objected, forgiveness of sin is reserved exclusively to God. After absolution the priest imposed "works" as penances, as if these were availing of salvation. The whole ritual, with the priest acting as judge in a setting officially understood as a tribunal in which faith (as Luther understood it) played no role, oppressed Christian consciences and held them captive to papal tyranny.

It was particular points like these that Seripando lifted from Lutheran writings. His procedure precluded a presentation of the system or synthesis from which the points were lifted. It judged them by the standard of a different system/synthesis and thus perforce indicated their incompatibility with that standard. The eight canons on penance that Cervini presented to the council on June 6 were, as in other instances, the result of this procedure. Only after three redraftings did the text on July 12 receive the approval of the General Congregation—but not the solemn approval of a Session.[15]

The council next engaged in debate over two issues closely related to penance—indulgences and Purgatory—upon which Charles V set great weight. In their Congregations, which extended over three weeks, thirty theologians delivered their opinions.[16] They all affirmed the existence of Purgatory as a state intermediate between heaven and hell, a doctrine denied by the Reformers, and similarly affirmed the legitimacy of indulgences, the spark that ignited the Reformation. Beyond these basic affirmations opinions differed widely.

The council did not pursue the issues further. In late July, it began work instead on the sacraments of extreme unction and holy orders. After that it turned to the Sacrifice of the Mass. At the very end of the month, August 29, Cervini asked the council's opinion on two controversial questions related to matrimony. First, were clandestine marriages valid? By these he meant marriages in which the spouses exchanged vows without the presence of witnesses. Erasmus satirized the practice in his colloquy "The Wooer and the Maiden" *(Proci et Puellae)*, in which the young man tries to persuade the young woman to say the fatal words, "I will be yours." The practice led to many widely recognized problems, caused especially when one of the parties, usually the man, later denied that vows had ever been exchanged.

Second, did an act of adultery free one, or even both, of the parties to marry again? This problem arose in connection with Jesus's words reported by Matthew, "Whoever divorces his wife, except for fornication [*fornicatio*, Vulgate], and marries another commits adultery" (19:9).[17] In the course of the debates in several General Congregations over the next two weeks a majority seemed to agree that clandestine marriages were valid and that adultery did not break the marriage bond.[18]

On September 10 the bishops were ready for a more general debate on six canons on matrimony, two of which dealt with those issues. That day, however, an event occurred many miles from Bologna that held grave consequences for the council and contributed heavily to its ultimate dissolution. Co-conspirators of Ferrante Gonzaga, Charles V's viceroy in the Duchy of Milan, accosted the Duke of Parma and Piacenza in his private chambers in the citadel of Piacenza and stabbed him to death. The victim was none other than Pierluigi Farnese, Pope Paul III's eldest son and the father of Cardinals Alessandro and Ranuccio. The next day by express courier from Bologna the council received word of the deed.[19]

What was the background to this shocking event?[20] As part of Paul III's large scheme for the enrichment and ennobling of his family, he had only two years earlier conferred upon Pierluigi the papal fiefs of Parma and Piacenza and created out of them a dukedom. The pope hoped the emperor would meanwhile confer the dukedom of Milan on Ottavio Farnese, Pierluigi's son and brother to the two cardinals. Charles had, instead, named Gonzaga his viceroy in Milan and, further, refused to acknowledge Pierluigi as the Duke of Parma and Piacenza.

Pierluigi, loaded with favors as soon as Paul had become pope, had an unsavory reputation, which included allegations that in 1537 he had raped the young bishop of Fano, Cosimo Gheri, who died shortly afterward. Once he was installed in his dukedom his autocratic and arbitrary rule made him powerful enemies within his own domain. Charles's refusal to recognize him aligned Pierluigi with France, a fact well known to Charles, who at least up to a point encouraged Gonzaga in his obsession to overthrow the upstart duke.

From the moment Paul III learned of the murder, he was convinced of the emperor's complicity, despite Charles's protestations of innocence. He found a confirmation for his suspicions when shortly after the murder Gonzaga occupied Piacenza and Charles made no effort to make him surrender it. His son's murder fed Paul's fears, sometimes bordering on paranoia, that the emperor was about to launch a military campaign against him and subject him to his will in all matters, secular and religious. Charles's troops had, after all, sacked Rome in 1527, an event the pope had witnessed with his own eyes, and there was now, with Charles's victory over Schmalkalden, little to prevent him from doing it again.

For the next two years the council and its fate were caught in the middle of a game of dare between these two leaders of Christendom. The new king of France, Henry II, saw in the situation a golden opportunity to drive an even deeper wedge between the two men, and he offered aid and comfort to the pope, thus further complicating the scene. The threats, intrigues, posturing, diplomatic maneuvering, rattling of swords, and genuine attempts to reach an accord that ensued are far too complicated and shifting to allow for even a summary retelling. The emperor never desisted in his demand that the council return to Trent, and the pope, despite occasionally seeming willing to allow it, never desisted in his refusal to make that happen. In all that transpired, however, both men, on occasion after occasion, backed away from the precipice of a full break in their relationship.

The legates were often and deeply involved in what transpired, but they were of course not the decision-makers. At Bologna itself they tried to carry on as best they could, but it was now more difficult than ever to accomplish anything. After a long discussion on September 14, for instance, the council decided by a unanimous vote to cancel the Session scheduled for the next day. To some extent the decision was a foregone conclusion because the previous week the legates had received word from Cardinal Farnese recommending proroguing, to which they had easily agreed.[21]

At the General Congregation on the fourteenth, just three days after receiving word of the assassination of Pierluigi, the bishops cited as one reason for the postponement the military preparations now under way to defend the Papal States. A further reason, however, was not to exclude from an eventual Session the large number of French bishops who were expected to arrive shortly, an indication of how tentative the membership in the council still was.

A French delegation did in fact begin to arrive a little while later.[22] The bishops among them joined the two French bishops already there, which brought the number of French prelates at Bologna to eleven. They therefore constituted a potentially powerful block, which might serve as the foundation for making the council a French council rather than, as the French had up to this point maintained, an imperial one. During the summer Henry II came to recognize that the move to Bologna provided him with a chance to show that he was opposed not to a council in principle but to a council under the emperor's aegis "in German lands." The French could not have arrived in Bologna at a more propitious moment to satisfy Henry's plan—when sentiments against Charles in Rome and Bologna had soared to new heights.[23]

Through the rest of 1547, the council trudged on, debating further aspects of sacramental doctrine and practice. It did not take long for disillusionment to seize the French bishops, who complained about "a council where nothing happens." They begged to be recalled. Only occasionally did the tedium break. On December 18, for instance, Del Monte received an important Brief from Paul III, in which the pope said that he did not want to respond to the emperor's petition, newly made, that the council return to Trent without first consulting the council itself. In it Paul mentioned Charles's promise that if the council returned, he would induce all Germans, "including the heretics," to submit to its decrees. The Brief was one of those moments in the complex interaction between Paul and Charles when the pope took action that at least on the surface seemed to be an attempt to meet the emperor's demand.

At the General Congregation the next day Del Monte read the letter and then laid before the council five conditions that he believed needed to be fulfilled before the council could give a reasonable answer: (1) the prelates remaining at Trent join the council at Bologna; (2) assurance be given that the heretics would submit to the decrees already enacted; (3) clarification be made as to how the council should proceed;

(4) assurance be given that all concerned could make a safe journey from Bologna to Trent and that, once there, be duly protected; (5) assurance be given that even after the return to Trent the council be free not only to move to another city if the situation warranted but, in addition, to declare itself concluded at the appropriate moment. As was to be expected, the council approved the conditions and enjoined the legates to send them as the council's response, which was the equivalent of refusing to move.[24] The response could not have been a surprise to Paul III nor displeasing. On January 2 the legates received word that Paul agreed with the conditions.[25]

The emperor had no intention of bowing to such stipulations, especially to the first, and resolved on his most drastic action to date, a formal protest against the legitimacy of Bologna. With that occurred the most exciting and dramatic moment of the Bologna assembly. On January 16 Charles's two agents Francisco Vargas and Martín Velasco appeared at the General Congregation, which was then discussing abuses of the sacrament of penance, and demanded a hearing. The council agreed to admit them.

Vargas asserted that the emperor found himself compelled for the good of the Christian religion solemnly to protest against certain persons who assumed the title of Apostolic Legates and against a meeting at Bologna that called itself a council but whose decisions were null and void. There followed for almost six hours a series of exchanges especially between Del Monte and the two imperial emissaries in which the usual arguments for and against the translation were repeated, with neither side giving an inch.

At the conclusion of his diary entry for the day, Massarelli prayed, "May almighty God in his ineffable goodness through the merits of the Passion of Jesus Christ, his only son and our redeemer, avert that today be the beginning of a great schism in the church of God."[26] For the next few days the council deliberated on its formal response to Vargas and Velasco, but by the time it was ready on January 20 to respond, the imperial emissaries had already left the city. In full consistory in Rome a few days later, on January 23, in the presence of Paul III himself, the imperial ambassador, Hurtado de Mendoza, delivered the same protest, a formal and solemn action that Paul had feared and very much wanted to forestall.[27]

An extremely dangerous moment in the relationship between the two men had been reached, but once again, they both recoiled from the prospect of a full break and sought ways to ameliorate the situation.[28] On February 1 the pope, scrambling to make peace and at the same time save face, in full consistory delivered his response. He engaged in a long justification of his actions regarding the council and regarding his relations with Charles, but, while making clear that he reserved judgment to himself, he conceded that he would review the question of the validity of the translation. He said, however, that he was ordering a moratorium on further deliberations at Bologna until he rendered his decision.[29]

That order was the beginning of the end. After it was received at Bologna not a single General Congregation was held. Over the next nineteen months, as pope and emperor sparred and no verdict on the translation was forthcoming, the prelates at Bologna twiddled their thumbs. Their anger and resentment mounted. One by one they slipped out of town not to return. By September the number had fallen to eighteen, just a few more than those still steadfast at Trent.

The death blow did not come, however, until September 17, 1549, a long two and a half years after the adjournment to Bologna. On that day Del Monte received word from Paul III to give the remaining bishops leave to return home. By this action the pope, strictly speaking, neither adjourned the council nor declared it concluded, but, as Massarelli noted in his diary, "Beginning today the Council of Bologna ceases to exist."[30]

A New Pope

Paul III died less than two months later. He had, as he dismissed the bishops from Bologna, proposed to convene a reform meeting in Rome in January, but his death in November made that impossible. The conclave to elect his successor opened on November 29. As was the custom, the cardinals swore to a number of "capitulations," which were agenda items they agreed to pursue if elected. Among them was the stipulation to reconvene the council. But no city was indicated. When Cardinal Pacheco left Trent to participate in the conclave, the others there began to disperse, which made it possible for Trent once again to be in the running as the location.

The rivalry between Charles and Henry dominated the conclave.[31] French and Francophile cardinals were outnumbered by the imperialists but still could muster enough votes to prevent the required two-thirds majority for any candidate Henry II opposed. When the conclave opened, the election of Reginald Pole, one of several cardinals favored by Charles V, seemed assured. But the French, dead set against him, were joined by others who had misgivings, which included suspicions about his orthodoxy on justification. Cardinal Giampietro Carafa, later Pope Paul IV, openly attacked him on that issue before a crucial ballot on December 5.

Pole's candidacy began to fail, just at the time the French party was strengthened by the arrival of four more cardinals, including the young Charles de Guise, who would play such an important role in the third period of the council.[32] With the defeat of Pole the conclave descended into deadlock. Destined to last well over two months, the stalemate was broken only when Cardinal de Guise, now the acknowledged leader of the French faction, and Cardinal Farnese, now, despite French leanings, leader of the imperialists, met and worked out a compromise in early February. De Guise favored Cervini, who Farnese knew was utterly unacceptable to Charles. De Guise therefore proposed Del Monte, who up to that point had garnered few votes in the many ballotings. Farnese reluctantly accepted him and then set energetically to work persuading others to follow suit. In the Pauline Chapel on February 7 the required number of imperialists fell into line, and Del Monte was elected. He took the name Julius III.[33]

As Del Monte had shown at Trent, he was a man of considerable ability. He was, moreover, not only honest and conscientious but steadfast in difficult circumstances. There was, however, another side to him. As his short pontificate wound down, he spent more and more time hunting, banqueting, gambling, or simply passing days in quiet leisure in the sumptuous residence he built for himself, the Villa Giulia. His relatives pursued him for favors. To their entreaties, despite his denunciations of the nepotism of his predecessors, he mustered only halfhearted resistance. But in that regard he was a model of restraint compared with Paul III.

His blind insistence on raising to the cardinalate a shifty teenager of low birth and questionable morals, whom he had brought with him to Trent when he was a legate, was the great scandal of his pontificate. Del Monte's obvious affection for the young man not surprisingly provoked salacious rumors about their relationship. After his death the cardinal's escapades and crimes continued to give great scandal. Although punished for his misdeeds, through the next five pontificates he eluded the severe penalties he deserved.[34]

Del Monte's election, the result of a hasty and uncomfortable compromise, was much more acceptable to Henry than to Charles, but it did not really please either man. The new pope's first task, therefore, was to reassure them and to follow a neutral policy in their regard, which was easier to profess than to practice. He felt, in view of the frayed and dangerous state of relations with Charles during Paul's last years, that his first task was to make peace with the emperor. Within a month he informed Charles that he intended to convoke the council and was willing to have it meet at Trent or even in a city in Germany, on condition that Charles assure him the authority of the Holy See and the reform of the Curia not be up for discussion.[35] He was a curialist down to his fingertips.

Like Paul III, he feared Charles's power and his potential for dominating all of Italy. He saw the council, as did just about everybody not in the emperor's camp, as potentially strengthening the emperor's hand.

Although he reconvened the council, he lacked enthusiasm for it and had learned from his experience as legate to be apprehensive about the directions it might take. Among the many ambivalences in his attitude regarding the council was his failure to apply pressure to the Italian bishops to attend, some one hundred of whom lived in Rome itself. From the beginning he was highly skeptical that any good could come from Protestant presence at the council.

In due course, however, Julius followed through on his promise to convoke, and he set May 1, 1551, for the opening day of the council—in Trent.[36] Charles, though hardly enthusiastic about the restriction on the agenda, was both surprised and pleased by the pope's initiative. He looked upon this unexpected turn of events as his last chance to persuade or force the Lutherans to attend and thus, he hoped, to lessen the religious and political tensions in the empire. By late summer, the Lutheran leaders had formulated conditions under which they would participate. They were conditions they knew that neither the pope nor the majority of bishops would ever agree to, such as the demand that they be allowed to vote on a par with the bishops, that the decisions already taken at Trent be considered null, that all decisions be based on Scripture alone, and that neither the pope nor his legates preside. That is where the matter rested for a while.

Just how the king of France would deal with Julius's decision was not at first clear, though everyone correctly anticipated a hostile reaction.[37] Julius did what he could to control the damage by reassuring Henry that the prerogatives of the French church, including the king's authority to nominate bishops, would not be questioned, even if the council proceeded to decree a "reform of the princes." He told the king that convoking the council, with the hope of saving Germany, was with him a matter of conscience. To no avail. It was soon obvious that Henry would follow an obstructionist policy. He threatened to hold a national French council in opposition to the pope's, which raised the specter of schism. More than that, as early as the summer of 1550, he contemplated an alliance with England, Denmark, Sweden, Poland, the Lu-

Discord between King of France (Henry II) and Charles V / and Henry & Julius

theran princes of the empire, and, possibly, the Republic of Venice to open hostilities once again against Charles. Most shocking, in early 1551 the Most Christian King entered into a military alliance with the sultan, "the infidel," whose forces pressed on Charles's eastern frontier.

The relationship between Henry and Julius reached a breaking point over another, though not unrelated, problem, the Duchy of Parma. Julius had given Parma as a fief of the Holy See to Ottavio Farnese, the son of the murdered Pierluigi. Ottavio, convinced that his mortal enemy, Ferrante Gonzaga, was with the emperor's backing laying claim to the territory, opened negotiations with France for military aid to vindicate his rights. If pursued, this course of action would lead to a war, which, among many other evils, would endanger the council. Julius reminded Ottavio that as a vassal of the church he could not enlist the aid of a foreign prince. When his cajoling, remonstrances, and threats had no effect, he determined to ally himself with the emperor against Ottavio. Henry in turn pledged to supply Ottavio with money and military resources.

In June 1551, a month after the council opened, Julius went to war against Ottavio and entrusted supreme command of the operation to Ferrante Gonzaga. The war, which dragged on for almost a year, did not go well for the pope. When French troops appeared in northern Italy Julius was forced to sue for peace. Henry set the conditions, which was a humiliation for Julius, but more to the point, the war jeopardized bishops' participation in the council. The war plus other contingencies had, moreover, emptied the papal coffers, which in turn severely limited the financial support the council needed to function.

Despite French threats Julius remained undaunted in his determination to hold the council. Even after the war broke out, he insisted the council go forward. For the solemn Session on May 1, however, only fifteen prelates showed up. This was the poorest showing for a Session in the council's history. Although all the bishops were from the emperor's domains, none were from Germany, for whose sake Julius had especially convoked the council.

In a departure from Paul III, Julius named only one legate to the council, Marcello Crescenzio. The legate was to be assisted by two nuncios—Archbishop Sebastiano Pighino and Bishop Luigi Lippomani—both of whom were well informed about the German situation.[38] The three formed an able team but not a team of equals. By his rank as cardinal and his commission as legate, Crescenzio outranked the others and held in his hands the effective direction of the proceedings.

From an old and distinguished family, he held a law degree from Bologna and had long been an important member of the Curia. His record was not unblemished. He had fathered an illegitimate daughter, whom he managed to marry off well, and had, except very briefly, never resided in either of the dioceses he successively held. But he was a close friend of Julius, who trusted him to keep the council on course and to forestall efforts by it to undertake a reform of the Curia. As with Paul III, so with Julius: that reform was to be in the hands of the pope alone.

In the Session on May 1 the few bishops present declared the council officially resumed. They also, after strong objections, agreed to Crescenzio's proposal, to set September 1 as the date for the next Session. The reason for the four-month hiatus was to allow the German and Italian bishops, as well as the Protestants, more time to arrive. Hope for French participation had by now evanesced.

As opponents of delaying the next Session for so long had feared, nothing constructive was accomplished during that long interval. Attendance grew by small increments. By September 1 thirty-four prelates had arrived. Spain provided the largest number, some of whom, like Pedro Guerrero, the archbishop of Granada, had excellent theological educations.[39] Italians were few compared with their earlier showings, mainly because the papacy was unable to provide subventions for the large numbers who truly could not afford the expenses entailed. Italians also feared traveling northward with the pope's war against Ottavio in progress.

Among German bishops, as well as others, skepticism was rampant that the council would accomplish anything. For the first time, however, bishops from Germany finally put in an appearance. They included the prince archbishops of Mainz and Trier, soon to be joined by the prince archbishop of Cologne—the three most important prelates in Germany, "Prince Electors of the Holy Empire," as the official council documents designated them. Other prelates followed, but the total never exceeded thirteen or fourteen.[40]

Work had yet to begin. At the Session on September 1 nothing was decreed except the date for the next Session, October 11, a further delay prompted, as the decree stated, by the "small attendance."[41] The Session was, however, hardly without excitement. As it was concluding Abbot Jacques Amyot appeared from among the onlookers and presented a letter and another document from Henry II, in whose name he said he was acting. He demanded the two pieces be read. With permission granted, Massarelli began with the salutation, "Henry, by God's grace, king of France . . . to the fathers of the Tridentine assembly." The single word "assembly" *(conventus),* interpreted especially by the Spaniards as an insult and a deliberate avoidance of the word council, threw the chamber into an uproar.

The scene seemed like a replay of Trent in January 1547, when the envoys of Charles V appeared and caused consternation. The legate and the others retired to the sacristy to decide how to respond, especially since the documents on the surface seemed to deny the legitimacy of the council. Rather than further antagonize the king, they decided to allow the reading, on the correct but lame excuse that in Latin *conventus* was sometimes a synonym for *concilium.*

Massarelli then read the letter aloud and Amyot the other document, the king's protest. Henry asserted that the pope, under pressure from the emperor, had broken the peace, which meant that he, the king, could not safely send prelates to the council. But more fundamentally, he could not do so because he regarded the meeting at Trent not as a general council but as a private assembly to promote the concerns of those for whom it had been convoked rather than the general interests of the church. For that reason the French church did not consider itself bound by any decisions the assembly might take.[42]

When the reading was finished, Amyot was told the council would formally reply at the next Session, scheduled for October 11. The king could not have made his position clearer nor publicized it in a more dramatic way. Still, he did not take the further and far more serious step of a formal protest in consistory in Rome as Charles had done. Henry's action lacked the solemnity of Charles's. Unhappy though the situation was, therefore, it was not so dire as four years earlier. At the council itself the upshot was simply a French boycott, deplorable but not calamitous.

The same could not be said of Henry's plans for a war against the emperor. At that very time he was negotiating an alliance with the Protestant princes. In an even broader perspective, the crisis between the king and the pope led in France to a resurgence of sentiments in favor of the autonomy of the French church vis-à-vis Rome and of the superiority of council over pope, which over time would coalesce into full-fledged Gallicanism.[43] Such sentiments were not, however, restricted only to France.

The Second Period: 1551–1552

The day after the Session on September 1 the council finally went to work, beginning with discussion of the Eucharist—initiated at Trent, continued at great length in Bologna, and now on the table once again. The same procedures were followed as before and the same problems and arguments debated, but different for the most part were the bishops and theologians, most of whom were facing the subject for the first time. Between September 8 and 16 twenty-five theologians spoke to them.[44] This was followed by nine General Congregations from September 21 to the 30.[45]

Among the interventions were those advocating granting the Eucharistic cup to the laity. Cardinal Madruzzo led them off.[46] He was followed by the archbishop of Mainz, Sebastian von Heusenstamm, then by the two envoys of King Ferdinand, one of whom was the highly respected theologian Friedrich Nausea, the bishop of Vienna.[47] Not everyone, however, was convinced by their arguments, including the legate. The reluctance was due in large part to the issue of church authority—had the church acted illegitimately in withholding the cup? The council decided to postpone action on the cup until the arrival of the Protestants.

By October 7 the document on the Eucharist was ready. Only at this point, just four days before the Session, did Crescenzio hand the council a draft of a reform decree, supposedly on the delicate subject of "obstacles to residence," which had been dealt with but only partially during the first period of the council. The text, composed by Crescenzio, altogether side-stepped the purported subject. On October 10 time did not allow for a clear surfacing during the General Congregations of the anger, especially of the Spaniards and Germans, at the legate's strategy on reform, which seemed designed to forestall debate on serious problems. The reform decree passed almost without change, but it fired resentment of the legate.

The Session on October 11 (officially Session 13) went smoothly—and lasted eight hours. Present, besides the presiding triumvirate, were forty-one prelates—twenty Spanish, thirteen Italian (plus the Italian general of the Augustinians), and seven Germans. Roughly the same proportion prevailed among the theologians. Present also were seven envoys—three from Charles, two from his brother Ferdinand, and two from the Duke of Brandenburg. Included in the formalities was, as promised, a long, conciliatory but firm reply to Henry II's protest.[48] The Session approved three decrees—on the Eucharist, on reform, and a final one postponing four articles on the Eucharist. To those decrees was added a safe-conduct to the council for the Protestants.[49]

Polemicists had fanned the memory of the burning of Jan Hus at Constance, which made repeated assurances of safe-conduct imperative. The safe-conduct stipulated that Protestants could freely discuss and propose to the council any topics they wished and on them "hold debate without any violent abuse or invective." Should they be accused of any crimes (a less reassuring note), they could name judges "favorable to themselves."

The postponement of the four articles, the decree stated, was to allow the Protestants to be heard on them. The articles were: (1) Is it divine law that for their salvation the faithful must receive communion under the forms of both bread and wine? (2) Does a person who receives under only one form receive less? (3) Has the church erred in allowing the laity to receive under only one? (4) Should little children receive communion? These questions were to be answered in the Session scheduled for January 25, 1552, but there was to be an intervening Session held on November 25.

The decree on the Eucharist made use again of the format of chapters and canons first employed for the decree on justification.[50] It consisted in eight of the former and eleven of the latter. The canons contain no surprises. Although framed negatively, they are most easily summarized by turning them around into affirmations. The first, if thus turned, affirmed the Real Presence. It was the foundation and presupposition for all the others. The second affirmed that Christ is present sacramentally through the transformation of both bread and wine into the body and blood, "which the church most appropriately [aptissime] calls transubstantiation." The others went on to teach that Christ is fully present in both forms and remains present in them even after the conclusion of the Mass, that Christ is legitimately adored in the Eucharist (as, the decree suggests, in Corpus Christi precessions and celebrations), that adult Christians are legitimately obliged to receive the Eucharist at least once a year, and, finally, that confession is required before communion if one's conscience is burdened with serious sin.

The chapters, as in the justification decree, were short, pastorally oriented instructions. A passage from the eighth reveals the positive tone the chapters tried to express. The passage is interesting, moreover, because it contained an exhortation to "frequent communion," which was a disputed issue among Catholics at the time and remained such into the twentieth century.[51] In it the council "enjoins, exhorts, begs, and entreats" all Christians to

> believe and reverence these sacred mysteries of his body and blood with such constancy and firmness of faith, such dedication of mind, and such devotion and worship that they may be able to receive frequently this life-supporting bread. May it be for them truly the life of the soul and the unending health of the mind; thus, strengthened by its force, may they be able after the journey of this wretched pilgrimage to reach the heavenly fatherland, there to eat without end the same bread of angels that they now eat beneath the sacred veil.[52]

Preceding the eight canons on reform was a long introduction reminding the bishops that they are "shepherds of their flocks, not oppressors, that they are . . . to love them as children and brothers." Bishops are to deal kindly with those who "through human frailty have fallen into sin." They must apply "gentle medicine," and even when they must apply the rod they must temper "strictness with restraint, judgment with mercy, severity with lenity." The introduction related, however, only peripherally to the canons, which dealt with legal technicalities arising from appeals from bishops' verdicts in criminal cases and from questions about bishops' rights when cases were filed against them. The decree avoided mention of every crucial issue on the reform agenda, including "obstacles to residence." It passed because bishops could hardly find fault with its provisions and had no time to organize opposition, but they felt duped.

A crisis was brewing. It fell to Francisco de Toledo, Charles's envoy, to mediate between the bishops and the legate. It was an unenviable task. The Germans were dismayed, the Spaniards furious. When Toledo presented to the legate a Spanish memorandum with thirteen points for action on reform, the legate, secure in Julius's support, reminded Toledo that only he had authority to propose materials for the agenda. When Toledo appealed to Charles for guidance, he was told to proceed with caution and, implicitly, to hold the bishops in check—reform was not to proceed with any diminution of papal authority. Charles was loath to be drawn into a replay of his conflict with Paul III.[53]

For the moment Toledo was able to calm fiery spirits. The crisis passed. But resentment of the legate was only one factor that by the middle of October made Trent an unhappy place. Prices had again soared to the skies. Food supplies were short, lodging scarce and often uncomfortable. The complaints were old, but the bishops were new. More serious was dismay about the council itself. Nausea, the bishop of Vienna, had arrived full of optimism, but by October he had plunged into a deep pessimism: the council moved at a turtle's pace; and it had so few in attendance that Protestants would mock it. To King Ferdinand he wrote, "It would be better if it had never been called."[54]

The excitement and anxiety over the arrival on October 22 of the first Lutheran envoys, from the Duke of Württemberg, briefly mitigated the gloom. Before engaging the council the two envoys decided to await the arrival of more Lutherans.[55] A month later an envoy came from Strasbourg, the renowned historian Johann Sleiden (Sleidanus), just in time for the Session on November 25, but both he and those from Württemberg had yet to say an official word. They were there but as if not there. In November the first Pole to take part in the council arrived, an archdeacon, Paul Głowoski, the procurator or vicar for the archbishop of Gnesen.

In preparation for that Session the council had ready decrees on penance and extreme unction (that is, last anointing). As with the Eucharist, little account was taken of the work accomplished in Bologna. For the first time in the council Calvin's name appears in the sources used to analyze and summarize Protestant positions.[56] The theologians went at the propositions derived from that process in their Congregations between October 20 and 30, after which, on November 6, the General Congregations began.[57]

A week later a deputation went to work to formulate the two decrees. Although bishops and theologians agreed that both rites were sacraments, and that penance consisted in three parts—sorrow for sin, confession of sin, and then some work of satisfaction, for example, saying some prayers—they were not so united or clear on other issues that had been raised. For penance the outstanding question was whether Christ had commanded secret (private) confession. The Protestants maintained, correctly, that there was no evidence for it until the Middle Ages. Some theologians at the council agreed with them, or at least that Christ did not command secret confession.[58] For extreme unction the problem was the lack of clear biblical basis. Some bishops insisted, moreover, that not all points on which Catholics disagreed with Protestants about these two sacraments were serious enough or clearly settled enough to be condemned.

November 25 was fast approaching. The deputation delivered its draft to the prelates, and on November 20 the General Congregation opened debate, which continued and concluded the following day. Crescenzio at the last minute that day delivered to the council the reform decree, his work and his alone, to be debated in a single General Congregation two days later, during which other business also had to be conducted. The document consisted in clarification of a few matters of episcopal rights and jurisdiction and a mishmash of disciplinary measures against clerical sins and sinners. Most of it was simply a reworking of already existing legislation. The Spaniards' memorandum on reform played no part in it.

The contents of the reform document, as well as the timing, sent the Spaniards into a rage. Toledo again had to step into the breach to plead with the legate to take at least some account of the reforms the Spaniards (and others, of course) demanded come to the floor and then to plead with the bishops to restrain themselves. The legate refused to give an inch. Toledo calmed the bishops somewhat by saying that he had informed the emperor of the situation and had again appealed to him for instructions on how to proceed, which the bishops could act upon in the weeks that intervened between the November and the January Session. The bishops, frustrated, had to bide their time.

The letters of the Spaniards to the court of Charles V were filled with bitter complaints about the legate, perceived as carrying out the will of Julius III, and about the consequent lack of liberty in the council.[59] Francisco Vargas, Toledo's assistant, who had delivered Charles's solemn protest at Bologna several years earlier, was hardly the most temperate among them. He wrote that the pope wanted nothing more than to suspend the council or, that failing, to end it as quickly as possible. The council was for Julius "a yoke from which he wanted to deliver himself."[60]

On November 23, two days before the Session, the General Congregation dealing with the legate's draft at first proceeded fairly smoothly, although Girolamo Beccadelli, the bishop of Syracuse, offered his opinion that the reform was "minimal."[61] The telling moment came later when Nicolas Psaume, the bishop of Verdun, commented, "This is a mere pretense at reform, superficial."[62]

The legate was much displeased. The next day he opened the Congregation by reprimanding "those fathers" who called the reform superficial. They did not know what they were talking about. When Psaume's turn to speak came he began to defend himself but was interrupted by the legate who told him to stick to the matter at hand. That was too much for Psaume, who shouted, "There's no freedom of speech in this council. I'll ask the emperor permission to leave, and he will grant it." Although the legate was eventually able to restore order and bring the meeting to its predetermined conclusion, the situation at the council was rapidly deteriorating.[63]

Adolf von Schaumburg, the archbishop of Cologne, began intimating in private conversations that he was considering going home, partly because of the tactics of the legate and partly because of disturbing news of Protestant military operations he was hearing from Germany. The archbishops of Mainz and Trier soon joined him in asking the pope's and then the emperor's permission to leave, an eventuality that both monarchs very much wanted to prevent. These three elector-archbishops stood as symbols for German participation, the great hope in convening this period of the council.

The Session on November 25, however, went off as planned and without untoward behavior. It approved two decrees, one on penance and extreme unction and the other on reform. The thirteen canons of the latter need no further comment.[64] The former decree is divided into two parts according to the two sacraments, each of which is further divided into chapters and canons.[65] The part dealing with extreme unction is relatively short and most notable for its firm and repeated insistence that the sacrament was instituted by Christ. In support of the assertion it quotes the Epistle of James (5:14–15) and then maintains that the matter and form of the sacrament have been handed down by an "apostolic tradition," a specification of what the council meant to include under "traditions." The text describes the comfort the sacrament is intended to provide:

> For the reality [res] of the sacrament is the grace of the Holy Spirit, whose anointing takes away sins and the remains of sin, if there be any, and comforts and strengthens the soul of the sick person by arousing great trust in divine mercy. Supported by this sacrament the sick person bears more lightly the burdens and trials of his illness and resists more easily the temptations of the devil, who lies in wait, and he sometimes regains his bodily health when it is expedient for the salvation of his soul.

The part of the decree dealing with penance is considerably longer. It is a compendium of the teaching on the sacrament that developed in the West beginning in the twelfth century, once the practice of private confession became widespread outside monasteries. No doctrinal decree of the council had up to this point betrayed such a strong imprint of medieval Scholastic theology and canon law.

The canons as usual identified the essential points of the decrees. The first asserted (as turned into a positive form) that Christ instituted the sacrament. Just as fundamental was canon 6, which asserted that "confessing secretly to a priest alone, which the Catholic church has always observed from the beginning," is in conformity with the command of Christ and is not a "human invention." The wording avoided asserting that Christ commanded secret confession, which took account of the reservations on this point of some bishops and theologians, but it committed the error of asserting that the church observed the practice "from the beginning." Other canons insisted on three indispensable components to a salutary reception of the sacrament—sorrow for one's sins, confession of them, and acts of satisfaction imposed by the priest—and on the divine command *(jus divinum)* to confess each and every sin.

Canon 9 asserted that the absolution the priest imparts is a judicial act and thus indicated that sinners present themselves to a tribunal in which they are subject to a judge. Late medieval writings on the sacrament described the priest's role as threefold—father, doctor, and judge. Different authors emphasized one or the other of these roles, but the presumption was that they were compatible and were all operative in how the ideal priest performed his function.[66] The council certainly did not intend to dismiss the first two roles, but even in the chapters it emphasized the judicial. It thus not only avoided dealing with the pastoral problem of the anxiety confession could induce, sometimes in acute forms as with persons as diverse as Luther and Ignatius of Loyola, but unwittingly contributed to it by its emphasis.

The chapters, relatively long, acted as usual as instructions, elaborating for the purpose of valid and devout practice on points made in the canons. They at times presented the consolatory effects of the sacrament properly received, as in chapter 3: "Of course, the meaning and fruit of this sacrament, so far as its force and efficacy are concerned, is reconciliation with God, which in persons who receive the sacrament with devotion is often followed by a peace and a serenity of conscience accompanied by intense consolation of spirit."

Nonetheless, the emphasis on obligation and the detailing of the conditions required for a valid confession are the overriding characteristics of the document. In neither the chapters nor the canons did the council try to simplify the confusing network of legislation regarding so-called reserved sins. The public and sometimes complex nature of certain kinds of sin—for example, cases of fraud or theft, where restitution might be required—had led to the practice of reserving absolution of them to the bishop or even the Holy See. But in the late Middle Ages popes had granted to the mendicant orders great "privileges" in this regard, which sometimes exceeded the authority of bishops to deal with such cases and further complicated the legislation. The mendicants' privileges were much resented by the bishops, but, more than that, they underscored the juridical character of official thinking about the sacrament and highlighted the fact that penitents presented themselves as in a courtroom in which they acted as the prosecuting attorney against themselves.

The decrees of November 25 were the last substantive legislation the council was to publish during this period. On January 25 the Session was duly held as scheduled, but, as had happened before, the decree called for a postponement of further decrees.[67] The previous month, however, the prelates and theologians had no idea that their labors thenceforth were to be in vain. They had therefore set themselves to address the Mass and the sacrament of holy orders, subjects debated at length in Bologna. From December 7 to the end of the month, forty-one theologians spoke, followed in January by the General Congregations of the bishops.[68]

By January 23 the council was ready to put the finishing touches on those decrees, but Crescenzio, under pressure from Toledo and Vargas, confronted directly the mode and measure of participation to be granted the Protestants, a problem that had been nagging at the council ever since they began arriving. With the Session on January 25 now on the horizon, the problem came to a climax. Would the Protestants be admitted to the Session? If so, under what conditions? Present at the council, besides Sleiden and the two envoys of Württemberg, were now envoys of the elector Maurice, Duke of Saxony, who had arrived on January 7.[69] Also present were six Protestant theologians.[70]

The Protestant demands were many, beginning with a new safe-conduct that would allow them full participation in the council as they asserted the Council of Basel had granted the Hussites in its safe-conduct for them. They also asked that the council delay the publication of the decrees scheduled for January 25 until more Protestant theologians arrived and that it not address new material until then.

But they had a much bigger agenda. They demanded, as mentioned, that they be given votes equal to those of the bishops, that the decisions already taken be reopened, that the council elect its own president, and that the pope be subject to its decrees—implicitly demanding the council declare its authority superior to the pope's. Thus the council would become, according to them, a true council.

Protestant demands of council [handwritten margin note]

Julius III had told Crescenzio that the Protestants were to be admitted only if they first agreed to submit to the council as it was presently constituted. Charles insisted that, while the council must hold fast to its authority, it grant the Protestants a hearing and an opportunity to defend their positions. Crescenzio, yielding to pressure from the imperial representatives, proposed that on January 24 a quasi-unofficial *(secreta)* General Congregation be held at which the Protestants could present their case. The Congregation would take place not in the Giroldo palace, as usual, but in a hall at the legate's residence. The bishops approved unanimously. Crescenzio thus tried to steer a midway course between the pope and the emperor. He wanted to forestall the Protestants' being heard, as they wanted, in the more solemn setting of the Session in the cathedral the next day, January 25.

The "Congregation" took place, and the Protestants were heard. Besides demanding a new and more absolute safe-conduct, they repeated now familiar themes, such as reopening debate on decrees already approved. Leonhard Badhorn, the envoy of Maurice of Saxony, flung at the assembled prelates the most comprehensive rejection of the council's work—Trent was *not* truly "a general, free, and Christian" council and had already committed many grave errors in doctrine.

Massarelli announced that after mature deliberation the council would respond.[71] The next day, besides a new safe-conduct, the council decreed a postponement of the publication of the decrees on the Mass and orders in the "definite hope" that more Protestants would arrive. The council would "receive them courteously and listen to them favorably" on condition they came not with the intention of "stubbornly attacking the Catholic faith, but of learning the truth." The text intimated that the German situation was the principal reason the council was being held: "This holy council . . . desires nothing more than to remove from the most illustrious German nation all disputes and schisms concerning religion and to take measures for the tranquillity, peace, and concord of that same nation."[72]

This safe-conduct was stronger and more detailed than the previous one. The Protestants could present their positions. Their safety was assured. Their envoys and all in their entourage would be treated with courtesy and respect. Beyond that, the document conceded little. The council would go on as before.

The episode makes absolutely clear that, thirty-five years after the outbreak of the Reformation, the problem was no longer disagreement over this or that doctrine. The Protestants had developed and appropriated an operational paradigm that was incompatible with the corresponding paradigm of the bishops and theologians at Trent. There was no possibility that the council would or could accede to the Protestant demands, just as there was no possibility that the Protestants would or could yield to the council as it was in fact constituted. Still, in the blind hope of accomplishing something, the council suspended further discussion until more Protestant theologians could arrive, a prospect expected shortly to be fulfilled.[73]

Francisco de Toledo, prescient, immediately saw in this suspension of activity the danger that it would be protracted and ultimately fatal to the council. After January 25 not a single doctrinal discussion was held, nor a single decree published. The pope had so severely reprimanded Crescenzio for letting the Protestants speak before they submitted to the council that the legate, deeply shaken, seemed for the first time uncertain of himself. But he and Toledo continued to tangle.

The pope complained bitterly to Charles V about the behavior of the Spaniards, whose program for reform challenged the extent of papal authority regarding episcopal appointments. He was particularly annoyed at Toledo. In the same communication on February 20, he warned the emperor that rumors were rife in Rome of a military alliance between the French king and the German Protestants and that, if war should break out, he saw no good purpose in continuing the council.

From January 22 to March 9 a delegation of Saxon theologians led by Melanchthon waited in vain in Nuremberg for instructions to proceed to Trent from Duke Maurice, who was still trying to conceal from Charles his conspiratorial machinations. But for Maurice the pieces had just at that moment finally fallen into place. On January 15, he signed the Treaty of Chambord with Henry II, firmly sealing their alliance and absolutely guaranteeing French military cooperation against Charles.

Even in this double-game situation, a few Protestant theologians made the journey to Trent. In early March, moreover, three "orators" (envoys) from King John III of Portugal also arrived, the first appearance of anyone from that nation. But the council was unraveling, and talk of its suspension was now common in Trent, in Rome, and in the imperial court. Uncertainty and anxiety hung darkly over it.

With no decrees prepared, the Session scheduled for March 19 had to be canceled, an unmistakable symptom of malaise.[74] Most troubling for the council's future, Charles V had finally become convinced that the Protestant mission to the council was useless, and he acknowledged that the pope would not give ear to reform proposals such as those of his Spanish bishops. From his viewpoint, therefore, the council had failed in the purposes for which he had insisted on its being convened and then reconvened. The final blow had been dealt to his "great plan." He let Toledo know that he saw suspension as inevitable but that he did not want the initiative to come from himself.

In mid-March some sixty bishops were still present at Trent, but in the previous month the archbishops of Mainz, Cologne, and Trier had left for home. Other German bishops began leaving. Not only was the council in the doldrums, but the German prelates were convinced they needed to defend their dioceses from the Protestant armies, now in open rebellion against the emperor. The king of France had, moreover, sent his troops to do battle on Charles's western frontier. The emperor had failed to grasp the seriousness of the threat until it was too late. The war was to be his undoing.[75]

In late March the legate took ill, and within a short while he lay mortally stricken, incapable of work.[76] He died about a month later. Even most of the Spaniards had given up hope of accomplishing anything. The end now seemed inevitable. When news arrived in Rome that on April 4 Augsburg had fallen to Charles's enemies, Julius III believed he could no longer delay taking action. The safety of Trent itself was now in question. The pope's brief of suspension bore the date April 15.

The two nuncios at Trent feared the reaction of the council if the prelates discovered the pope had suspended it without consulting them. They decided, presumably in consultation with the stricken Crescenzio, to keep the papal brief secret until the council deliberated on the matter.[77] In a General Congregation on April 24, Pighino outlined the difficulties of continuing the council. Madruzzio, the first to speak, urged suspension, and he was followed by many others agreeing with him.

In the General Congregation two days later a majority voted for the suspension. Only at this point were the bishops informed of the papal brief. On April 28, in Session 16 of the Council of Trent, the council solemnly ratified a suspension for two years but stipulated at the same time that the council be reconstituted as soon as conditions allowed.[78] The decree passed by a majority of forty-five votes to twelve.

The Lost Decade

Four months later Charles V had to sue for peace with Maurice and his allies. The concessions he made through his brother Ferdinand in the Peace of Passau foreshadowed the terms of the Peace of Augsburg, 1555, in which Lutheranism was granted legitimacy and local rulers empow-

[handwritten marginal note at bottom of page:] Revival 2 failed due to infighting between Charles V & Henry II of France who declared war on Charles; discord between Julius III & Charles; inability to accommodate the German Lutherans etc

ered to determine the official religion of their territories, a provision later designated with the tag *cuius regio, eius religio.* Even contemporaries grasped the deep significance of these happenings: Germany was divided, presumably permanently, according to religion, and Charles V's power was broken. Charles abdicated and divested himself of his realms, leaving the empire and the traditional Habsburg lands to his brother Ferdinand. He left everything else to his son Philip II—Spain, Naples, Milan, the Low Countries, and the Spanish dominions overseas. Even without the empire Philip was, like his father, by far the most powerful man in Europe.

In Rome these events were watched with acute anxiety and a correspondingly great sense of impotence. Meanwhile, shortly after the suspension of the council, Julius had announced in consistory his plans for a wide-ranging reform of the church and the Curia. After a flurry of activity, the bull *Varietas Temporum* was drawn up. Although publication was expected in early 1554, the bull never appeared. Julius, curialist that he was, lacked passion for reform and feared its consequences. He died on March 23, 1555, just as the Peace of Augsburg was being negotiated.

After a short but contentious conclave reformers were able to break the deadlock with Marcello Cervini. Just what the former legate would have accomplished as Pope Marcellus II is a matter of pure speculation because he died within three weeks of his election. A similarly brief and contentious conclave elected Giampietro Carafa, who took the name Paul IV.[79] The new pope, a vigorous seventy-nine years old, came from a powerful and distinguished Neapolitan family. He had, as mentioned, helped found the Theatines, an austere religious order of priests, and was known as a fearless and uncompromising reformer. He was also known for his passionate opposition to the Habsburgs. He held Charles V responsible for the spread of Lutheranism and deeply resented the Spanish-Habsburg domination of his native Naples. In 1555 he threatened to excommunicate both Charles and his brother Ferdinand for the concessions made to Protestants in the Peace of Augsburg.

It would be difficult to imagine anyone more zealous for the good of the church, but Paul's intransigence, his political prejudices, and his unmitigated confidence in his own judgment destroyed the possibility of a constructive reign. For the first time in Rome he constructed a ghetto for the Jews, forced them to live in it, and imposed upon them other demeaning restrictions. He saw heresy in the slightest deviation from his own narrow orthodoxy, which led to his putting Cardinal Giovanni Morone, a leading member of the College of Cardinals, on trial for heresy and imprisoning him in Castel Sant' Angelo.[80] He ordered Cardinal Reginald Pole, now the archbishop of Canterbury, back to Rome for the same fate, but Pole delayed and died in the meantime. It was no coincidence that both these prelates were partisans of Habsburg policy.

Paul infused the Roman Inquisition with a new and fiery zeal, and he broadened the scope of the crimes it could investigate. In 1559 he published the first papal *Index of Prohibited Books*. The papacy was somewhat of a late-comer in the Index-enterprise. Between 1544 and 1556, for instance, the theological faculty of the University of Paris published six, and in roughly the same period the University of Louvain three. Between 1547 and 1559 the Spanish and Portuguese Inquisitions published three each, which in their impact were much more important than those from the universities.

Two features were special about the *Index* of Paul IV. First, it established an institution that operated without interruption until the middle of the twentieth century and that became a distinctive feature of modern Catholicism. Second, Paul's *Index* was so extreme that it elicited from the Jesuit Peter Canisius, certainly not known for being soft on heresy, the cry that it was a scandal. Whereas the council in its decree on Scripture left open the question of vernacular translations of the Bible, the papal *Index* forbade publishing, reading, or possessing them without the written permission of the Roman Inquisition. When Paul died that very year, pressure mounted from all sides for a mitigation of its stipulations, a phenomenon that affected deliberations at the reconvened council.[81]

Although Paul IV was scrupulously careful in making worthy appointments to the College of Cardinals, he made mistakes, one of which was colossal. Reformer though he was, two weeks after his election he named to the College his nephew Carlo, an intelligent but devious and scheming young man, upon whom Paul began more and more to rely for advice. Carlo, well aware of his uncle's hatred of the Spaniards for their control of Naples, had little difficulty persuading him to join in a military alliance with Henry II against Philip II. The alliance ended in 1557 in a costly and humiliating defeat for the pope. Only toward the end of his pontificate did Paul become aware of the nefarious schemes of Carlo and other nephews, whom he then banished from Rome. Paul's successor took more drastic action against the nephews and had Cardinal Carlo and his brother, Giovanni, the Duke of Paliano, executed for their crimes.[82]

Paul's war with Spain and the ongoing war between Henry II *France* and Philip II eliminated of course the possibility of resuming the council. Even had the political situation been more propitious, Paul almost certainly would not have done so. Horrified that Protestants had been admitted and granted a hearing at Trent, he saw the council as an extravagant and extremely dangerous waste of time. If there was to be a council, it had to be more directly under papal control.

On January 20, 1556, soon after his election, Paul announced to the cardinals his intention of creating a new commission on reform.[83] He was bold enough to confront them with the word many feared the most, simony. He actually accomplished a radical reform of the Datary, which cost him two-thirds of his personal income. A member of the failed commission under Paul III and a witness to the quiet demise of the commission established by Julius III, Paul was determined his would succeed. His plans for it grew with each day, it seems, and gradually escalated from a commission to a large, multinational gathering modeled on the Fifth Lateran Council, that is, a council in Rome under the immediate presidency of the pope.

Outside Rome that prospect encountered resistance from almost every quarter and ridicule from not a few. Even if Paul had lived longer, the plan, ever more grandiose, almost certainly could not have succeeded. The failure of yet another "papal reform commission" fueled the widespread conviction that the papacy could not and would not reform itself. Paul on his own, however, forced some changes on the Signatura and the Penitentiary, two of the papal offices whose practices were most often criticized for their venality, and thus he showed that strong hands could at least modify embedded patterns.

The Romans grew to hate Paul IV. In mid-August 1559, as the pope lay dying, the city erupted into a fury. A mob broke into the headquarters of the Inquisition, destroyed records, freed the prisoners, and set the place on fire. Another toppled Paul's statue on the Capitoline hill, cut off its head, and, after exposing it to mockery, threw it into the Tiber. The rioting lasted for a week. Paul was buried at night in Saint Peter's the day after his death. Guards were stationed over the grave.

Some forty cardinals took part in the ensuing conclave, which lasted four months.[84] Included in that number was Giovanni Morone, whom the cardinals had voted to release from prison with rights restored shortly after the death of Paul IV. Divided between French and Spanish factions, the conclave was further complicated by yet another faction led by the still powerful Carlo Carafa and made up of cardinals named by his uncle. Not to be underestimated was the influence of ambassadors to the Holy See, especially the Spanish ambassador, Francisco Vargas.

The leading candidate was Cardinal Ercole Gonzaga, the future papal legate to the reconvened council and the brother of Ferrante Gonzaga, the enemy of Ottavio Farnese. Another important candidate was Cardinal Pedro Pacheco, who from 1547 to 1549 had held out at Trent against the transfer of the council to Bologna. From September 5 to December 25 the cardinals debated, negotiated, made and broke deals, especially after it became clear that Gonzaga could not be elected. Meanwhile the situation in the city grew desperate as money ran out to pay the 3,000 soldiers and 400 cavalry hired to keep order during the conclave.

Exhausted and on the verge of desperation, the cardinals finally compromised by turning to Gian Angelo de' Medici, who had been sick during much of the conclave and received little support. He was Milanese and not related to the famous Florentine family of the same name. On him, finally, agreement was reached. Elected on Christmas day, he took the name Pius IV. In character and outlook he could hardly have been more different from his predecessor.

Early in life, before receiving holy orders, the new pope had fathered three illegitimate children. With a degree in law from the University of Bologna, he served under Paul III as a governor in the Papal States and as commissioner with the papal military trying to hold the Turks at bay in Hungary and Transylvania. The absentee archbishop of Ragusa, he was nominated to the cardinalate by Paul III in 1549.

As pope he at once reversed some of Paul IV's policies. He moderated the influence of the Inquisition and established a commission to revise and temper the draconian *Index* of his predecessor. The Roman populace received him with jubilation for these measures and also for promising them peace, justice, and an ample provisioning of food. He won special favor by reducing the price of grain.

Pius IV was as affable in personal dealings as his predecessor had been dour and intimidating. He loved literature, enjoyed the jokes of his jester, and indulged his relatives seeking favors, appointing some dozen to remunerative positions. Among his first acts was nominating his nephew, Carlo Borromeo, age twenty-one, to the College of Cardinals. He then named Carlo administrator of the diocese of Milan, the richest and most important diocese in Italy, and two years later took the obvious step of naming him archbishop of Milan. He did, however, keep him in the Curia, where he invested him with multiple responsibilities, some of which were lucrative. As his uncle's secretary, Carlo would play perhaps an even more important role during the third period of the council than had Alessandro Farnese during the first.

Little, therefore, in the first months of the pontificate seemed to augur well for the cause of church reform, but there was another side to Pius IV. He was a hard worker, and he developed an extraordinarily productive relationship with his devout nephew, Carlo. He reached out in friendship to the Habsburgs—Emperor Ferdinand I and his nephew, Philip II, the hated enemies of Paul IV. Like all the cardinals, he had sworn as part of the capitulations at the beginning of the conclave to convene a council.[85] Cardinals once elected tended to adopt a free and easy interpretation of capitulations they had sworn to uphold, and Pius in his first months seemed to be following this path. But in early May he let it be known unequivocally that he intended to live up to his promise.

To move ahead he of course needed the cooperation of the great rulers. In the decade that had elapsed since the suspension of the council, the religious and political situation had changed radically. All the major protagonists of the first two periods were dead, as were many of the bishops and theologians. A whole new cast of characters now dominated the scene. Elizabeth had successfully claimed the throne of England, an event that proved decisive for securing England for Protestantism. In Scotland, Mary Stuart returned from France in 1560 to find her kingdom so firmly in Protestant hands that in the chapel of her own palace she hardly dared allow Mass to be celebrated. Beginning in the 1550s in Poland, that is, in the large Polish-Lithuanian Commonwealth, Protestantism in its Calvinist form was gaining ever more adherents, especially among the rich Polish, Lithuanian, and, to some extent, Ruthenian gentry. The Scandinavian countries were by this time solidly Lutheran.

Philip II, though extraordinarily powerful, was perceived by France as a lesser threat than his father had been. At the Treaty of Cateau-Cambrésis signed on April 3, 1559, the year Pius IV was elected, Philip and Henry II agreed to lay down their arms, thus ending the Habsburg-Valois conflicts that had troubled European peace for almost forty years. Both monarchs were ready to turn their attention to other affairs. In Spain Protestantism had established no beachhead, thanks principally to two factors—the vigilance of the Spanish Inquisition and the notably high caliber of the episcopacy.

Like Philip, Emperor Ferdinand I did not pose the threat to France that his more powerful brother had, but he was by no means a monarch of second rank. The Peace of Augsburg, the landmark victory for the Lutherans, brought an uneasy but operative cessation of military hostilities in the empire. This situation hardly strengthened Ferdinand's hand, but at least he did not have to expend his resources on the field of battle. Moreover, he held other important titles in his own name, such as king of Hungary, king of Bohemia, and archduke of Austria.

By the time Pius was elected at the end of 1559, France was already by far the most unstable of the three great Continental powers. On July 10 Henry II died from a wound inflicted in a tournament celebrating the Treaty of Cateau-Cambrésis, an event that deeply unsettled the political situation. He was succeeded by his teenage son, Francis II, the husband of Mary Stuart, whose policies were guided by the House of Guise. Francis himself died eighteen months later. In December 1560, the throne therefore passed to his brother, Charles IX, ten years old. The transition signaled the emergence of the queen mother, Catherine de' Medici, as regent and virtual ruler of the realm, an efficacious challenge to the former ascendance of the Guise.

Regencies almost by definition foster intrigue and political unrest, *France* but in France at this time the religious question turned the situation into a crisis of such major proportions that civil war loomed. Among the nobility and the upper bourgeoisie Calvinism had made great gains, and its adherents were aggressive in their beliefs. The Huguenots, as they were known, threatened to form a military alliance not unlike the earlier Schmalkaldic League. They were most obviously different from the Lutherans in that they drew notoriety to themselves by uncompromising iconoclasm, which resulted in the desecration of churches, the smashing of altars and statues, and the burning of sacred paintings.

To many outside observers France seemed inexorably heading to Protestantism. In March 1560, just months after Pius's election and still during the reign of Francis II, Charles de Guise explained to the pope that the French situation was in need of immediate remedy, that a general council would take time to prepare, and that therefore a French national council was required in the meantime. Later that month the

French court issued a formal announcement of a meeting of the Gallican church, whose purpose was not only reform but also religious reconciliation.

Pius was alarmed. Was France about to go its own way? Could de Guise be trusted? The pope's determination to convoke the council and to have it meet at as early a date as possible stemmed largely from his fears for France. He believed that a general council would forestall the French council by providing the incontrovertible alternative to it. Before he could move ahead with his plan, however, he had to win the support of the rulers. For almost the entire year 1560 he negotiated with Philip II, Ferdinand I, and the still reigning Francis II, that is, with the Cardinal of Lorraine.

On the surface the prospects looked good. In the Treaty of Cateau-Cambrésis, both Philip II and Henry II had agreed to support the convocation of a council. The treaty meant, moreover, that for the first time since the council had convened in 1545, the European rulers were at peace among themselves. When Francis II succeeded his father, he accepted the terms of the treaty, which meant supporting, at least in principle, a general council. Both the French and the imperial courts let it be known, however, that they believed the Council of Trent had up to this point caused more harm than good.

Difficulties emerged. Conditions were set down. The French pleaded the prior necessity of a national council. Not surprisingly, the location of Pius's council again became a point of contention. As usual, the French court raised strong objections to Trent, and even Ferdinand opposed it as a place whose very name was hateful to his Lutheran subjects. Philip held out for it. The pope finally won agreement for Trent. Underneath the question of location, however, lurked a new and deeply troubling substantive issue. Was this council to be a new one or a continuation of the old? Francis and Ferdinand argued for the former, Philip for the latter.

At stake was the status of the decrees approved in the first two periods. Those decrees had never been ratified by the papacy, which meant, at least in some eyes, that their final status was still tenuous. By convoking a new council, the pope would, it seemed, automatically place them once again on the table for further discussion, revision, and even rejection. For the French court, now grasping at the possibility of doctrinal reconciliation with the Huguenots, and for Ferdinand, worried that the implicit confirmation of the already enacted decrees would antagonize the Lutherans and stir them to military action, a new council was the order of the day. Despite the experience of the second period of the council, Ferdinand still harbored hopes that the Lutherans could be persuaded, if conditions were right, to attend a new council and thus ease religious tensions.

The prospect of reopening debate and thus throwing into jeopardy decrees so painfully hammered out was for the pope a specter of nightmarish proportions. Moreover, like virtually everybody in his court, he thought that prospects of reconciliation through a council were unrealistic in the extreme. What the council could do was shore up Catholic belief and practice in lands where that was still possible. Pius could not, however, risk losing French and imperial support, which meant he was willing, probably sincerely but without expectation of success, to make overtures to the Protestants. As he moved resolutely ahead with his determination to convoke the council, he tried to allay fears and win confidence. Although he never openly and directly opposed the idea of a brand new council, he had no intention of going along with it.

When his bull of convocation lifted the suspension of the council, it thereby would seem to make clear that in the pope's mind the council was to take up where it had left off a decade earlier. The point was implicitly underscored by the decision to hold the council at Trent. But the bull never explicitly made that point, and it sedulously avoided the word "continuation."[86] Although the pope in other official documents stated his position clearly, the wording of the bull was sufficiently ambiguous to allow that the council was a new beginning.[87] In any case, on November 29, 1560, Pius signed the bull *Ad Ecclesiae Regimen,* announcing the opening of a council at Trent on Easter Sunday of the next year, less than five months later.

5

The Council Resumes, 1562–1563

Easter Sunday, April 6, 1561, came and went. At Trent only four bishops had arrived and not a single legate. The next nine months came and went. But by January 18, 1562, when the council officially declared itself assembled, the number present had grown to about one hundred. It continued to grow, eventually more than doubling, which made this period by far the best attended of the three.

Pius IV surely realized how unrealistic April 6 was as an opening date. At least a month was required for word to reach bishops and their sovereigns that a council had been summoned. Then rulers of both large and small states had to make up their minds about how ardently or coolly to support the project and about how many and which bishops to send—if any. Bishops themselves had to make arrangements for an absence of undetermined duration but almost certainly for at least a year. Then they had to make the journey, which for bishops in places like Spain and Portugal could take many weeks. Why, then, the early date? To put the French on notice that the council was not a distant prospect but a reality about to happen.

The pope set about in great earnestness to invite, entice, cajole, and threaten prelates and others to attend, and he sent his agents far and wide to accomplish that goal. Most surprisingly, he included in his scope the schismatic churches of the East, dispatching legates to the Coptic patriarch in Alexandria, to the Greek Orthodox patriarch in Constantinople, and to the Armenian patriarch in Antioch. None of these efforts bore fruit. His several attempts to reach the Russian patriarch in Moscow were obstructed by the Poles.[1]

On December 1, 1560, he sent a letter to the Lutheran princes of Germany inviting them to send envoys to the council.[2] In early February two papal legates to Germany, Giovanni Francesco Commendone and Zaccaria Delfino, appeared before a gathering of princes in Naumburg to ask their support for the council. They received a firm negative, based especially on the premise that the pope had no authority to convene such a gathering.[3] When later that year the legates approached individual princes, they received the same response.

Their efforts with the Catholics met with failure as well. The universities of Louvain, Cologne, Freiburg, and Ingolstadt all turned down the invitation to participate. The bishops, cowed, it seems, by the possibility of a Protestant military offensive, protested that leaving their dioceses would make them vulnerable to Protestant military and propaganda offensives. They pleaded that taking part in the council would provide grounds for such actions against them. Some seemed simply to lack the psychic energy to embark on such a doubtful venture as the council. Commendone's judgment in his report to Borromeo, on April 25, 1561, was scathing: "The Protestants are wide awake; the Catholics fast asleep. One has the impression that not the Protestants but the Catholics believe in faith without works, so little effort do they make to prevent the complete breakdown of Catholicism in Germany."[4]

Emperor Ferdinand had to resign himself, therefore, to the virtual absence of German prelates at the council. He did not for that reason lack influence. He was able to make his authority strongly felt through his envoys—Count Sigismund von Thun, Anton Brus von Müglitz, the archbishop of Prague, and Georg Draščovič (Draskovic, Draskovich, etc.), the bishop-in-exile of Pécs (German, Fünfkirchen). The Duke of Bavaria, Albrecht V, also eventually sent an envoy, Sigismund Baumgartner. High in the priorities of both monarchs was concession of the Eucharistic cup to the laity and relaxation of the discipline of priestly celibacy.

Bishops in the Catholic cantons of Switzerland were, like others, skeptical about whether the pope really intended the council to take place. They worried about the expenses they would have to bear if he did. Not until the middle of 1562 did the bishop of Basel send a procurator to Trent. No others followed. Nonetheless, the seven Catholic cantons sent two envoys, a layman and Joachim Eichhorn, the abbot of Einsiedeln.

The nuncio Berardo Bongiovanni had meager success in Poland. The bishops pleaded that they could not leave home amid such a dangerous religious and political situation. No bishop, only the abbot of Sułechow, made it to the council in time for its opening. Later, however, the king sent an envoy, and one of the legates named by the pope to preside at the council was a Pole.

After earlier efforts failed in Scotland, the Jesuit Nicolaus Floris (Goudanus) was finally able in disguise to reach a bishop in the summer of 1562, only to realize the situation was hopeless.[5] In May 1561, the nuncio Girolamo Martinengo, bearing the invitation to the council for Queen Elizabeth, was denied entrance to the kingdom on the grounds that the presence of a nuncio in England was illegal and could give rise to unrest.[6]

What about France?[7] Pius had distrusted Charles de Guise since the accession of Francis II, and he worried even more about the French situation now that the cardinal had been displaced by the queen mother as the power behind the throne. Catherine began to play a double game, ostensibly preparing to send bishops to Trent but in fact going ahead with the national council. On June 12, 1561, a royal decree was sent to the bishops telling them that the Gallican church was to assemble at Poissy on the outskirts of Paris to elect those to be sent to Trent and to deal with other matters "of great importance" about which the queen wished to consult them.[8] The decree was worded so as to reassure Philip and Pius that King Charles—that is, his mother—was abiding by the agreement of Cateau-Cambrésis, but it was in fact a call for a national solution to the religious problem. In July Catherine made clear that the assembly at Poissy was open to "all subjects" who desired to be heard, which was an invitation to the Huguenots.

Both Catherine and de Guise were still under the illusion that the Huguenots could be persuaded to compromise if the Catholics showed the same willingness. De Guise thought the Eucharist was the only serious issue on which there was disagreement and that the meeting at Poissy would bit by bit win the Huguenots for the Catholic cause. The Huguenots, now fully aware of their political strength and in no mood to dilute it, were convinced that, with Scripture alone as the foundation stone for the discussions, they would emerge victorious. The stage was set for stalemate.

On July 31 the meeting opened. With the boy-king present, the royal chancellor Michel de L'Hôspital addressed the gathering with a speech emphasizing the right and duty of the crown to provide for the needs of the church. Present were six French cardinals, forty-five French archbishops and bishops, and eventually a Huguenot delegation headed by Theodore Beza from Geneva and Peter Martyr Vermigli from Zürich. Although opposed to this assembly, Pius, forced to tolerate it, sent Cardinal Ercole d'Este of Ferrara as his legate.[9]

Before the arrival of the Huguenots, the Catholic prelates debated church reform. On August 12 Charles de Guise delivered an address in which he made a deep impression by his strong insistence on the duty of episcopal residence. The bishops got to work and drew up a set of articles on reform whose centerpiece was precisely that duty but that went on to demand, for instance, that bishops preach to their flocks and adopt a modest lifestyle. These articles helped shape the proposals for reform that the French eventually brought with them to Trent. They are an important but often overlooked aspect of the meeting at Poissy.

In the meantime, however, the attempt to arrive at agreement with the Huguenots failed completely. With that, the queen ordered a list drawn up of twenty-six bishops to be sent to the council, a ploy to reassure Philip II that France was not drifting into Calvinism and thus to forestall his sending his armies to prevent such a calamity. Not only were no bishops sent, but Catherine called another colloquy with the Huguenots to meet in her own quarters at the Château de Saint-Germain-en-Laye beginning on January 27, 1562. At Trent nine days earlier the council had officially opened without a single French bishop present.

The assembly of Saint-Germain broke down almost as it began. The first item on the agenda was the veneration of images, which Catherine considered a matter where easy agreement could be reached. To her dismay it aroused such passionate feelings that the colloquy had to be terminated, which further exasperated the political situation. Civil war seemed ever more imminent. With France unable to resolve the religious problem on its own, participation in the council at Trent began to seem the only alternative.

Portugal gave promise of better results. The nuncio Prospero Santacroce received assurance from King Sebastian that he would send a good number of bishops, which was a promise well meant but difficult to fulfill. Bartolomeu dos Mártires, the devout Dominican archbishop of Braga, arrived in Trent on May 18, 1561, the first non-Italian to do so, and a few months later the king nominated Fernando Martin Mascarenhas as his envoy to the council. Although in numbers the Portuguese delegation remained small, these two men played important roles as the council unfolded.

The support of Philip II for the council, at first hesitant, soon became unwavering, and he chose two dozen of his best-educated and most exemplary bishops to send. Those bishops, often spurred on by the fervent reformer Pedro Guerrero of Granada, seized a leadership role in the council in their single-minded determination to carry through a thorough reform of the church, which they believed had to begin with "the head." They were eventually aided and abetted in this goal by Count Claudio Fernández de Quiñones Luna, Philip's envoy, who, however, did not arrive until the council was well under way. In the meantime Fernando Francisco d'Avalos, Marquis of Pescara, performed the function but only intermittently because of his duties as the governor of Milan. The Spaniards hoped to be reinforced in their reform efforts when and if bishops arrived from France. They had to wait almost a year after the council opened for those reinforcements to appear.[10]

Pius himself applied pressure, sometimes greater, sometimes lesser, to the many bishops of the Papal States and to the many from other parts of Italy, especially the "poor prelates" from the Kingdom of Naples, who resided in Rome. He was reasonably successful. The other Italian states such as the Grand Duchy of Florence and the Republic of Venice eventually bestirred themselves and sent both bishops and envoys. The result was that, in contrast to the second period, the overwhelming majority of bishops for this period were from Italy. Of these the largest number were indebted in one form or another to the favor of Pius IV and were therefore disinclined to support any reform that might impinge upon papal prerogatives. Known at the council as the *zelanti* (the zealots), they constituted the counterpoint to the Spaniards. Also among the Italians, however, was a smaller group from northern Italy in which the Spaniards found allies.

Meanwhile on March 10, 1561, Pius named five legates to lead the council, all of them cardinals.[11] The late date of their appointment confirms that the pope was not serious about opening the council on April 6. This fivesome—it cannot be called a team—was an uncongenial mix of personalities and perspectives. At its presidency was the prince-bishop of Mantua, Ercole Gonzaga, who, as mentioned, had come close to being elected pope in the recent conclave. Connected through the marriage of a niece to a nephew of the pope and through the marriage of a nephew to another relative of Pius, he at first enjoyed the pope's confidence.

His mother was Isabella d'Este, one of the great and most learned women of the Italian Renaissance, who saw to it that her sons received excellent educations. Gonzaga was, therefore, intellectually engaged and had broad interests, which included theology. He was a conscientious bishop, an effective administrator of the Duchy of Mantua, and widely respected for his integrity and fairness of judgment. Not a saint (he had fathered five children), he had worked intelligently and effectively for the reform of his diocese, much influenced in this regard by his friendship with Gasparo Contarini and Gian Matteo Giberti, the reforming bishop of Verona. His high social rank, his gifts of mind and personality, and his comfort in a leadership position enhanced his authority at the council.[12]

He worked well with Girolamo Seripando, the former prior general of the Augustinians who was now archbishop of Salerno and his fellow legate, whom he often consulted for his opinion on doctrinal and theological matters. Seripando had of course played an important role in the two previous periods. Besides his theological training he brought to the group much needed experience as to how the council functioned. As archbishop he seemed a model of what reformers were calling for. He and Gonzaga formed a coherent core within the fivesome.

The third most important member was Ludovico Simonetta, a canonist who, as the bishop of Pesaro, had been present during the first period of the council. Since 1549 he had been a member of the Curia, to whose authority he was ardently committed. Just a year before naming him legate, Pius had made him head of the Datary, a papal office reformed by Paul IV but notorious for venality. Simonetta, not Gonzaga or Seripando, was the legate whom Pius came most to trust and to whose reports from Trent he gave the most credence. Those reports, kept secret from the other legates, were highly critical of Gonzaga and

Seripando and undermined their authority in Rome. When he arrived at Trent, Seripando entered in his diary the simple words, *miserere mei*— "[Lord,] have pity on me!"[13] His words were prophetic. Simonetta soon assumed the mantle of unofficial and indefatigable leader of the *zelanti*.

Stanislaus Hosius (Hozjusz) was a Pole, the prince-bishop of Warmia (Ermland) since 1551, when he took the lead in the Polish episcopate by his writings and decisive actions against the Reformation. More a diplomat, organizer, and polemicist than a theologian, Hosius, somewhat like Reginald Pole in the first period, had a less prominent profile at Trent than Gonzaga, Seripando, and Simonetta. He tended to side with Simonetta on controversial issues, but he worked with the other legates in a more collegial fashion.

The last of the five was Markus Sittich von Hohenems, a nephew of Pius IV by his sister Chiara, who had married into the noble German family of Ems. Poorly educated (he barely understood Latin) and more at home with soldiers than with theologians, he was utterly unsuited for such an important post. Although he had previously received no sacred orders, his uncle in 1560 named him, at age twenty-seven, bishop of Cassano and, the next year, just in time for the legateship to Trent, cardinal. Sittich's ecclesiastical career was itself an affront to the bishops at Trent keen on reform. He wielded little influence during the short time he was there.

This was the fivesome designated to lead the council. Not surprisingly, it broke down completely in less than a year. By then the council was in full and seemingly irresolvable crisis, so severe that the strain contributed to the deaths of Gonzaga and Seripando within weeks of each other. At that point the council seemed to be, once again, a lost cause. In desperation Pius turned to Giovanni Morone, whom he named head legate, and transferred to him the confidence he had earlier placed in Simonetta. This decision, brilliant, was absolutely determinative in the history of the council. Morone, the former prisoner of the Roman Inquisition, saved the situation and was perhaps the only person who could have done so. His consummate diplomatic skill meant that, despite all odds, the Council of Trent was able to recover from the crisis, pick up momentum, and finally on December 4, 1563, declare its business accomplished.

Six Frustrating Months

On January 18, 1562, the council finally opened with a solemn ceremony in the cathedral of Saint Vigilius, which constituted the first Session of this period (Session 17 of the council). Present were four of the legates (Sittich arrived later), the Duke of Mantua (nephew of the cardinal), some one hundred archbishops and bishops, five abbots, four superiors general of mendicant orders, and over fifty theologians. Present also were the faithful Angelo Massarelli, again acting as secretary for the council, and Gabriele Paleotti, the head of the council's official legal advisers, who would play an important role in this period, kept a diary that complemented Massarelli's, and was later the reforming bishop of Bologna. The council eventually grew to such a size that the General Congregations could no longer be held in the Palazzo Giroldo. A special hall in the form of an amphitheater had to be constructed in the Renaissance church of Santa Maria Maggiore. The city of Trent was already bursting at the seams, with lodging ever less available and ever more expensive.

The legates were pleased at how smoothly the opening Session went. The council approved the official decree declaring itself begun. In the decree, however, was contained the provision that the legates propose the agenda *(proponentibus legatis)*.[14] The legates failed to reckon with the potential seriousness of the fact that in his written ballot Guerrero qualified his approval with the objection that that stipulation was "unnecessary and inappropriate." In this he was joined by three more Spanish bishops. The issue was not going to disappear.

In any case, the council now had to go to work. Despite the fact that for months Gonzaga and Seripando, as well as an increasing number of bishops, were present in Trent before the council opened, they, like their predecessors, made little preparation for how to proceed. The logical starting point was discussion of the Mass and of the sacraments of holy orders and matrimony, which the second period had not been able to finalize in a decree. But such a beginning would be a direct signal that the council was a continuation. The legates decided that it would be best to begin with a neutral subject and suggested to Borromeo that it might be revision of Paul IV's *Index*.

Although Pius had established a commission in Rome to undertake such a revision, he now directed the legates to have the council take it up.[15] The *Index*, universally criticized as unreasonable in the extreme and impossible to implement, had to be tempered. Seripando, who had been a member of the Roman commission, now set to work drafting a decree on the revision that included inviting to the council, with safeconduct guaranteed, all those authors whose books were slated for censure so that they could defend themselves.

Even before the council formally began, however, Guerrero demanded of the legates that in the opening Session the council declare itself a continuation.[16] The legates were able to sidestep this threat when it became clear that in this instance Guerrero had neither a mandate from Philip II nor the unequivocal backing of other Spanish bishops. The legates took note, however, that the Spaniards, and Guerrero in particular, had not come to the council meek as lambs.

The first several General Congregations were largely taken up with formalities, which included the question of whether or not to begin with the revision of the *Index*. Many objections were raised to addressing that subject, which included the scarcity of books in Trent upon which judgment would have to be made, the inefficiency of such a large gathering trying to deal with an issue that by definition descended to so many particulars, and, finally, the waste of time this enterprise entailed in view of the more important and urgent matters the council had to face. Despite the objections, by February 12 the council had implicitly accepted the revision as the first order of business, and the legates created a deputation of four members to draw up a draft document laying out principles. Five days later the deputation presented to the council its document, which in the main incorporated the points Seripando had earlier sketched.

When the debate opened on February 20, strong voices were raised in favor of inviting those censured and absolutely guaranteeing their safe-conduct so that, as Giambatista Castagna, the archbishop of Rossano insisted, the same fate not befall them as befell Hus at the Council of Constance. According to Castagna the return to the church of those separated from it was the first business of the council—*principale negotium.* He asked that the decree be conceived in a way that would make clear to "the repentant that the council was a place where they would find forgiveness and a place where the others would find it a school of true faith and saving teaching."[17]

Opposition to such provisions emerged quickly from the ranks, and the version accepted for the Session on February 26, while it invited those concerned to come to the council, where they would be kindly heard, was too weak to please those who still hoped a reconciliation was possible. Nonetheless, the 127 bishops present for the Session easily approved the decree, which essentially mandated a commission to revise the *Index* and then report back to the council.[18]

At the General Congregation on February 17, the legates announced the eighteen members of the commission, which was to be headed by Anton Brus von Müglitz, the archbishop of Prague. This commission worked diligently for the next year and a half. Its task was to moderate the extremes of the earlier *Index*. By the time the council concluded it had a revision ready, but in those rushed final hours it was unable to submit it for debate. The council decreed to transmit it to the pope for later action.

In the meantime, the legates decided to begin the more substantive discussion with a draft decree not on doctrine but on reform. Seripando had earlier asked a group of five Italian bishops to draw up a memorandum on the subject, with special care given to revitalizing the ministry of bishops in their dioceses. From the ninety-five articles the bishops produced, he chose eighteen as the most important. These were further reduced to twelve, the first nine of which dealt with episcopal reform. The council received the draft on March 11.[19]

Reformers among the bishops all shared the opinion that the decree on residence enacted in the first period that threatened severe penalties for noncompliance had had no palpable effect. Nothing had changed. Ten years after the decree passed, 113 bishops were in residence not in their dioceses but in Rome, either in the Curia, in cardinals' households, or in other venues. Neither in Rome nor elsewhere was the decree taken seriously. Since penalties did not work if loopholes persisted, another solution to the problem had to be found. One such solution was to declare the obligation of residence to be a law of God, *jus divinum.*[20]

The first of the twelve articles asked the council to consider the means necessary to oblige bishops to reside in their dioceses unless prevented by "just, honorable, and compelling reasons and in the interest of the church." In the original memorandum article 32 stated that, if no other means could be devised for securing that end, the council should declare the duty required *jure divino,* by divine law, but the document the bishops received omitted that highly controversial expression.

Proponents of *jus divinum* believed that residence was so constitutive of the episcopal office that even the pope could not dispense from it. A number of reputable canonists and theologians of the era, such as Cajetan, held this interpretation of the residence obligation. Others, however, such as Ambrosius Catharinus, also a Dominican like Cajetan, held that the obligation was simply canonical, that is, a church law.[21] If that was the case, dispensation from it could be granted for any reasonable cause.

Underneath this issue lay a fundamental question that had profound ecclesiological implications: did bishops receive their powers from God by virtue of the rite of their consecration or from the pope by their appointment? That question surfaced explicitly months later in the debate on holy orders. Bishops who believed in the *jus divinum* subscribed to the former of the alternatives, the others to the latter.

Even though *jus divinum* did not appear in the document the bishops received, it was impossible to keep it from hitting the floor of the council, which at this point began to divide into two factions, each holding passionately to its position. The first, which favored the *jus divinum,* comprised almost all the non-Italian bishops but also included a number of Italians close to Seripando, such as the Humanistically trained and devout Ludovico Beccadelli, the reforming archbishop of Ragusa.[22] The second, which held residence to be merely an ecclesiastical law, was almost exclusively Italian and led by Simonetta. It maintained that a declaration of *jus divinum* was contrary to the practice of the church, which had consistently allowed dispensations; would hamper the proper functioning of the Curia; and infringed upon papal authority.

On April 7 the debate opened on the first four of the twelve articles. Guerrero spoke that day and insisted that the council examine the basis for episcopal residence and, if that basis was *jus divinum,* that the council declare it such.[23] The next day Bartolomeu dos Mártires, the exemplary and much admired archbishop of Braga, seconded him.[24] The gauntlet had been thrown down. On this matter bishops felt keenly and were not hesitant to speak their minds, sometimes at considerable length, which resulted in a debate extending over nine General Congregations, the two weeks from April 7 to April 20.[25]

Even after such a large expenditure of time, it was still unclear where the bishops as a body stood. If any progress were to be made, the deputation responsible for formulating the decree had to be given guidelines. The legates agreed to pose before the council an orienting vote— or a "straw vote," as this procedure is sometimes called today. Although there was a precedent for such a procedure in the first period, in the General Congregation on April 3, 1546, it was an unusual practice, open to challenge. In any case, the question, straightforward, was presented to the council on April 20: should the council declare the duty of residence a divine ordinance?[26]

The question was straightforward. The answers were not. While sixty-eight prelates cast affirmative votes and only thirty-five negative, another group of thirty-five referred their vote to the pope, who certainly did not favor *jus divinum*. In that case, the vote was sixty-eight affirmative and seventy negative.[27] At this point, however, the pope had not in fact made a public statement of his position. Although on the surface the vote was indecisive, the council in fact seemed headed for deadlock.

Matters only got worse. Simonetta's letters to Rome alarmed the pope and sowed distrust of Gonzaga and Seripando.[28] They depicted the Spaniards and their sympathizers as plotting the downfall of the Curia and as ultimately intent on declaring the council superior to the pope. Pius on May 11 sent a harsh letter "to the legates" expressing his displeasure at the way they handled the issue and informing them that he intended to send two more legates, the most palpable sign of his distrust of Gonzaga's leadership. Although generically addressed, the letter was obviously aimed at him and Seripando.

In a letter to Gonzaga under the same date Borromeo confirmed the pope's great displeasure and plan to send more legates. He also wrote to Simonetta to inform him that the pope was resolved that the council "not in any way treat the article, 'Is residence of divine ordinance?'" The letters betrayed how thoroughly the pope and the Curia bought Simonetta's depiction of the article's proponents as enemies of the Curia intent on its "ruin."[29] They also betray how the ghosts of Constance and Basel haunted papal policy and struck fear into the hearts of those responsible for it.

At Trent word spread quickly that Gonzaga and Seripando had fallen from favor and that they had been replaced by Simonetta as the person of trust. The very day Gonzaga received Borromeo's letter, he responded that he would leave Trent when the new legate who would assume the presidency arrived.[30] His departure under such circumstances would create an international scandal with profound political and ecclesiastical repercussions.

Pius thus was forced to abandon the plan for more legates and to temper his reaction by insisting simply that the residence question be postponed to a later date. The sad result of this incident was that the atmosphere at Trent was further poisoned with bitterness between two clearly defined factions and, especially in the Spanish camp, with bitterness toward Rome and the conviction that the pope was opposed to a real reform of the church. To make matters worse, it soon became known that the "right-minded" bishops received letters from Rome praising them and even sometimes granting them new privileges. Meanwhile, the legates found it ever more difficult to work with one another. The situation was grave.

But the council moved on, taking up six of the remaining articles on reform but postponing discussion of two dealing with clandestine marriages. The possibility of reaching an agreement on all but the most banal issues receded ever further into the background. The Session on May 14 decreed only that it was postponing decrees until the next Session, scheduled for June 4. The legates informed Rome that they were postponing the residence question until the council took up the sacrament of holy orders. They assured the pope that they would try to handle the issue in a way pleasing to him.[31]

The Spanish bishops, frustrated and angry, threatened to lodge a solemn protest at the June 4 Session, which included the threat of leaving the council as a group. The legates were walking a tightrope. They were able to restrain the Spaniards at the last moment only by their promise to resume debate on residence later, in connection with holy orders. A public confrontation at the June Session was thus avoided, but the council was once again forced to issue a decree postponing action "because of various difficulties arising from different causes."[32] The council was almost paralyzed.

In the meantime further complications ensued. The legates, under pressure from the Spaniards, considered publishing a decree affirming that the council was a continuation of the earlier periods. But on May 18 the French envoy to the council arrived. After the failure of the meeting at Saint-Germain-en-Laye and what now seemed to be an inevitable war with the Huguenots, the French government finally decided to send a delegation of bishops to Trent. Long before the bishops arrived, however, the French envoy Louis de Saint-Gelais, seigneur de Lanssac, made his entrance into Trent and was soon followed by his two colleagues— Arnaud du Ferrier and Guy du Faur. Lanssac immediately got in touch with the envoys of Ferdinand, and they agreed to resist a declaration of continuity. A crisis over the issue was avoided only when the leading Spanish diplomat at the council withdrew his insistence on it.

With the June Session behind them, the Spaniards' tempers began to cool somewhat for two reasons. They learned in unequivocal terms that Philip did not want a confrontation with the pope, even though he still stood by the council as a continuation. Then Gonzaga renewed to them—publicly, at the General Congregation on June 6—the promise of taking up the question of residence again when holy orders were discussed.[33] Meanwhile, Gonzaga's nephew in Rome let him know that new criticisms of him were rife there. With that Gonzaga had had enough. He sent to Pius his resignation.[34]

The resignation had an effect. Pius, probably at Borromeo's urging, refused to accept it and realized he would have to deal more circumspectly with Gonzaga. He sent to the council Carlo Visconti, a trusted friend and the bishop of Ventimiglia, to investigate the relationship among the legates and to report back his findings. The report seems to have tempered somewhat his confidence in Simonetta. Thus, with the resignation refused, with the controversy over residence for the moment off the table, and with the continuity question somewhat attenuated, the council was able to move ahead. All parties were eager to break the stalemate.

At this time Ferdinand's envoys handed the legates a memorandum on reform from the emperor.[35] In it he recommended that, among other things, the council consider the following: introduction of the vernacular into the liturgy, preparation of a catechism, founding of schools for the training of the clergy, creation of an *Index* of *recommended* (rather than forbidden) books, and, most urgent, mitigation of celibacy and granting the Eucharistic cup to the laity. The legates therefore felt secure in proposing the cup as the next item on the agenda. A deft move! The issue had been debated at the last period. Its reintroduction now was a backhanded way of insinuating that the council was a continuation. Ferdinand could hardly object to its being debated.

At the General Congregation of June 6 when the legates introduced five articles on that issue, Gonzaga announced that the council would next consider "the sacrifice of the Mass," another subject debated both in Bologna and in the second period. The announcement raised no objections. All at once the legates had, without recourse to an explicit decree, accomplished their goal of moving the third period along as a continuation of the previous two. June 6, 1562, was, therefore, an important day in the history of the Council of Trent.

By this time all parties had quietly acknowledged that there was no possibility of Protestant participation in the council, which turned therefore in an even more single-minded fashion to the business of Catholicism itself. The number of bishops had now grown to almost 150, the theologians to about 70. It was at this point that the plenary meetings of the council moved to the amphitheater in Santa Maria Maggiore.

Debate on the five articles on the cup began as usual with the Theologians' Congregations, which consumed the rest of June. As the days moved on, with the same arguments repeated again and again, sometimes at great length, the number of bishops in the council hall thinned considerably.[36] But before they got their turn, the council on June 27 admitted Sigismund Baumgartner, the envoy to the council of Duke Albrecht V of Bavaria.

According to the standard protocol for such occasions, the envoy, in this case a layman, addressed the council to convey to it the concerns of his sovereign.[37] To that extent there was nothing special about what happened on June 27. Baumgartner's speech deserves mention, however, because it so clearly pinpointed the concerns of the duke (and also, clearly, of the emperor) and is thus symptomatic of the difference

FIGURE 4 *The Council of Trent* (Pasquale Cati, 1588–1589). The fresco depicts a General Congregation of the council assembled in the Renaissance church of Santa Maria Maggiore in Trent. The feminine figures are an allegorical personification of the Church of Rome. The central figure with the tiara represents the papacy, triumphing over heresy at her feet. The other figures represent the four cardinal virtues (fortitude, justice, prudence, and temperance) and the three theological virtues (faith, hope, and charity). (Altemps Chapel in the church of Santa Maria in Trastevere, Rome. Courtesy of Getty Images.)

in priorities between Catholic leaders in northern and Mediterranean Europe.

Citing information garnered from an extensive visitation of Bavaria in 1558, Baumgartner painted a dark picture. The vast majority of the parish clergy was ignorant and infected with heresy. Out of a hundred only three or four were not secretly married or keeping concubines, to the great scandal of the faithful. The envoy pleaded for implementation of three remedies to prevent further slippage from the Catholic faith.

The first was granting to Bavaria, Bohemia, Moravia, and Austria permission for communion under both forms. The second was reform of the clergy, to be accomplished through two measures: enforcing a stricter discipline upon them as laid down in the traditional canons and, to remedy their ignorance, establishing schools for their training. Baum-
2 gartner thus for the first time brought "seminaries" to the floor of the council in an authoritative way.

The third remedy, related to the second, was permission of the
3 clergy to marry. Baumgartner made the point that in German-speaking lands devout and faithful Catholics had come to the conclusion that "a chaste marriage is preferable to a tainted celibacy"—*castum matrimonium contaminato coelibatui praeferendum.* The situation would deteriorate further, he predicted, unless, in accordance with the custom of the early church *(primitivae ecclesiae),* well-educated men who were married were admitted to holy orders. They would be able effectively to preach the Word of God: "It is, after all, not a divine law that requires priests to be celibate. As is clear from the historical record, married men were admitted to holy orders—and not only to the dignity of priesthood but even to the exalted heights of the episcopacy."

As with seminaries, Baumgartner for the first time put this urgent issue directly before the prelates. The council, in accordance with its practice, issued a formal acknowledgment of his address, but then moved on to the business at hand, which in this instance happened to be Baumgartner's plea for the Eucharistic cup. The council would not be allowed, however, to forget the other two issues.

Some months later Duke Albrecht through two envoys he sent to
Rome asked the pope directly for permission for the cup and for permission for "upright and learned married men to perform certain ecclesiastical duties, especially preaching the divine word."[38] Pius responded
to the first request by saying that it was being considered by the council,
and he did not want to interfere. The second he referred to the legates,
asking them to send him their opinion as quickly as possible. The legates consulted four theologians, who in their response said it was against
the tradition of the church and, in their opinion, inexpedient "even for
these calamitous times."

For six General Congregations, beginning on June 30, the bishops
got their turn to speak. Although there was general agreement about the
basic doctrinal issues, fierce controversy broke out over the two articles
on the practical question of whether to allow the cup to the laity, at least
in certain regions. The bishops were divided. Some, especially the Spaniards, were passionately opposed. Among the legates Hosius and Simonetta supported them, Gonzaga and Seripando sympathized with the
other side. Resolution seemed impossible. Finally, with the concurrence
of the council, the legates decided to restrict the decree to the doctrinal
teaching and to reserve the two contested articles "for examination and
decision at another time, at the earliest opportunity."[39] It was highly
uncertain whether at that "earliest opportunity" the council would be
better able to achieve consensus.

To accompany this doctrinal decree a reform decree was of course
required. Only on July 10 did the bishops move to that subject. They
worked from a draft decree whose origins were the twelve articles they
had received four months earlier, on March 11. They harshly criticized
aspects of the text, but with the article on residence missing, they were
in basic agreement with the sensible but safe provisions that for the
most part dealt with benefices and administrative responsibilities of
the bishops. The nine canons on reform passed easily at the July 16 Session.[40]

Canons 3 to 8 each described bishops as "acting even as delegates of the Apostolic See" *(tamquam apostolicae sedis delegati)*, an expression that will now occasionally recur in reform decrees of the council. On the surface it seems to consolidate the position of the *zelanti* that all of the bishops' authority derived from the papacy, a position the reform party strenuously opposed. As subsequent controversy in the council shows, however, the reformers had by no means surrendered their position. How, then, is the expression to be understood in context?

Among the "hindrances" that kept bishops from effectively exercising their authority in their dioceses, and hence provided them with an excuse for not residing in them, were, as mentioned, the many privileges and exemptions not only of the mendicant orders but also of cathedral chapters, archdeacons, and other institutions. Many of the privileges and exemptions had been granted by the papacy, but others came from other sources. If bishops in certain of these cases were to do what the council prescribed, they had to have the clout that preempted appeals to higher authority of any kind, which is what the "delegates" expression was meant to provide. In these instances, therefore, the expression had a limited and altogether practical intent and was not a statement of ecclesiological principle. Despite what the wording might seem to imply, the provision was intended to strengthen episcopal authority, not weaken it.[41]

At the Session the four chapters and four canons on the Eucharist also passed as easily as the reform canons. They affirmed (1) that receiving under both forms was not necessary to salvation, (2) that the church had not erred in allowing under only one form, (3) that Christ is present "whole and entire" under each form, and (4) that it is not required that children receive communion before they "reach the age of discernment," that is, before an awareness of what was entailed in receiving the sacrament.[42]

Neither the doctrinal nor the reform decrees marked bold steps forward. Yet they showed that, after six months of stagnation, the council was finally capable of action, even if only at a minimal level. The question loomed: would the council ever be able to rise above that level?

Smart money was on the negative. The council was making a career of dodging the hard issues. In Rome, however, the fact that the council had taken action evoked satisfaction and gave rise to the hope that this dangerous assembly could be concluded in a few more months.

The Mass, Soft Reform, and the Eucharistic Cup

The council trudged on. After the Session on July 16, the legates delivered to the theologians in question form thirteen articles on the Mass, which were then debated for two weeks in the presence of the bishops.[43] The articles were essentially a reworking of those debated in 1552 but now with less sensitivity to the problems raised by the Protestants. A deputation of bishops meanwhile went to work and on August 6 presented to the council a draft document of four chapters and twelve canons, in which the guiding idea was that in the Mass a "true and proper" sacrifice is offered in which Christ's sacrifice on the cross is represented, its memory recalled, and "its saving power applied to the forgiveness of sins that we daily commit."[44] The document then asserted that at the Last Supper Jesus offered his body and blood to the Father under the forms of bread and wine, which identified the meal as a sacrifice related to the sacrifice on the cross.

By the time the decree was reformulated after the bishops' interventions, it received almost unanimous support at the Session on September 17.[45] It was an answer to Lutheran assertions, as the theologians at Trent understood them, that the only true and saving sacrifice was Christ's sacrifice on the cross, of which the Mass was a mere commemoration, and that making the Mass a sacrifice turned it into a "good work" by means of which Catholics believed they merited salvation, instead of being saved by "faith alone."

The decree contributed an important element in the council's teaching on the Eucharist. That teaching suffered, however, from the piecemeal approach suggested by the fact that the council expressed it over the course of several decrees instead of one. The approach was due

to the disruptions the council suffered and to the vagaries of its procedures but, more fundamentally, to the limitations of the Scholastic theology of the Middle Ages, which never formulated in a satisfactorily
synthetic way the indivisible unity of three aspects of the Eucharist—
sacrifice, Real Presence, and communion or "supper." The Eucharistic
practice of the Middle Ages reflected the problem: most Catholics received communion no more than once or twice a year, and those few
who received it more often generally did so outside Mass.[46]

An arresting feature of the decree on the Mass from a twenty-first-
century perspective is its stance regarding vernacular liturgy, found in
chapter 8 and again in canon 9. The chapter stated: "Although the Mass
is full of instruction for the faithful, the council fathers did not think it
advantageous that it should everywhere [*passim*] be celebrated in the
vernacular." The canon repeated the idea in negative form, "If anyone
says . . . that the Mass should be celebrated only in the vernacular . . . let
him be anathema."[47]

With these few words, the council in essence decreed simply that
Latin was legitimate. It went no further, and, despite what is often attributed to Trent in this regard, it certainly did not condemn vernacular
liturgy or rule it out as unfitting. One of the ironies of the council is
that it approved this provision without controversy, whereas it agonized
time and again over what today seems a far less radical question, the
Eucharistic cup. One of the few prelates to comment on the vernacular while the decree was under discussion was the bishop of Krk, the
large Adriatic island then a Venetian possession. He informed the council that "in the church of the Holy Sepulcher in Jerusalem Masses are
celebrated in every language under heaven."[48] Long before the council
ended, however, Latin was such a badge of identity for Catholics that
it prevailed unquestioned. It became a non-negotiable issue, allegedly
written in stone by the Council of Trent.[49]

The decree contained other provisions relating to liturgical performance. It affirmed the legitimacy of Masses in honor of the saints. It
affirmed in chapter 4 that the Canon of the Mass (the central Eucharis-

tic prayer in the Roman Rite), of which "for many centuries" the church had made use, was "free from error and contains only what savors in the highest degree of the holiness and devotion that raises the mind to God."[50] Justifying the Canon was necessary because for Protestants it encapsulated the Catholics' erroneous teachings about "offering" the Mass.

Chapter 5 was in effect a manifesto against the radical spiritualization of religion that prevailed in some Protestant writings and religious services:

> Since human nature is such that it cannot easily raise itself up to the meditation of divine realities without external aids, holy mother church has for that reason duly established certain rites, such as that some parts of the Mass should be said in quieter tones and others in louder, and it has provided ceremonial such as symbolic blessings, lights, incense, vestments, and many other rituals of that kind from apostolic order and tradition, by which the majesty of this great sacrifice is enhanced, and the minds of the faithful are aroused by those visible signs of religious devotion to contemplation of the high mysteries hidden in it.[51]

The chapter assumed in human nature a close relationship between the corporal and the spiritual and was thus able to justify material enhancements of divine worship, a feature that strikingly set Catholic worship off from most of its Protestant counterparts and also that, more broadly, promoted two profoundly different cultural appreciations that would persist through the centuries.

To this doctrinal decree on the Mass was added another, a quasi-appendix, entitled "Things to be observed and avoided in celebrating Mass," the work of a deputation headed by the able Beccadelli. Well before the council local synods especially in Germany and France had recognized the problems and tried to grapple with them. There was, therefore, considerable documentation available to the deputation and considerable agreement in the council that abuses were widespread.

[handwritten margin notes: "Permitted the vernacular at mass, but encouraged Latin. Discouraged polyphonic church music"]

Priests, for instance, omitted prayers central to the rite, such as the Preface and the Our Father—and even the entire Canon. They introduced prayers that were unfitting or superstitious. More general were the textual discrepancies in the many editions of the liturgical books, the result of scribal or typographical errors and of local interpolations, some of which seriously distorted the meaning of the original text.[52]

The first draft the deputation prepared, comprehensive and detailed in its scope, was rejected by the legates out of fear that it would occasion long debate, which would mean postponing the Session scheduled for September 17.[53] It was therefore revised, and then revised again into a blander and more general decree, easily approved.

The decree made no mention of the problems of the liturgical books, nor did the council at any point specifically deal with them. Despite what is often said, there is no "Tridentine liturgy" in the sense that the council did something more than, first, assume the Roman Rite was to continue to be standard unless another ancient rite prevailed in a given region or religious order, and, second, in its final Session commend to the papacy a reform of the missal and breviary of the Roman Rite to eliminate the abuses that had crept into them and thus provide a standardized text.

Embedded in the decree, however, was a sentence exhorting the bishops to "keep out of their churches the kind of music in which a base and suggestive [*lascivum et impurum*] element is introduced into the organ playing or singing, and similarly all worldly activities, empty and secular conversation, walking about, noises and cries, so that the house of God may truly be called and be seen to be a house of prayer."[54]

In the original draft the deputation asked specifically whether polyphonic music should be forbidden because it "appealed more to the ear than to the spirit and served the looseness of morals more than religion."[55] The revised version omitted mention of polyphony but expanded on the quality of music that was appropriate—conducive to devotion and of sufficient simplicity to allow the words of the sacred texts clearly to be heard and understood.[56]

The final version was more general than either of the earlier ones and abandoned any mention of polyphony and any words that might be construed as referring to it. The change may have been due solely to the general effort to simplify and shorten the decree. But shortly after the council ended the story sprang up that Palestrina's masterpieces, especially his "Mass of Pope Marcellus," were known at Trent and that their effect on influential prelates there led to the final wording and thus saved polyphony for the church.

There is no foundation for the story in the official council sources, but the sacred polyphony of the Flemish composer Jakob van Kerle was almost certainly heard at the council as the musical setting for a series of prayers for the success of the council. It is not certain that Palestrina's Mass was heard at Trent, but his music was surely known to some of the prelates, who, it may be assumed, would have been loath to condemn it.[57]

To complement the decree on doctrine a reform decree of course was needed. Only on September 10, just a week before the Session, did the legates present the bishops with a draft, put together under their direction. Although it ranged more widely, it focused on spelling out bishops' responsibilities. Like the correlative decree of the previous Session, it skirted controversial issues. At the General Congregations a few voices were raised against it on that score, but the majority let it pass with little comment of substance, bowing to the pressure of time. The legates seemed to be employing the tactic Crescenzio used in the second period of introducing reform at the last minute and thus forestalling substantive action.

On the eve of the Session, all the envoys at the council, except those from the Republic of Venice and the Duchy of Florence, visited the legates to make known their displeasure with the decree, which according to them took little account of the real needs of the church and was unworthy of the council. They asked that in the future they see the text of reform decrees before they were distributed to the bishops. Their visit was an ominous display of the pressure the envoys could bring to bear when they acted in concert, which they had never done before, and it served as a warning about the role they might play in the future. The visit implied deep dissatisfaction with how the legates handled their right to control the agenda.

The Spanish bishops had presented to the legates their *libellus* or memorandum detailing the reforms they advocated, and Ferdinand's envoys had done the same. When the French arrived, they also brought with them their memorandum. Among the grievances of these bishops, diplomats, and their rulers was their perception that the legates paid no attention to these documents, and they wanted such disregard of them to change.

Although the legates had to bear the brunt of the criticism for the limpness of the reform decrees, they knew what would pass and what would not pass in Rome. The pope still did not understand how explosive the situation had become at Trent and how powerful were the forces resolved to bring about a more radical reform than he envisaged. He would, to his dismay, soon find out.

Even with its limitations, however, the decree embodied what had long been developing as a basic orientation of the council: providing bishops with a job description that would shore up their authority as chief administrators of their dioceses. Canon 4 stipulated, for instance, "Both ecclesiastical and lay administrators of the fabric of any church, even a cathedral, or of a hospice, confraternity, almshouse, charitable lending house [*mons pietatis*], or other pious establishment of any kind, are bound to give an account of their administration annually to the bishop of the diocese."

Besides these three decrees, the council published at the Session on September 17 its long-awaited, much postponed decree on the Eucharistic cup, the last of the council's decrees related to the Eucharist. Pius IV had let the legates know that he was not opposed to allowing the cup for those areas of Europe where it promised to help retain Catholics in the fold. On August 21, therefore, the legates placed the issue before the council in terms of allowing German Catholics to receive under both forms.

On August 27 Georg Draškovič, the exiled archbishop of Pécs and one of Ferdinand's envoys, delivered before the council an impassioned plea supporting the decree. The general debate, heated, began the next day and lasted until September 6. Most of the Italian and Spanish bishops opposed the concession, most of the others favored it.[58] Although the former constituted a strong majority, pressure, political and emotional, was strong from the other side. The legates had to find a way out of the dilemma. The council simply could not once again postpone a decision.

Finally, on September 15, just two days before the Session, the legates proposed that the council refer the matter to the pope.[59] No other solution seemed possible. It was a disappointment to the members of the imperial party, who pleaded for a decision from the council itself. In their eyes remanding the matter to the pope was an abrogation of responsibility on the part of the council and weakened its authority. Nor was the decree pleasing to the other side, which knew the pope was open to granting permission. Both parties had to be satisfied with less than perfect—far less than perfect! The decree stipulated simply that the pope would "in his unrivaled wisdom judge what will be best for the Christian community and most salutary for those requesting the use of the chalice."[60]

The final decree on September 17 set holy orders and matrimony as the agenda for the next Session, to be celebrated on November 12. These were the last two sacraments needing debate, and their resolution would, as far as the legates were concerned, go far toward concluding the council's doctrinal agenda. The council at last seemed to be moving at a reasonable pace, and hope of ending it before Christmas was optimistic, perhaps, but not altogether unrealizable. It was not to be.

The Great Crisis

A full ten months would elapse between the Session on September 17, 1562, and the next on July 15, 1563. During that long period the council suffered through a bitter and complicated crisis that seemed impervious to resolution. The frustrations and antagonisms that had long been evident rose to the boiling point, and all attempts by the legates and others to reduce the heat only served to increase it. The occasion for the eruption of the crisis was debate on holy orders and, once again, on episcopal residence. The council addressed the former beginning on September 23, the latter not until December 10. The two subjects were inextricably related to each other, not least because both raised the issue of *jus divinum*.

Since bishops were the ministers of the sacrament of holy orders, the document on the subject perforce dealt with the character and prerogatives of their office. In its essence the decree was foreseen as both a vindication of the sacramental character of the rite and an affirmation of the hierarchical structure of the church, two teachings denied by Protestants. The articles the legates delivered to the theologians were substantially the same as those debated during the second period, in January 1552, but with one slight change. It was that change that set off the conflagration.

The original article 7 of 1552 distinguished the office of priest from bishop as of *jus divinum,* but the legates had stricken the inflammatory expression from the version the council now received, a futile effort to prevent controversy. The very absence of the expression, however, called attention to it. The article, which was intended to express the wrong or heretical Protestant position, read, "Bishops are not superior to priests, nor do they have any special claim to be able to ordain them; or, if they have such a claim, it is the same as that had by the priests; any ordinations done by them without the consent of the people are invalid."[61]

After the Congregations of Theologians expressed their opinions on the articles, a deputation went to work and after a few days delivered to the bishops a draft document, which included seven canons that roughly corresponded to the seven articles. Canon 7 slightly expanded article 7 but left it essentially unchanged, without mention of *jus divinum.*[62] On the first day that the bishops addressed the draft, October 13, there were already unmistakable signs that controversy was brewing.

Guerrero, for instance, insisted that canon 7 had to state clearly that it was by divine ordinance that bishops possessed their authority and that priests were subject to them. From that point forward the controversy devolved through complicated theological and canonical arguments into the question of the relationship of the bishops to the papacy: what powers were the bishops' in virtue of their office, as conferred by the rite itself of their episcopal consecration (therefore *jure divino*), and what in virtue of delegation from the pope?

The Spaniards and the others who demanded that *jus divinum* be inserted into canon 7 were intent on enhancing episcopal authority and saw this article as crucial in attaining their goal. The bishop was the linchpin in the reform of the church that they so passionately desired. They argued that Christ instituted the office of bishop and made the Apostles the first to hold it. The bishops possessed the full authority of that office, therefore, not by delegation from the papacy but by divine ordinance.[63] Their position was close to that ratified in Vatican Council II in the mid-twentieth century.

The Italian "zealots," led by Simonetta, once again saw their opponents' arguments in favor of the *jus divinum* as an attempt to subvert papal authority, and they portrayed themselves as the faithful and intrepid champions of that authority. They employed different arguments to sustain their position, of which the most revealing was that Christ made only Peter a bishop, after which Peter then passed on episcopal authority to the other Apostles.

As the debate continued all through October, the two positions hardened, each resistant to compromise as reformulation after reformulation of canon 7 was rejected. The atmosphere grew ever more sour. At the end of the month Seripando, utterly distraught by a situation that he had made every effort to ameliorate, wrote to Borromeo, "No letter could possibly convey to you how difficult things really are here." In his desperation he confided to Borromeo that he believed the only remedy was to translate the council to another city where the pope himself could preside.[64]

The Session scheduled for November 12 had to be postponed, as debate on holy orders continued, with interruptions, through the month and well into the next. It had to be postponed yet again and again, as prospects of its ever taking place evanesced. Matters only got worse when on December 10 the bishops opened discussion on the decree on residence.

But in the middle of the previous month an event occurred of extraordinary significance for the council: the French delegation, so long promised, finally arrived in Trent—12 bishops, 3 abbots, and 18 theologians, under the leadership of Charles de Guise, "the Cardinal of Lorraine." The legates, the envoys, and some 130 bishops went to the Porta Santa Croce to meet them and accompany them into the city. The Cardinal of Lorraine, flanked by Gonzaga and Seripando, rode at the head of what amounted to a triumphal procession.

From this point forward no figure at the council, with the exception of course of the legates, played a more determining role than de Guise. Not yet forty years old, he had already had in France and on the international stage a striking career, of which we have caught a few glimpses. Intelligent, high-born, well-educated, and stunningly handsome, an eloquent and compelling speaker, he was also devout and genuinely concerned about church reform. He led a similarly devout, concerned, and well-educated party of prelates and theologians.

Born to lead! To few persons of the era could those words be more appropriately applied than to Charles de Guise. Fully aware of his gifts and his exalted social and ecclesiastical rank, he expected to be treated accordingly and was sensitive to slights. Although at Trent he became the leader among the reformers, with whom his sympathies certainly lay, he tried to act as a mediator in ways he believed helpful to the church at large and to the now desperate situation of the church in France.

Despite the jubilation at Trent over the arrival of the French delegation and of de Guise in particular, under the surface considerable ambivalence and misgiving reigned. Apprehension was nowhere more pronounced than in Rome. Pius IV had convoked the council particularly out of concern for France, but he, like all the popes of the period, knew that official repudiation of the Pragmatic Sanction of Bourges did not at all mean that conciliarist sentiments were dead among French bishops and theologians. For the French the principles upon which the Council of Basel had functioned were the ideal. For the pope they were an abomination. Pius feared French participation in the council as much as he wanted it.

Long suspicious of de Guise for his promotion of a national council in France, he had become more suspicious once he learned that after the failure of Poissy de Guise had made contact with German Lutherans. De Guise hoped to play the Lutherans off against French Calvinists, but the fact, not the motive, was what struck the pope. The *zelanti* at the council shared these fears and suspicions of the French in general and of de Guise in particular, and with grave misgivings they saw how jubilant the arrival of the French made the Spaniards.

The French brought with them a memorandum of thirty-four articles on reform, which in early January they presented to the legates. The *zelanti* took it as another ominous sign. As a dispatch from Trent to the Duke of Ferrara put it: the *zelanti* up to this point thought the Spaniards were almost as bad as the heretics, but now, in comparison with the French, the Spaniards seemed like saints.[65] The legates in the meantime received instructions from Rome that they were not to accord de Guise any special treatment, which prompted him to complain that they treated him like an enemy.[66]

The opening words of the decree on residence presented to the council a few weeks after the arrival of the French were close to a platitude: "By virtue of human and divine law, all those who hold office in the church, especially offices to which the care of souls is attached, are bound to give an account to God of how they carry out their duties."[67] The text was careful not to say residence itself was required by divine law but only that divine law required bishops to fulfill their responsibilities. But the very mention of *jus divinum* set off the zealots, who argued that the original decree on residence of 1546 was all that was needed. From the outset of the discussion of the document, therefore, the council divided along predictable lines.

Through December and the ensuing months the council considered and rejected a number of formulations of the contested issues without coming close to resolution.[68] The General Congregations became ever more tense and embittered, with sharp, sometimes insulting words exchanged. Meanwhile the pope at every opportunity offered him sided with Simonetta and the *zelanti,* which left Gonzaga, Seripando, and now de Guise marginalized and their efforts toward a solution sabotaged. Rumors spread that Pius intended to suspend the council, and they grew more credible with each passing day.

High on the agenda of reformers at Trent was reform of the College of Cardinals. In early January word arrived that the pope had raised two young Italian princes to the cardinalate—Federigo Gonzaga, a nephew of the legate, eighteen years old, and Fernando de' Medici, the son of Duke Cosimo of Florence, barely fourteen years old. The news added to the reformers' gloom and confirmed their suspicion that the pope, despite his promises, was not to be trusted on the crucial issue of "reform of the head."

Indicative of the depth of the crisis was the fact that in January Emperor Ferdinand transferred his court to Innsbruck to be able to monitor the council more closely. He called to Innsbruck four theologians, to whom he submitted a series of questions formulated out of an oral and written report by the imperial envoy at Trent, Archbishop Draškovič, whom he had also summoned to Innsbruck. The first question, not surprisingly, was whether, under the present circumstances, the council should be suspended or even declared concluded. The questions went on to ask how the freedom and independence of the council could be guaranteed, how it might be put in working order again to effect the reform of the church, and so forth.

Draškovič was pessimistic. He believed the council had arrived at such a serious impasse that suspension was the only course. He complained with bitterness that the freedom of the council was compromised because not only every decree and every canon but every little phrase and clause had to be reviewed in Rome. If the emperor still believed the council should continue, he should take measures to ensure its freedom.[69] Francisco de Córdoba, a Franciscan and one of Ferdinand's theologians, observed in his responses to the questions that "there are two councils going on in the church. One is the council at Trent, and the other the council in Rome with the pope [and the cardinals]. They are somehow at war with each other."[70]

At this point, while the theologians as well as Duke Albrecht of Bavaria were still in Innsbruck, de Guise took it upon himself to journey there to inform the emperor about the situation. He told Ferdinand that three things had to happen. First, the pope had to allow not only freedom of expression in the council but also freedom in formulating its decrees, so that "what is decided is not just what Rome finds expedient." Second, so that the numerical domination of the council by bishops from the Kingdom of Naples and the Papal States be overcome, more bishops needed to be ordered to the council from Spain, France, and, if possible, from Germany. Finally, the right of proposing agenda for the council must be extended beyond the legates to the envoys and the bishops. De Guise, like Draškovič and many others, feared that, unless the legates' right was broken, the French, imperial, and Spanish reform memoranda were destined for the dustbin. For the immediate future, he urged Ferdinand to come to the council himself and, besides that, to arrange to meet with the pope to thrash out the problems.

De Guise concluded his report by asking what was to be done to avoid a schism if the pope decided to suspend the council. He suggested that in that eventuality, the emperor in collaboration with the kings of France and Spain call together leading bishops and other learned men to draw up a memorandum for the pope of the things they agreed needed to be done. The aim would be to secure the peace, unity, and well-being of the church and, if confirmed by the pope, to ensure the submission of the faithful to the authority of the Apostolic See.[71]

De Guise spent a week at Innsbruck. His success was notable, due in part, surely, to what Ferdinand had heard from Draškovič and the theologians. As a result of these conversations the emperor sent instructions to his envoys at the council to work closely with de Guise for the council's independence and for the reform of the church. He also instructed them, however, to avoid any discussion of the relative authority of pope and council and to make sure that in the council's decrees the authority of the pope not in any way be diminished.

Ferdinand sent two letters to Pius IV under date of March 3. They were the most palpable and important result of the consultations at Innsbruck. The first was officially public, the other, though also official in the full sense of the word, was equivalently "for his eyes only."[72] In the first he warned the pope of the potentially catastrophic consequences of suspending the council and urged him, among other things, to guarantee the council's freedom. He stated, further, that he was ready to go to the council himself to deal with the problems there and urged the pope to be ready to do the same. The letter was a formal and official warning to the pope that the emperor was ready to act in his capacity as Protector of the Church, and it was thus interpreted in Rome. Ferdinand was careful to send the legates a copy, an unmistakable sign of the public character of its warning.

Serious though the first letter was, the second, incomparably longer and more specific, was more so. Though respectful and deferential, it did not mince words. Ferdinand began by reminding the pope that both of them were old men in frail health and soon would face the judgment seat of God. There they would have to answer for the decisions they made. After that sober reminder of the briefness of the time they had before them, Ferdinand confronted the pope with the reality of the situation at Trent.

The letter amounted to a compendium of concerns and grievances widespread at the council: the reform of the church had to begin with "the head," that is, with the Roman Curia; papal elections had to be reformed so as to eliminate simony and every "illicit machination"; measures had to be taken to ensure that only worthy men were named cardinals and bishops; the pope should not try to win and guarantee for himself and his successors privileges with no foundation in Scripture, the Fathers, or the councils of the church; the council at Trent must have full freedom—in other words, Pius must eliminate the blockage that had resulted from having a council in Rome and a council in Trent operating at the same time. Finally, the pope should appear in person at the council. Ferdinand vowed that he would ensure his safety.

Indicative of the frankness of the letter was Ferdinand's analysis of the motivation of the Italians at the council who opposed the *jus divinum* on episcopal residence. He divided them into three groups: the first consisted in the bishops who hoped to become cardinals, the second, the "poor bishops" dependent on the pope's liberality, and the third, bishops who already enjoyed a comfortable income. Prelates of the last group, he averred, probably voted according to their conscience, but the other two took their stand out of concern for their own advancement and convenience. The accusation of papal complicity with those two groups was hardly veiled. Ferdinand, while skirting direct engagement with *jus divinum,* implored the pope to do everything in his power to ensure that bishops resided in their dioceses.

Ferdinand's envoy in Rome delivered the letters to the pope on March 8. Pius immediately recognized that the emperor was threatening action that could turn the crisis at the council into a political bombshell of the first order. Behind the letter he saw the hand of de Guise. A week later, to add to the pope's woes, the Spanish envoy handed him a letter expressing the grave concerns of Philip II, especially the fear that the pope was contemplating suspending the council. Although this letter was much less pointed than Ferdinand's, it possibly shocked him more deeply because he had been assured by the nuncio in Madrid that Philip stood firmly behind him.[73] A direct intervention in the council by Philip was more dangerous, if possible, than one by Ferdinand. The pope could not now dismiss as a paranoid's dream the specter of the three great powers—Spain, France, and the empire—making common cause and taking matters into their own hands.

Just before Ferdinand's letter was delivered to him, he had received another shock, news that at Trent in the night of March 2–3 Cardinal Ercole Gonzaga had died.[74] The legate's illness was short, his death unexpected. Then two weeks later Cardinal Girolamo Seripando also died. There can be no doubt that, though Seripando had not been well for months, both men, unstinting in expenditure of their talents and energy, were victims of the strain the council imposed upon them. With their deaths the council lost the two leaders most concerned to hold it together.

In these first weeks of March 1563, therefore, the crisis point had been reached. The fate of the Council of Trent hung in the balance. The resolution of the crisis, no matter what form it might take, held immense implications for the future of Catholicism. All eyes were turned to Pius IV, who found himself at the epicenter of a potential maelstrom.

[handwritten notes]

Sources of disharmony:
1. ↑ influence by Pope Pius IV on the Council in Trent
2. Criticisms re this from King of Spain, France & Ferdinand, Emperor of the crumbling empire
3. Ongoing practices b) simony by Pope et al.

6

The Council Concludes

On March 7, the very day word arrived in Rome of Gonzaga's death, Pius IV announced the appointment of Cardinal Giovanni Morone, an old and trusted friend, to succeed Gonzaga as "first president." As legate Morone had the advantage over his predecessor of enjoying the pope's unqualified trust. The ablest and most seasoned diplomat Pius had at his disposal, he was known to the emperor and respected by him since 1536, when, as a very young man, he was papal nuncio to Germany. Now, at this difficult moment in the relationship between Pius and Ferdinand, Morone's good standing with the emperor further recommended him to Pius, who quite sensibly entrusted him with conveying to Ferdinand his response to the two letters.

This was the second time Morone had been nominated as legate to Trent. In 1542, Paul III had designated him to open the council. Morone dutifully went to Trent, where he and his fellow nuncio awaited the arrival of the bishops, but the outbreak of war between Francis I and Charles V made the opening impossible. In the meantime he assumed other important posts in papal service. Morone had met Cardinal Contarini at the religious colloquy in Regensburg in 1541 and entered into a brief but close friendship with him. This association led to his being identified with the suspect *spirituali* and, as mentioned, imprisoned for heresy by Paul IV.

As a master diplomat Morone was able to maneuver first this way and then that as difficult situations required, which helps account for the fact that his character remains elusive. Although devout and deeply concerned for the good of the church, he cannot be numbered among those seeking a radical reform of the system. No one, however, is more responsible for bringing the Council of Trent to conclusion than Morone.[1]

His nomination, therefore, is no mystery. More surprising is the speed with which Pius acted. For some time, of course, he had considered—or threatened—sending more legates and therefore had plenty of time to ponder ideal candidates. Not least among the reasons for the haste, certainly, was the pressure he anticipated to nominate the Cardinal of Lorraine, who at this point was the leading candidate of virtually all those assembled at Trent except the *zelanti*. De Guise was the very last person Pius wanted to lead the council. Two years earlier, when Pius first decided to reopen it, he wanted Morone to serve as legate, but, for reasons unclear, Morone declined. This time he accepted.

Besides Morone, the pope named Cardinal Bernardo Navagero, a Venetian patrician who before being raised to the cardinalate by Pius IV in 1561 had had a distinguished career in the diplomatic service of *La Serenissima*. Pius ostensibly meant him to replace the long-absent Sittich. With Seripando's death two weeks after Navagero and Morone were named, however, the number of legates was again reduced to four. Immediately upon his arrival at Trent Morone towered above the other three. Navagero stood very much in his shadow, Hosius never had a particularly strong profile, and, because of the pope's confidence in Morone, Simonetta's influence began to wane. At the end of the month Pius responded to the message he had received from Philip II. He reminded the king that he relied on him as his "right arm" for support in the venture of the council. While defending his policies, he assured Philip that he intended to see the council through to a good conclusion and work for a "severe reform." The pope did not hide his own grievances. Because the Spanish envoy to the council, Count Luna, still had not arrived, the Spanish bishops had been allowed to behave almost like enemies of the Apostolic See, and the French bishops were interested only in reform, not at all in doctrine.[2] Pius's response was a success. His promise to continue the council and work for reform quelled the storm that had been brewing in Madrid and won Philip again to the pope's side.

Morone and Navagero arrived at Trent on April 10. Six days later Morone set off for Innsbruck, where his task was to convince the emperor of the pope's determination to work for reform of the church, to persuade him to instruct his envoys to support the legates, and to dissuade him from casting his lot with the French and Spaniards. In response to Ferdinand's urging that the pope come to Trent, Morone pleaded Pius's frail health, a genuine excuse, though certainly not the only reason Pius did not want to face the council. He insisted that reform of "the head" was the responsibility of the pope alone, not the council.

Morone remained at Innsbruck for a full three weeks, a striking indication of how important he considered these negotiations, which were difficult and protracted. It was, however, time well spent. Morone's achievement was that he won Ferdinand's agreement, though qualified, on the essential points. In particular he defended the exclusivity of the legates' right to propose agenda. That was a major achievement because Ferdinand had become convinced that through that provision the pope had so shrunk the freedom of the council that reform was impossible.[3]

Even with Morone's relative success on this point at Innsbruck, at Trent the legates' right continued to be a source of contention to the very end of the council.

On a related issue, Morone argued against a proposal that the bishops vote not individually as at present but "according to nations," a measure meant to offset the power the Italians wielded by their overwhelming majority. Most important, he restored the emperor's trust in the pope's goodwill, in his commitment to reform of "the head," and in his determination to see the council through to the end (no suspension!). He thus dispelled the great threat that for months had hung over the council.[4] Since January the council's headquarters had been located neither in Trent nor in Rome but in the imperial court at Innsbruck. Now the center shifted back, at least in large part, to Trent.

The visit was a diplomatic triumph for the papacy, wrought by Morone. The seemingly inevitable disaster that threatened Pius IV just weeks earlier had been averted. Even though the emperor had not given way on every important point, especially regarding papal conclaves and the appointment of cardinals, for the most part he had modified his positions. As subsequent events showed, however, he fully intended to use his authority to make sure the council did its duty regarding reform. In particular, he continued to insist on reform "of the head," even though he desisted from using that expression.

Pius could not have been more pleased. In a letter dated May 19 Borromeo reported to Morone how gratified his uncle was with the outcome. In his whole pontificate, reported Borromeo, the pope had never been more satisfied with "one of his ministers." In this case his satisfaction was all the greater because of the difficulty of the undertaking and its crucial importance "for the conservation of the Apostolic See." The pope was confident, moreover, that Morone would bring the council to a "swift and salutary" conclusion.[5] The confidence was not misplaced. Once Morone took hold of the reins at Trent, he guided that difficult and fractious body with extraordinary skill, enabling it once again to take action on the questions facing it.

The French Find Their Voice: March–June 1563

Since the deaths of Gonzaga and Seripando, de Guise had by sheer virtue of his personality filled the leadership gap, even though he complained that Simonetta and Hosius treated him like "some little bishop or other." But his prestige suffered two heavy blows: Pius had not, as he and others anticipated, named him legate, and Morone had not invited him to accompany him to Innsbruck. De Guise had no idea how deeply Pius IV distrusted him. On May 23 the pope through Borromeo instructed Morone to play a duplicitous game with de Guise: to flatter him and show him every sign of respect but at the same time to conspire with Simonetta to get bishops "friendly to us" to embarrass him in public and cut him down to size. No surprise that this part of the letter was written in code.[6]

These were not, then, happy days for the Cardinal of Lorraine. In late February he received word that his brother, Duke François de Guise, had been assassinated, an event that further complicated the political scene in France and further jeopardized the future of Catholicism there. Despite all, however, de Guise did not step back from what he saw as his responsibilities at Trent.

A new duty was imposed upon him on May 10 with the arrival at the council of a brief letter from Mary, Queen of Scots.[7] In it the queen explained that because of the "troubled times" *(inuria temporis)* she had been unable to send prelates or envoys to the council. She said that the "Cardinal of Lorraine, my beloved uncle," would inform the council in detail about her situation and about the depth and constancy of her devotion to the Holy See. After Masarelli read the letter aloud, de Guise in a long oration did as he was enjoined. The incident served as a sharp wake-up call to members of the council from the Mediterranean countries that the radical upheavals set off in northern Europe by the Reformation were far from ended.

Another strong personality had meanwhile at last arrived in Trent, where he would from this point forward play an important role. In the

General Congregation on May 21 Count Luna made his formal entrance into the council chamber and took his assigned place. He would prove a sharp thorn in the legates' side. The long interval between Philip's naming him for the office and his arrival was due in part to a bitter dispute with the French over precedence among the envoys, settled at last by an uneasy compromise.

Whatever his personal feelings about the protocol arrangement, Luna did not let them keep him from close contact with de Guise and Draškovič. The three formed a potentially powerful force, but, though they agreed on certain principles, they often disagreed on particulars and thus dissipated the collective influence they might have had. Meanwhile, the number of envoys continued to grow. Eighteen were now ascribed to the council.

Until early May the council still seemed to be almost comatose. Although from February 9 until March 22 a series of Theologians' Congregations debated eight articles on the sacrament of matrimony, no General Congregations followed them up. When the theologians concluded their interventions, Hosius and Simonetta decided to suspend substantive operations until Morone arrived from Rome. Morone arrived but then left for Innsbruck. In the meantime the contested issues on holy orders and episcopal residence hung suspended in an ominous limbo.

On May 12, five days before Morone's return from Innsbruck, the bishops went to work again in a General Congregation and took up seventeen long canons concerning "Abuses in the Administration of the Sacrament of Orders," the reform counterpart of the doctrinal decree that was in abeyance.[8] In early February a deputation in which the French influence was strong had gone to work on the document. When it was finished, the legates sent it to Rome, where the pope objected to the first canon because it seemed to limit his freedom in nominating bishops. Once the envoys got their copy of the document, Luna and Mascarenhas objected to the same canon because it seemed to limit the freedom of their sovereigns. In both instances the legates refused to change the document on the grounds that the deputation was an official organ of the council. If they interfered with its functioning, they argued, people would say that the council was not free. The document arrived on the floor of the council unchanged.

At this time in the history of the church bishops were chosen principally in three ways: nomination by the pope, nomination by a sovereign (in France, Spain, Portugal, Poland, and Hungary), or election by a cathedral chapter.[9] The canon did not directly challenge these modes. The requirements it enjoined for the candidates were, however, so stringent that they very much reduced the pool from which they could be drawn and thus seemed to limit especially papal and royal freedom of choice.

The deputation obviously saw this canon as crucial to accomplishing the preeminent goal of the council, the reform of the clergy, higher and lower, by ensuring that only worthy candidates fill those ranks. The first plank in that reform platform had to be bishops, who, as the first canon stated, should be "of the right age, good character, and appropriate learning." The title of the canon was "On the Scrutiny Required for Candidates to the Episcopacy" *(De Examine Promovendorum Ad Ecclesiae Cathedrales).*[10]

The scrutiny, which the canon laid out in elaborate, almost painstaking detail, was to be thorough, public, and severe. A nominee's name and date of birth were to be announced from the pulpit of the cathedral and parishes of the diocese and posted publicly for fifteen days, to make sure everybody was fully informed. Clergy and laity were to report any reasons they knew of why the candidate should not be advanced to the episcopate. The candidate himself was required to provide weighty and distinguished witnesses to his character, who would be questioned by the presiding archbishop and others, and to present full documentation regarding his academic degrees and other qualifications. He would himself undergo an examination by the archbishop and others present, and he was to deliver a sample sermon.

Many of the remaining sixteen canons dealt with relatively technical matters of procedure, but they all breathed this same determination to ensure by means of careful scrutiny a worthy clergy through all the stages of clerical profession, that is, from tonsure and so-called minor orders, such as lector and doorkeeper, to subdiaconate, diaconate, and, finally, priesthood. The goal was to be accomplished by a discipline that was as strict as it was clearly laid out.

Among these canons was one of extraordinary importance for the future clergy of the Catholic church. That was canon 16 (final version, canon 18), which mandated that every diocese was to provide a seminary for the education especially of poor boys for the priesthood. It is difficult to exaggerate the canon's long-range influence. Within a century of the council, Sforza Pallavicino, the Jesuit who wrote a history of Trent to counter Paolo Sarpi's antipapal account of it, asserted that that canon alone made up for all the trials and tribulations the council suffered through eighteen years.[11]

The canon did not come out of the blue. The draft was textually dependent upon canon 9 of the National Synod that Cardinal Pole as apostolic legate had convoked in England in late 1555.[12] There were, moreover, precedents for such an institution in a few dioceses, and, at the urging of no less a person than Cardinal Morone, the Jesuits had in 1552 opened in Rome their Collegium Germanicum for young men from the empire who wanted to be priests, an important precedent on an international scale.[13]

Almost since their founding religious orders prescribed generally exigent courses of study for their members and saw to their ascetical training as well. But the preparation of candidates for the secular clergy followed haphazard and often minimal patterns. The result was wide disparity in their level of education even within a particular diocese or locality. In the cities clergy tended to be better educated than those in small villages. Boys or young men from wealthy or middle-class families might for at least a few years attend a university or one of the Humanistic colleges run by the recently founded Society of Jesus. Some few, especially if ambitious for ecclesiastical advancement, won university degrees in canon law. Learned clergy were not lacking, therefore, but they were notably fewer among the secular clergy than in the religious orders. In some places the educational level was deplorably low, with priests barely able to pronounce the Latin of the Mass and other rites, let alone understand what they were saying. Whatever education they had they acquired informally from the parish priest, who may have been little better educated than they. Pastoral skills such as preaching and how to hear confessions they also learned, if at all, through imitation of a local priest.

The canon aimed at remedying the situation by providing at least the bare essentials for boys from whom sometimes little was to be expected beyond correct administration of the sacraments and basic preaching, even if this last meant reading sermons prepared by others. The canon's provisions were generic, not specifying length of training or levels of proficiency required. This left the door open for institutions of meager ambition and for others with higher aspirations.

The council never intended to require every candidate for the priesthood to attend such an institution, which was an almost fall-back alternative for those who could not do better. From this modest seed, however, eventually sprang institutions of considerable sophistication. Although outside Italy implementation of the canon was slow, its influence eventually was ubiquitous in the Catholic world. At the time of the council the word "seminary" was applied indiscriminately to several types of institutions, but the council's usage gave impetus to its being applied almost exclusively to institutions preparing students for ministry.

The seminary, to some extent an update of the medieval cathedral school, was to be located at the cathedral so as to initiate the students into the practical operations of church life and provide moral protection. The council was thus as intent upon ensuring that priests of the future give example of an upright life as it was that they be sufficiently educated. The final version specified that the bishop punish with severity "the difficult and incorrigible and those who spread bad habits," and he was to expel them if necessary. He was to require the seminarians to attend Mass every day, confess their sins at least every month, and receive Holy Communion as often as their confessors judged appropriate.

Boys admitted to the seminary were to be at least eleven or twelve years old, know how to read and write, and be of good character. Although established primarily for poor boys, the seminary was not to exclude others, provided that they paid their own expenses. The draft document devoted considerably more attention to the academic training of the seminarians than did the one finally approved, and it held up a higher standard. In the draft the seminary was to include a grammar school, to which boys who were not candidates for ordination were also to be admitted, a provision dropped in the final version.

Regarding the seminarians' schooling the final version reads: "They should study grammar, singing, keeping church accounts and other useful skills; and they should be versed in Holy Scripture, church documents [*libros ecclesiasticos*], homilies of the Fathers [*sancti*], and the practice of rites and ceremonies and of administering the sacraments, particularly all that seems appropriate for hearing confessions." Besides being less detailed and less exigent about the academic program, it devotes much more attention than the draft to how these schools were to be financed, which was through levies imposed on the cathedral chapter and other clergy. Otherwise there is little difference of note between the two versions.

When the draft of the seventeen canons hit the floor of the council on May 13, the bishops rose to the subject, about which they could not have been more concerned and passionate. De Guise led off the first day.[14] His thinking on the matter was much influenced by the learned Humanist theologian Gentian Hervet, present at the council, who just two years earlier had published a work on church reform. He was also influenced by Claude d'Espence, also present, who in 1561 published a large commentary on the First Epistle to Timothy, a "pastoral epistle" that established standards for the choice and behavior of leaders of the

Christian community in the church of the apostolic era. D'Espence's message: return to the practice of the early church.

For three hours de Guise held the attention of his audience as he developed his theme: the church had to break with its contemporary practices, especially nomination by secular rulers, and let itself be guided by principles found in the early church. He proposed a radical program that espoused election of bishops by people and clergy. As became clear in the subsequent debate, he voiced the opinion of many French bishops and theologians at the council.

He met immediate resistance. Canon 1 on the scrutiny required for episcopal candidates did the same, for it seemed a milder version of de Guise's position. Cardinal Ludovico Madruzzo, the nephew of the Madruzzo who first hosted the council, was the first to speak the next day. In an indirect rebuttal of de Guise, he called for laws that were realistic and capable of implementation.[15] Pietro Antonio di Capua, the bishop of Otranto and a staunch zealot, was next. He predicted that canon 1 would cause, not cure, abuses. And what, he asked, would happen to the nomination rights of the kings of Spain and Portugal in this new order of things?[16]

Guerrero, as well as other reforming bishops, came roaring to the defense of the fundamental aim of the decree, but even he admitted that canon 1 in its present form would be difficult to implement. The essential goal, no matter how it was accomplished, was to ensure that the bishops chosen would be true pastors of their flocks. It was possible, he insisted, for monarchs to retain their nomination rights and still ensure that bishops be worthy of their office.[17] On this point the vast majority of the bishops agreed with him.

In the course of the month-long debate the glaring difference between the French and the rest of the council became clear. The French, in their desire to restore the discipline of "the primitive church," a radical *ressourcement,* here moved on a different plane from their colleagues at the council. Their political situation was also different from the others' and provided them with an argument to support their theological stance. Nominally ruled by a boy-king but in fact by his mother, they chafed under the situation, which gave them added reason to disavow the royal nomination rights guaranteed the French crown in 1516 by the Concordat of Bologna. Claude de Sainctes, the abbot of Lunéville, reviewed for the council how inconsistent those rights were with the earlier tradition of the church. He asked how bishops could defend the church's rights against rulers when they owed their position to those very rulers. And how unseemly, he exclaimed, that a boy or a woman have the right to name a bishop![18] The council had already heard such sentiments expressed by de Guise.

As the days and weeks moved on, it became clear that canon 1 was dead in the water—*Primus canon non placet* became almost a mantra as it was repeated by bishop after bishop. Besides objecting to it for restricting nomination rights, the bishops argued that its provisions were far too complicated, that the significant role it gave to the laity was improper or impracticable, and that what was needed was not a list of new provisions but the strict implementation of the good laws already on the books. When Diego Laínez, the superior general of the Jesuits, a papal theologian for the first two periods of the council, argued that just because the election practices of the early church were good for that era was no argument that they were good for the present, practical-minded bishops welcomed his words.[19]

The council in its final decree simply bypassed the issue of nomination rights, whether by pope, monarch, or chapter. The debate revealed, however, that, aside from canon 1, the bishops were in the main satisfied with the other canons, including the canon on seminaries. It also revealed how genuinely committed they were, despite their differences, to ensuring a better-educated and more pastorally effective clergy in the future.

Once the debate ended on June 16, the deputation, now expanded with fourteen new members, went to work. In its revision it retained most of the original canons, though it shortened and simplified some and made other small changes. The major casualty was the original canon 1, which simply disappeared and was replaced by another. Although the final document made careful provision for the scrutiny of candidates for the orders leading up to and including priesthood, it made none for bishops.

The council took up the scrutiny of candidates for the episcopacy again, however, in its general reform decree ratified much later at the Session on November 11. At that time it stipulated that, in consideration of the variety of circumstances that prevailed in different places, provincial synods should draw up a formula in keeping with local needs and traditions to ensure adequate scrutiny of candidates for the episcopacy. In a separate canon it then made extremely detailed regulations about the careful attention required before the appointment of pastors of parishes.[20]

Morone Takes Hold: The Deadlock Broken June–July

An even more important change in the final version of the document was the new canon 1, which now dealt with the stumbling block, episcopal residence. The original draft had for obvious reasons altogether skirted that burning issue. For the Spaniards and the French, however, it was inconceivable to speak of "Abuses in the Administration of the Sacrament of Orders" without speaking of this problem. Gonzaga had, after all, publicly promised that the council would deal with it when it took up this sacrament. The moment had arrived. The council had to take action—the reformers would not tolerate another decision not to decide.

Morone, returned from Innsbruck and recovered from a bout of illness, now faced his first great challenge in dealing with the assembly at Trent. He had quickly grasped how serious the problem was and how ominous the consequences if a compromise could not be found. He had drawn up a revision of the text proposed to the council in December that asserted conscientious performance of episcopal duties was of *jus divinum* but did not explicitly and specifically apply the *jus divinum* to residence itself. The shift was, however, important: from law to conscience, from a regulation to a sense of personal responsibility. After heated debate, this was the version that prevailed. As finally approved by the council, it substituted, in deference to the zealots, *divinum praeceptum* for *jus divinum,* essentially a cosmetic change. The text began:

> All to whom care of souls has been entrusted are subject to the divine command [*praeceptum*] to know their sheep, to offer sacrifice for them, to nourish them by preaching God's word, by administering the sacraments, and by the example of good works of every kind, to have fatherly care for the poor and of all others who are wretched, and to be devoted to other pastoral duties. As none of these roles can be fulfilled by those who do not stay with and watch their flock, but desert them like hirelings, this holy synod charges and exhorts them to remember the divine commands to rule and feed them with faithful wisdom.

For the Council of Trent, therefore, the ideal bishop and pastor was not simply an administrator of sacraments and an officiator at liturgies, but somebody active in preaching and in caring for his flock, especially the poor, in a variety of ways.

The decree went on: "this holy council declares that all by any name or title who are in charge of patriarchal, primatial, metropolitan, and cathedral churches of any kind whatsoever, even if they are cardinals of the holy Roman church, are bound to reside personally in their church or diocese, and there to fulfill the duties of their office, nor may they be absent except to the degree and on the grounds that follow."[21]

The decree then specified the conditions for legitimate absences and the complete loss of revenue for illegitimate ones. The last paragraph of the decree made the same provisions for "all those of lower rank," that is, priests, who have the care of souls. With such provisions the council made clear the connection between benefice and performance of the duties it entails. If you don't do the job, you don't get the money.

Strong though the decree was, it was not strong enough for those insisting on *jus divinum,* and it certainly did not shut the door to papal dispensations. Nor were the zealots satisfied. The inclusion of cardinal bishops signified for them that the council was entering the forbidden territory of reform of the Curia.

Morone was astute enough to realize that, though he himself insisted with the emperor and with the council that reform of the Curia was reserved to the pope, the reservation could not be absolute, especially in this matter of residence. Moreover, there were cardinal bishops, including de Guise and Madruzzo, who were not members of the Curia, which meant the provision could not be construed as being directed exclusively at the Curia.

In this instance Morone won the support of Pius IV. This was a major breakthrough. In consistory on July 30 the pope explained to the cardinals that he had intended to deal with their reform himself, but since some princes wanted the matter handled by the council, he had agreed. He reassured the cardinals, however, that the legates would look out for their interests and thus tried to sweeten the bitter and unwelcome message.[22]

To the end a few Spaniards continued to oppose this compromise, but the battle for a radical statement on *jus divinum* had been lost. Like the canon on the establishment of seminaries, this canon, despite its limitations, had a great impact on the future of Catholicism. Popes and others exploited its loopholes, but the hundreds of bishops present at the council went home with a lesson learned for themselves and for the priests in their dioceses. Their example and the example of others not present at the council, such as Carlo Borromeo, the papal nephew who set a dramatic pattern in Milan as a residing bishop and who, especially after his canonization, became the star exemplar of what the council intended, began the slow process of making the legislation a living reality.

Morone meanwhile put Egidio Foscarari, the talented and evenhanded bishop of Modena, to work on finding an acceptable formula for the doctrinal decree on holy orders, with its own issue of *jus divinum* and the authority of the pope.[23] On June 8 Foscarari had a version ready, which he presented to leading Spaniards and French figures at the council. That same day Morone called to his quarters five of the leading *zelanti,* as well as three canonists and a few others. The *zelanti* rejected the text for the usual reasons. The next day Morone proposed a reformulation, which was again rejected, and the day after that yet another. On June 11 he convoked a much larger meeting of members of both parties, during which de Guise and Pietro Antonio di Capua, the fierce zealot, fell into a bitter argument over the relationship between council and papacy, the forbidden topic.

Negotiations, difficult and frustrating, continued for several more days, until an agreement was reached by all except for a few hard-core *zelanti.* The differing parties agreed to affirm the hierarchical structure of the church and not touch on the question of whether the bishops' authority derived immediately from God or from the pope. Chapter 5 contained a cautious assertion of papal primacy.

By bringing together a select body of leaders Morone had hit upon a procedure that would continue to serve him well. Through it he was able to hammer out agreements that smoothed the way for the interventions in the General Congregations and almost ensured a certain outcome. His success in moving the council along was in large measure due to this approach, though it did not please all prelates. For Morone, however, diplomat and pragmatist, it worked, and that was sufficient justification for employing it.

In this case, with the agreement, fragile though it was, in hand, Morone acted quickly. On June 19 he sent the formula and the decree on residence to Rome. He explained that these were the best solutions that could be achieved and that he had to have the pope's agreement to go ahead with them. Such an agreement, he knew, would take the wind out of the sails of zealots who were still resisting. From the pope he asked a clear response. A qualified answer would inevitably draw the council into a debate on the relative authority of pope and council, the nightmare that at all costs had to be avoided.[24]

To the great frustration of the legates, the pope, despite their repeated pleas for a response, took his time. A canonist, he did not like ambiguous legislation, which was a fair criticism of the text, and he had other reservations as well. Meanwhile at Trent the agreement reached on June 19 fell apart, even as time was running out to ready the texts and have them approved by the council in time for the Session scheduled for July 15. That Session, already postponed so many times, could not be postponed yet again. Not to hold it would be a blow to Morone's leadership. When the papal response finally came, it was too late. Morone had had to take action.[25]

On July 4 the legates had met with de Guise and a few Spanish prelates. They proposed again that the question on the origin of authority be completely bypassed. Otherwise, as Paleotti observed in his comments on the meeting, "Many Italian prelates would object that too much was attributed to the bishops, too little to the pope, while many Spaniards would object that too much was attributed to the pope, too little to the bishops." De Guise asked the legates to prepare several versions of the critical chapter 5 and canons 6 and 7. Four versions were quickly produced and handed to de Guise and Madruzzo, the only two cardinals at the council besides the legates. De Guise then got the Spaniards to agree to the fourth formula, in which chapter 5 was incorporated into chapter 4.[26]

Two days later, Morone gathered in his quarters about fifty council leaders: the four legates, the two cardinals, all the envoys who were clerics, plus some forty bishops. After a lively discussion, which generally concerned details of wording, the prelates agreed to support the document and the revised version on residence. Paleotti commented, "All were filled with great gratitude to God, who has given us hope of putting these many difficulties behind us and of being able to hold the Session."[27]

That day, July 6, 1563, marked a turning point in the council, freeing it to move forward. Morone had succeeded in attaining what for ten months had seemed impossible. He was not intimidated by the *zelanti,* and he had for the most part persuaded the Spaniards and the French, as he had Ferdinand, of the pope's goodwill and resolve to reform the Curia. Just as important, he had won de Guise as a working partner in the quest for a solution.[28] As Paleotti said in connection with the success of the July 6 meeting, "All recognized how committed Lorraine was to making sure we could hold the Session and how concerned he was to reconcile the different parties, although up to that time many believed his attitude was quite different." Even the pope began to recognize that de Guise was not the wild card he had imagined and began to cultivate his cooperation. Had Charles de Guise thrown in his lot with Luna instead of Morone, the history of the last phase of the Council of Trent would look altogether different.

A few days later the long-awaited response to the June 19 letter arrived from Rome, "which did not altogether approve" the formula sent there. Paleotti commented that Rome's displeasure "did not bother us" because the version approved on July 6 was different from the one sent to Rome.[29] Morone and his supporters moved ahead.

The two decrees, doctrinal and reform, faced another hurdle, however, when on July 9 they were presented on the floor of the council. Guerrero and others insisted on divine origin of the episcopacy and on *jus divinum* for residence. Draškovič said he agreed with Guerrero but "for the sake of concord" he approved the decree, a sentiment expressed by others. Laínez, who had consistently sided with the *zelanti,* perhaps best articulated why the compromises were to be accepted: "Opinions differ among Catholics as to whether episcopal residence and jurisdiction are of divine law and from Christ. The way to deal with this situation is not to condemn one of the opinions because to do so would be to condemn a lot of Catholics. It is safer in such cases to remain silent. We can for the sake of concord accept these decrees, even though their wording is sometimes ambiguous."[30]

The result of the day was that an overwhelming number of prelates voted in favor of both the doctrinal and the reform decrees. The doctrinal decree, designed as counterpoint to Protestant teaching, in essence asserted that holy orders was a sacrament instituted by Christ, that the

Note 3RD council concentrated on
reform within the church rather than + concerns
THE COUNCIL CONCLUDES rebuttal to Protestant concerns 223
since Prot were absent.

church was a hierarchical structure, that once a man was ordained a priest he could not become a layman again, that bishops were of higher rank than priests, and that bishops nominated by the pope were true bishops. Once again, the decree was a minimal statement, a succinct reaffirmation of long-held teachings. It abstained from any mention of papal primacy.

The General Congregation lasted for six hours. It was worth it, Paleotti said, because of the happy outcome. On July 14 the bishops cast their votes on the decrees in preparation for the Session the next day. As anticipated, the decrees passed easily, but such a large number of Spanish bishops, led by Guerreo and supported by Luna, still objected to canon 1 on residence in the reform decree that the legates feared they would either boycott the Session or raise a protest during it. Their fears were misplaced. The Spaniards did neither. At Session 23 the next day eleven cast votes against canon 1, "non placet," but otherwise the vote on both decrees, which included the canon on seminaries, was virtually unanimous. The deadlock had been broken. The council was free to move on.[31]

Matrimony and the "General Reform"
July–November

Spirits rose in Trent and in Rome over the resolution of the crisis and over the prospect of the council's finally completing its tasks. From this moment forward Pius IV dunned Morone with letters prodding him to end it as soon as possible. To ensure that the council moved along in ways agreeable to himself, Pius informed Morone that he was willing to send more bishops from Rome, thus increasing the Italian majority that was already two-thirds of the total membership—a move that surely would set off howls of protest from the non-Italians.[32] He worried about escalating costs and feared that the longer the council lasted the greater the danger of further crises. His fears proved prescient.

Much as Morone, too, wanted to end the council, he realized that could not happen until certain outstanding issues were resolved. On the doctrinal agenda the council still had to address not only the sacrament of matrimony but also those other issues, urgent in northern Europe, that touched directly upon the daily lives of rank-and-file church members—Purgatory; obligatory fasting and abstinence; the veneration of the saints, of their images, and of their relics; and, finally, indulgences, the spark that had set off the Reformation but that up to this point had hardly been mentioned in the council chambers.

The new council president also realized that in the view of the non-Italians especially, the council had scarcely begun to address reform "in head and members." The Spaniards, the French, the emperor, and others had, as mentioned, submitted detailed memoranda to the legates about what they wanted from the council in this regard. These memoranda, to the dismay of envoys and bishops, still rested inert on the desks of the legates. They had to be addressed. Dealing with them would, besides satisfying the interested parties, also dissipate the storm still brewing over the legates' control of the agenda.

Of the issues still facing the council, matrimony seemed to promise a relatively easy resolution. The members of the council were agreed, as the debate subsequently showed, on two essential points: matrimony was a true sacrament instituted by Christ, and the church had the right to impose impediments to its valid celebration. Moreover, this was not the first time the council had examined the subject. In addition to the debate on it at Bologna a decade before, earlier that very year the theologians had at great length discussed the articles on marriage presented to them by the legates.[33] The groundwork had therefore been laid, it seemed, for a smooth passage. As had happened so often in the past, however, the road to resolution turned out to be much rougher than anticipated.

Only on June 21 was the deputation constituted to formulate the decree, which the prelates received a month later in the form of eleven canons and a short statement on clandestine marriages.[34] Clandestine marriages emerged almost immediately as the most troublesome subject. The bishops agreed that abuses were rampant in marriages entered into without witnesses and that they led to major problems in pastoral practice. Especially troublesome was the ease with which one of the partners could later deny that an exchange of vows had taken place and thus go on to contract a further marriage. As early as 1215 Lateran Council IV forbade them.[35] Nonetheless, the church recognized them as true marriages, and they continued to take place.

The theological problem was this: if the consent of the spouses constituted the sacrament, how could the church legitimately declare a thus-consented-to union invalid? Did the church, in other words, have the power and the authority to impose a condition on the validity of marriage that intruded on the partners' exchange of vows, the constitutive element of the sacrament? How could the church declare invalid in the future marriages that in the past had been recognized as valid, even if forbidden? It was over questions like these that the council fretted, with strong opinions expressed on both sides of the debate.

Among Christians the rituals surrounding marriage had gradually evolved through the centuries from family observances conducted in the home. Bit by bit priests began to play a part—at the invitation of the parents or the spouses, to bless the couple or the ring or the marriage chamber or the marriage bed. The church itself became ever more interested in having priests present to ensure that the consent was free and that the spouses were not close blood relatives. By the twelfth century at least part of the marriage rituals had in some places begun to be celebrated inside the parish church. Even at the time of the council, however, practices differed widely across Europe.[36]

On the opening day of the debate, July 24, the French envoy, Arnaud du Ferrier, laid a petition before the council asking for a declaration on two points: that the presence of the pastor or another priest and three or more further witnesses be required for the validity of the marriage bond and that the consent of the parents be required for the validity of marriages of minors.[37] The petition differed from the statement the bishops had in their hands, most notably by requiring a priest as witness. This provision would be incorporated into the final document, a change of landmark significance. The provision about minors was in substantial agreement with the document the bishops were examining, but the final decree affirmed the validity of marriages without the parents' consent.

When debate ended after a week, the legates realized that in the matrimony decree the canons and the declaration on clandestine and minors' marriages had to be revised. The revised version of the decree contained not only twelve doctrinal canons and the declaration on clandestine marriages but, as well, eleven more provisions ("reform articles") on matrimony. This entire document went through two more revisions before it was finally approved three months later. The part that encountered by far the most resistance was the declaration on clandestine marriages, known by its opening word, *Tametsi* ("even though"). As late as the third revision, for instance, it still gathered 50 negative votes out of a potential 190. Moreover, all through the debate two of the legates— Simonetta and Hosius—had sided with the opponents to the decree.[38] Because of the disagreements especially over *Tametsi* and the fact that the council had scarcely begun to address a correlative reform decree, the Session scheduled for September 16 had to be postponed—not a good sign—and rescheduled for November 11.

No single provision of the entire council affected the Catholic laity more directly than *Tametsi,* which was finally approved in time for the Session on November 11. The approval and implementation of *Tametsi* meant that in the future the church recognized no marriage between Catholics as valid unless it had been witnessed by a priest. Since the requirement of a priest applied to all marriages, those between minors were of course included. *Tametsi* condemned, however, the view that parental consent was required for validity, and thus struck a blow for Romeo, Juliet, and Friar Lawrence.[39]

Implemented only with a great deal of local variation over a long course of time, *Tametsi* strongly reinforced the church's claim of determinative authority over marriage and constituted the decisive step in putting the institution firmly under ecclesiastical aegis:

> Even though there is no doubt that secret marriages entered into by the consent of the partners are true and valid marriages . . . nevertheless, the holy church of God has for excellent reasons always detested and prohibited such marriages. . . . Hence, this council orders that in the future . . . the celebration of marriage must take place in open church, during which the parish priest will, by questioning the man and woman, make sure of their consent and then say "I join you together in marriage, in the name of the Father and the Son and the holy Spirit," or use other words according to the accepted rite of each province. [If for good reason no public announcements are made of the forthcoming marriage] let the priest at least celebrate the marriage in the presence of two or three witnesses.

Tametsi concluded:

> Finally, the holy synod exhorts couples to make a careful confession of their sins and to approach the most holy sacrament of the Eucharist with devotion before they marry, or at least three days before they consummate the marriage. The holy synod earnestly desires that, if any provinces have praiseworthy customs and ceremonies in this matter over and above those here mentioned, they should by all means be retained. So that such salutary precepts may not escape anyone's notice, the council orders all local bishops to see that this decree is promulgated to their people as soon as they can, and is explained in all the parish churches of their dioceses. This should be done as soon as possible in the first year [after the council], and then again as often as they think expedient.[40]

The final set of documents on matrimony approved on November 11 contained other important provisions, such as the doctrinal canons condemning the view that matrimony is not a true sacrament, that polygamy is divinely sanctioned, and that heresy, continued absence, and adultery break the marriage bond.[41] The reform canons that followed *Tametsi* dealt for the most part with ecclesiastical regulations concerning the sacrament. Two are particularly revealing of what was perhaps the council's central concern—that marriages be entered into freely. Canon 9 castigated as "the height of wickedness" any violation of that freedom and forbade "temporal lords and officials" to force anybody into marriage in order to gain control of their wealth or inheritance.

Canon 8 decreed that no marriage could be considered valid between a kidnapper and his victim as long "as she remains in his power. But if, after being separated from him and settled in a safe and free place, she consents" to marry him, he can take her as his wife. He and all who connived with him, however, are henceforth to be held in public disrepute and be ineligible for public office.

During the long discussions on matrimony, clerical celibacy received remarkably little attention from both theologians and bishops despite the pressure from the emperor and the Duke of Bavaria to address the issue. However, in a lengthy speech on May 20 covering many topics, Draškovič reminded the bishops of the grave scandal priests caused because of their sexual misconduct, and said, "If you want young priests, let them get married first." Otherwise, only older men should be ordained, presumably because they would have better control over their sexual desires.[42] A month later Laínez implicitly answered him by saying that youth was not the problem but poor education: give the young the right education, and they would make good priests, a sentiment that, for all its questionable assumptions, correlated well with the decree on seminaries.[43] In the General Congregations that was virtually the extent of the discussion. For better or for worse, celibacy lacked urgency as an issue for bishops from Mediterranean countries.

During their Congregations earlier in the year, however, the theologians had discussed issues related to celibacy, but rarely at any length. They unanimously agreed on the spiritual superiority of celibacy to matrimony, but they held diverse opinions on whether celibacy was a church law or intrinsic to the priesthood, and therefore whether the pope could dispense from celibacy a priest already ordained. They held similarly diverse opinions on whether it was advisable to ordain already married men for certain troubled areas of the church. For the most part, however, their opinions were conservative.[44]

In his intervention the Spanish Dominican Juan Ludeña, for instance, engaged in a long, fictive, and tedious dialogue with Calvin over marriage and celibacy in which, though he conceded that in the present circumstances good reasons existed for dispensation from celibacy for married men, better reasons counseled against it.[45] Other theologians, such as Sanctes Cinthius, a German Dominican, and Lucius Anguisciolo, an Italian Franciscan, asserted, on the contrary, that ensuring the continuation of the faith was more important than the law of celibacy.[46]

Although the introductory chapters to the final doctrinal document on matrimony did not mention celibacy, two of the twelve canons that follow dealt with it. Canon 10 condemned the view that marriage was a more blessed state than virginity or celibacy. Canon 9 condemned the view that clerics in holy orders or religious who had taken a solemn vow of chastity could contract marriage and that such marriages were "valid in spite of church law and the vow." This was a minimal statement, more juridical than theological, that sidestepped the deeper questions raised by the theologians. It was the council's only pronouncement on a problem that had exploded with the Reformation and become a grave concern among Catholics in northern Europe. After the council the matter ended in the lap of Pius IV.

Morone had long been busy with another crucial matter, a general program for reform of the church. From the national memoranda he had drawn up a set of forty-two reform articles, which he sent to Rome in a letter dated June 4.[47] In the letter he cautioned that this was a first draft that he had not himself had time to examine carefully, but it would give His Holiness an idea of what was developing at the council. From Borromeo came the reply that the pope, without at this point wanting to go into detail, was pleased.[48] For Morone this was the signal that he had a relatively free hand in constructing this important instrument. He continued to engage Paleotti as his close collaborator and, indeed, as the chief architect in formulations of it. Both men were convinced that for the reform to carry the day in the various realms of Christendom after the council it had to be based on the national memoranda.[49]

Once he had the nod from Rome, Morone delivered the forty-two articles to the envoys and in reply received sharp criticism, in which the objections were not always consistent. Not surprisingly, they particularly contested the article on "reform of the princes," which was for the most part a unilateral rewrite of church-state relations emphasizing the exemption of the church from secular jurisdiction and abolishing all previous "privileges" of the princes. The article was a contemporary version of the implications of the traditional ecclesiastical concern for the "freedom of the church," that is, the freedom of the church to conduct its affairs apart from the oversight or especially the domination of the laity, or "the secular arm," an ongoing and contentious issue since the Investiture Contest of the eleventh century. But the envoys also complained that crucial items such as the reform of the cardinals, the reform of papal conclaves, and similar issues concerning "the head" were notable for their absence.

In view of the criticism the articles were reduced to thirty-six. On August 20 they were delivered for the first time to the bishops for their consideration, without at this point having been formally introduced onto the floor of the council. By this ploy Morone hoped to anticipate problems and thus avoid endless wrangling in the General Congregations. The article on reform of the princes stirred up a storm. Through his envoy the emperor communicated his severe displeasure. For Morone as well as for many of the prelates, guarding bishops from violations of "the freedom of the church" was as fundamental to reform as ensuring that prelates performed their pastoral duties. The bishops from the Kingdom of Naples felt oppressed by their Spanish overlords ("the barons"), but bishops from other places—France in particular—also felt strongly in the matter. In view of the sharp objections from the envoys, however, Morone saw to it that the article was revised in a milder form. The tensions were escalating to an alarming degree. Was the council gliding into another major and seemingly insurmountable crisis? On September 3 the legates delivered to the bishops for debate twenty-one of now thirty-five reform articles.[50] When the debate opened a week later, Morone apologized that the article on the princes, now number 35, was not included but promised that it and the remaining articles would be delivered within a few days. In fact the envoys, especially Count Luna, were applying heavy pressure to the legates for more drastic revision of article 35 or for its deletion altogether, whereas some bishops threatened to leave the council if the article was suppressed. Luna challenged once again the legates' control of the agenda. The situation grew so serious and divisive that Morone was forced to consider the possibility of suspending the council.[51]

On September 14 the bishops received the remaining articles.[52] This long document defies summary, each article of which was technical in its language and detailed in its stipulations. For the most part the articles, which constituted a full job description for bishops, were elaborations of principles of episcopal reform ratified in the first period, Sessions 5 through 7, and were particularly designed to enhance bishops' authority over the personnel and institutions of their dioceses.

Among the more important provisions were the mandates to hold annual synods, to visit the institutions of their dioceses every second year, to see to the repair of churches, to act responsibly with church funds, and to put into action the care of souls that had been committed to them, which meant in particular fulfilling their most characteristic duty (episcoporum praecipuum), which was preaching the "sacred Scriptures and the Law of God," an echo and reassertion of the stipulation about preaching in Session 5.

Pastors of parishes also had the obligation to preach to their flocks or, if they were unable to do so or otherwise impeded, to provide preachers. "Metropolitans," that is, archbishops, should summon provincial synods every three years. The decree forbade "even cardinals" to hold more than one benefice attached to the care of souls. Underlying all the provisions was the concern expressed in canons 1 and 18 that only the more worthy candidates be chosen for the offices of bishop and pastor. In those two canons appeared the process of scrutiny for the two offices described earlier.

The document required that anyone taking part in the first provincial synod after the council swear obedience to the Roman Pontiff and accept all the council had decreed.[53] It also mandated that those receiving a benefice that entailed the care of souls make "public profession of their orthodox faith." On the basis of these provisions Pius IV drew up a document after the council that came to be known as the "Tridentine Profession of Faith" *(Professio Fidei Tridentinae).*[54]

Article 35, still long and detailed, was divided into twelve headings. Addressed to "Catholic princes, whom God ordained to be the protectors of the faith and the church," it insisted on the exemption of the clergy from secular courts and jurisdictions. It forbade rulers to impose taxes on the clergy, to confiscate church property, or to prevent the publication of papal or episcopal documents. It insisted on the immunity of church buildings from incursions by secular police or military personnel. These were traditional claims but never before marshaled in such a coherent fashion. The article said nothing about rulers' rights to nominate higher clergy.

The debate on the articles lasted from September 11 to October 8. De Guise led off the first day, once again insisting that bishops be elected by their clergy, as in the early church, and, though he was a cardinal himself, complaining that not a single article concerned reform of the cardinals. On September 22 the legates gave du Ferrier, the French envoy, permission to "make a few remarks."[55] The envoy's "remarks" turned out to be fierce invective against the reform work of the council thus far and against the present document in particular. For 150 years the Most Christian Kings of France had begged the popes for reform of the clergy, he complained, and nothing had happened. The document the prelates now held in their hands was no reform at all. It was not based on the Bible and the early discipline of the church and said not a word about exemptions, dispensations, papal financial exactions such as annates, or similar matters.

Although du Ferrier's "few remarks" were in general badly received because he seemed to impugn the work the council had accomplished, they struck a sympathetic chord with many bishops. The situation continued to be precarious, with speculation over the fate of article 35 a festering wound. As the debate drew to a close on October 8 Morone got the council to agree that for the next Session, scheduled for November 11, it would limit itself to the first twenty-one articles, which would postpone action on article 35. That day the legates appointed a deputation of eighteen bishops to draw up the draft. Of the ten Italians among the eighteen, half were leading *zelanti,* a fact that did not go unnoticed.[56]

A month later, after further debate on the decrees concerning marriage, the bishops got the text of the now twenty canons on reform. When discussion opened it was heated.[57] The bishops had many suggestions and gave vent to passionately held grievances. Some protested that the revised text was weaker than the original. But no party was strong enough to effect significant changes in the text.

Among the aggrieved prelates was certainly Martín Pérez de Ayala, the bishop of Segovia.[58] In his intervention he let loose with a blanket denunciation of the text similar in some ways to du Ferrier's. According to him the document was "insufficient and inefficacious," nothing more than a "pretended reform" that did not touch the real abuses in the church and that said virtually nothing about widespread simony in the distribution of benefices. He went on, however, to attack as radically flawed the process that produced the text, which took place not in open discussion on the floor of the council but in a committee in which the Italian faction that had consistently impeded all attempts at reform was given a determining voice. It was an attack on Morone's leadership.

Pérez demanded that his objection be entered into the official acts of the council.[59] His speech had no follow-up by others, but it expressed sentiments widely felt especially among the non-Italians.

Meanwhile, cardinals in the Curia swamped certain bishops with letters expressing their dismay over the reform and its potential as "a calamity for the Curia and a diminution of the cardinals' dignity." They urged bishops to get the council suspended, if necessary, in order to obviate this eventuality. They wanted, according to Paleotti's bitter assessment, to make sure that "nothing solid be enacted that might diminish the cardinals' luxury and high standards of living [*luxum fastumque*]."[60]

Among the cardinals trying to influence the outcome, Alessandro Farnese went further than the others. He criticized Morone directly for his support of the reform and warned him that it had hurt his chances for election in the next conclave.[61] Morone in his turn complained sharply to the pope about the letters, saying that from Rome he expected support, not more problems.[62]

The debate drew to a close on November 10, the eve of the Session. Most of the articles received an overwhelming number of positive votes, but several saw so many negative votes that the legates in cooperation with leading prelates reworked them, out of fear that the Session would be disrupted by protests or give cause for bishops to register their displeasure by leaving the council. With the military situation in France now dire, some French bishops had in fact already left.

Morone's concern about the Session was not misplaced—it was the most difficult of the whole council. Although the decree on marriage passed, a number of prelates suggested qualifications of aspects of it. The reform decree suffered even more qualifications and calls for reworking.[63] At the end Morone announced that the decrees had been approved by almost everybody but that changes would be made wherever a majority asked for it. After the Session Paleotti went to work and a few days later received approval of the revisions from the deputation, and the council ratified the decrees in the final Session.[64]

With Mass, the sermon, the reading of the decrees, the voting, the voicing of qualifications, and other formalities the Session on November 11 lasted eleven continuous hours. It exhausted everyone. The final act of the Session was to set December 9 for the next one, in which would be treated "the remaining articles on reform already expounded, other matters concerned with reform, and, if it seems opportune and if time allows . . . some matters of dogma."

This was a big agenda to be accomplished in a month. Morone's agenda was even bigger, for he had long been planning that the December 9 Session would be the final one and conclude the council, a goal that Pius IV, almost obsessed with it, urged upon him with ever stronger language. Yet the council had not even touched upon the reform of the religious orders, which was high on the agenda of many bishops, the reform of the *Index*, on which the commission had long been working, the reform of the liturgical books, and the construction of a catechism. Beyond those difficult matters lay the burning and more directly pastoral issues, especially in lands where the Reformation was strong—indulgences, Purgatory, the laws of fasting, and the veneration of saints and images.

The Hectic Final Weeks

Shortly after the Session on November 11, Morone gathered a group of about twenty-five leading prelates and proposed that the council conclude on December 9 or shortly thereafter. The pope wanted it, he told them, a majority of the bishops wanted it, and no obstacle to it was to be expected from the secular authorities. De Guise seconded Morone's proposal and added that the situation in France had become so desperate that half of the French bishops had already left for home and that he himself could not possibly stay beyond the December Session. Morone's proposal carried the day, but not everybody was convinced that it was feasible or desirable. Count Luna led a relatively small but determined group to slow down a process that could not be other than rushed and dangerously superficial.

On November 15 Morone made the same proposal to the full council. He recounted for the group how much had been accomplished and, while admitting that the results were not perfect, tried to forestall objections by reminding the bishops that "we are just men, not angels."[65] With 130 positive votes the proposal easily carried the day and set off a scramble to make arrangements for departure. The "poor prelates" joined in the excitement, for the legates guaranteed them the money they needed to make the journey home. The prospect of actually ending the council acted like a shot of adrenalin that energized the bishops to move the agenda along swiftly. They were now inclined, for better or worse, to glide over problems that in different circumstances would have entangled them for weeks. The result was a massive production of legislation, much of which, though of considerable importance, received no discussion on the floor of the council.

From November 15 to 18 the bishops dealt with the remaining articles on reform.[66] They made many suggestions for improvement but none of major import. As the debate began, they received a radically revised and reduced article 35.[67] Now just a paragraph long, it had originally run several pages. It consisted basically in an exhortation to the "princes" to protect the church from its enemies, to observe the appropriate boundaries regarding ecclesiastical property and persons, and to act as dutiful leaders of the Christian community. It made its way easily through the council, partly because of the press of time and partly because the bishops realized, as Morone reminded them, that they would later need the princes' help in implementing the council and that now was, therefore, no time to antagonize them.[68] In the final version of the document it became number 20.[69]

But there was more to it than that. Ferdinand's and especially Philip's envoys had applied heavy pressure to Morone to tone down the document, and he felt compelled to acquiesce. Moreover, as Paleotti acknowledged, Morone also saw that his acquiescence helped buy the princes' support for a swift end to the council. Pressure on the bishops "from the City," that is, from Pius, not to obstruct the legate's program also accounts for the bishops' acceptance of this radically mitigated statement. Paleotti, the principal author of the original version, was bitter about the new one, which he assessed as a reduction of the article "to a vague formula of almost meaningless words."[70]

Aside from the chapter on the princes, this set of reform articles consisted mostly in further specifications of bishops' duties and authorities. It began:

> Those who accept the episcopal ministry should recognize what their function is and realize they have been called not to personal advantages, not to riches or to a life of luxury, but to toil and solicitude for the glory of God. For there can be no doubt that the rest of the faithful are more readily aroused to the practice of religion and innocence of life if they see those set over them absorbed not in what is of the world but in the salvation of souls and their fatherland in heaven. . . . They should order all their conduct in such a way that others may be able to look to them for an example of moderation, modesty, continence, and of the holy humility that so much commends us to God. . . . This holy council wholly forbids them to try to improve the living of their relatives and household from church revenues. . . . [These stipulations] also apply to cardinals of the holy Roman church.[71]

Those words set the tone for what followed, much of which consisted in technical ordinances regarding lawsuits and benefices, that is, regarding just and proper administration of ecclesiastical goods and properties.[72] But there are interesting exceptions. Chapter 3, for instance, enjoined that "the sword of excommunication be wielded with great reserve and caution," and chapter 19 decreed that "the detestable practice of dueling . . . must be wholly wiped off the face of the Christian world."[73]

These two sets of reform decrees constituted Morone's "General Reform." Approved in the last two Sessions of the Council of Trent, they were compromises, falling far short of what more ardent reformers wanted, especially regarding the reform of the cardinals and the Roman Curia, yet going further than the *zelanti* wanted. That the decrees had the impact they did on the improvement in episcopal performance after the council was due, as mentioned, perhaps more to the example of bishops who became convinced of the ideal the council held up for them than to the intrinsic efficacy of the decree's provisions.

From November 23 until November 27 the council turned to the documents on the reform of the religious orders, male and female.[74] In most cities and dioceses the mendicant orders, now supplemented by the Jesuits, dominated the pastoral ministry. While some bishops deeply resented them, others were grateful to them. Any attempt to curtail the orders' pastoral "privileges," a long-standing goal for many bishops, touched upon the authority of the papacy, which had conferred the privileges upon the orders. Yet the basic question remained: why take up residence in your diocese to supervise its ministry if so much of the ministry falls outside your control?

There were other problems. Was there not a confusing number of orders following a confusing number of "Rules" or ways of life, each claiming to be superior to the other? Should not the number be reduced—even to the point of putting all religious under two or three Rules? The public and often bitter polemic of the Observantist branches of the mendicant orders against Conventual branches broadcast to the world at large their real or alleged laxity and failures in discipline. Satires about the orders' foibles flowed easily from the pen of Humanists like Erasmus. Should not the council look into such matters?

The women's orders or convents presented different problems. They were in most cases under the supervision of the male branch of the order. If that branch were by definition lax, what more could one expect from the convent? More palpable was the problem of families forcing daughters against their will into convents, often at a young age. Many convents had as few as four or five members, considered far too small for a proper religious life, whereas others had far too many. Some were too poor to sustain the nuns, which led to nuns' living off gifts of friends and relatives, which introduced a disparity of lifestyles within the same convent. And then there were rumors and proven cases of sexual misconduct in convents. What action should the council take?

On November 20 the bishops were handed two documents, one dealing with men and the other with women, which were later condensed into a single decree, *Decretum de regularibus et monialibus*. They began debate three days later. Nothing is known about the deputation that drew up the documents. Surely, however, the superiors general of the orders were somehow engaged in it. As far as the religious orders were concerned, the debate got off to an excellent start when de Guise praised them for their ministries in France and for their courage and steadfastness, to the point of martyrdom, in the present religious conflict. They should keep their privileges.[75] After him Giovanni Trevisan, the patriarch of Venice, proposed, regarding women's convents, "Let their superiors reform them."[76] Thus without fireworks went the four-day debate, in which bishops proposed only technical revisions of the text. The notable exception was the archbishop of Braga, Bartholomeu dos Mártires, who wanted to eliminate the Conventual branches altogether because the members "lived badly."[77]

The decree is long, addresses a number of technical canonical issues, and, again, is less radical than many reformers called for. It lays down general principles, beginning with the most basic: the members should faithfully observe their Rule, especially the three vows of poverty, chastity, and obedience. More specifically, no religious, male or female, was to possess private property, and each was bound to observe common life. Every effort should be made to ensure that the election of superiors be done properly, freely, and by secret ballot, "so that the names of voters are never disclosed." The decree acknowledged bishops' supervisory authority over the public ministry of religious, but did not directly engage the delicate question of the regulars' "exemptions."

The decree stipulated age qualifications for superiors of women's convents and prohibited anyone from being superior of more than one at the same time. Bishops were obliged to ascertain whether a young

woman entering a convent was "free or forced or under immoral pressure, and whether she understands what she is doing." The decree imposed an anathema on anyone forcing a woman to enter a convent
against her will, which was unfortunately a deeply rooted problem that
this stricture did not eliminate.[78]

Chapter 5 is perhaps the most stringent of the whole decree. It
"commands all bishops, calling the divine justice to bear witness and
under threat of eternal damnation, to ensure the enclosure of nuns in all
monasteries subject to their jurisdiction." Bishops were to make use of
secular authorities in enforcing obedience to the decree, and "secular
princes" were to provide whatever aid was needed to that end.

This chapter must be seen as an aspect of the Observantist movement in religious orders still vigorous at the time of Trent. For women's
monasteries strict cloister was an important feature of faithful observance, and reformers like Teresa of Avila on their own promoted enclosure before the council enacted its decree. What was unclear in the decree was whether cloister applied only to nuns *(moniales)* in the strict
sense of the term, that is, to members of the older religious orders with
solemn vows, or applied more broadly to "virgins" living or working together and engaged in some form of social assistance in the public
sphere, as in certain confraternities.[79] After the council enclosure began
ever more commonly to be imposed on the latter group and frustrated
the purposes for which the women had joined together. For many convents, moreover, observance of the decree entailed severe hardships, financial and other, that were not provided for in the decree.[80]

The bishops finished debate on Saturday, November 27, and they
still had not seen even a line of text dealing with indulgences, Purgatory,
and other important issues. If the council was to end on December 9,
only nine working days were left. No one, of course, was more aware of
the problem than Morone, but he had not directly addressed it until after the Session on November 11. His first impulse was to have the council remand those items to the Holy See for action after the council. The
idea met with opposition from the imperial envoys who insisted that

the council itself had to assert Catholic teaching on Purgatory and indulgences; otherwise "the heretics" would see in the council's failure to do so an implicit admission of the church's error or wrongdoing. De Guise absolutely insisted that France had to have a decree from the council, not the pope, on the veneration of images because of the council's greater authority in France, which is where the decree was most urgently needed.

Although these issues all had practical and pastoral aspects to them, up to this point in the council they had generally been considered doctrine on the rare occasions when they had been raised. But to treat them now as doctrine would require employing the full apparatus of the council's procedures, beginning with the Congregation of Theologians. If that apparatus moved into motion, the council could not possibly end on the appointed date. It might be prolonged for months.

On November 13 Morone won approval in a gathering of council notables to treat them as reform, to have the decrees drawn up by special deputations (without previous debate in General Congregations), and to have them thus presented to the council. This was a big shortcut, but it would still allow bishops to debate the decree and, it was hoped, allow the council to finish on December 9.

Two days later the legates set up three deputations consisting of prelates and theologians to formulate decrees on Purgatory, indulgences, fasting, and the veneration of saints, images, and relics. Nothing is known about the work, if any, of these deputations. By Sunday morning, November 28, two weeks after they had been constituted and produced no palpable results, de Guise had had enough. He appeared in Morone's quarters and demanded categorically that the council issue decrees on Purgatory and the veneration of images.

Morone moved into action, and the next afternoon, after another large consultation that morning, constituted a new, sizable deputation, made up in part of members of the deputations of November 15, charged with formulating in short order all three decrees. That afternoon the deputation went to work in the quarters of Cardinal Charles de Guise.

Morone meanwhile had to deal with the strong resistance from Count Luna on the rush to finish the council. The legates' letters to Rome are filled with the problem of dealing with him.[81]

The deputation under the direction of de Guise continued working the next day on its huge task, but that night two separate couriers arrived from Rome with the alarming news that Pius IV had taken so seriously ill that his life was in question. If the pope died and the council had not officially declared its business finished, it would automatically be suspended. Not only would it suffer the delay of a possibly long conclave, but its very existence would be in jeopardy because there was no guarantee the new pope would reconvene it.

The prospect of the pope's death provided Morone with the best possible instrument for overcoming the last resistance to ending the council as soon as possible. The next morning, December 1, he convoked all the envoys and made clear how dangerous the situation was. That day, moreover, he received a letter from Rome, written of course before the pope's illness, demanding that the conclusion of the council not be postponed a single day, no matter how strong the opposition from Luna or anybody else.[82]

The following morning, December 2, he called together about fifty leading prelates, who almost unanimously agreed that that afternoon the remaining materials, including the revisions of the decrees on general reform and religious orders, should be presented to the bishops in a General Congregation, and that the final Session of the council should take place immediately thereafter, on December 3 and 4. Both days were required for the Session not only because of the vast quantity of new materials but because the council would also have to give its final approval to all the decrees enacted since the first Session, in 1545, so that the French, virtually absent from the first two periods, might give their formal assent.

In the General Congregation that afternoon the bishops in principle got the opportunity to comment on the materials presented to them, but because those materials were so vast, not all of them could even be read to the assembly. This meant a second, brief Congregation had to be held on the morning of December 4 before the Session itself opened in the cathedral so that the reading could be completed. There was virtually no time for discussion in either of these Congregations, which meant they were simply rubber stamps.

At the Congregation on the afternoon of December 2, Morone asked the crucial question, whose answer was a foregone conclusion: during the Session the next day did the fathers want to decide whether or not to conclude the council? Despite Luna's strong opposition, Morone, as expected, received an overwhelmingly positive response.[83] The Congregation had hardly concluded when a courier arrived from Rome with news that the pope had improved and was out of danger. At this point, however, there was no turning back.

Under this intense pressure of time, de Guise's commission had to produce texts on the subjects committed to it, an extraordinarily difficult and perforce rushed task. The decree on Purgatory in an introductory clause stated simply that on the basis of Scripture and ancient tradition the church taught that Purgatory existed and that souls detained there could be helped by prayers. It then, in this short document, exhorted bishops to see to it that the doctrine was preached and explained to the faithful in clear and correct fashion and to ensure that anything smacking of venality or superstition be eliminated from Christian practice regarding it. Thus, although the decree in fact made a doctrinal statement, its orientation was to pastoral practice.[84]

The decree "On Invocation, Veneration, and Relics of Saints, and on Sacred Images" was much longer.[85] It directed bishops to see to the proper preaching on these subjects. Regarding the invocation and veneration of saints it rejected as impious calling into question that the saints, "reigning together with Christ," do not pray for those still on earth or have no care for them. Regarding relics it enjoined bishops to teach that the "holy bodies" of saints and martyrs were "living members of Christ and temples of the Holy Spirit and due to be raised by him to eternal and glorious life" and therefore deserved respect and veneration.

By far the longest part of the decree dealt with the veneration of sacred images, a subject that first received solemn church ratification in the Second Council of Nicaea, 787, in reaction to the violent outburst of iconoclasm in the Eastern Empire. Nicaea essentially declared two things: sacred images were legitimate, and they were helpful for instruction and devotion. Trent went a step further by declaring that they should be free of all "sensual appeal" *(lascivia),* false doctrine, and superstition. For this statement on images the deputation drew heavily on a document formulated by theologians of the Paris Faculty of Theology for the Colloquy of Saint-Germain, in January 1563, which Charles de Guise had brought with him to Trent. The *lascivia* in the Tridentine text was a reworking of *impudica et lasciva* in the Saint-Germain text. De Guise must therefore be considered the principal architect of the council's statement on images.[86]

The decree on indulgences was short. It declared, incorrectly, that they had been in use in the church "from the most ancient times" and anathematized those who asserted that they were useless or who denied the church's power to grant them. Then, after enjoining that "moderation be used in granting them," it acknowledged that their abuse had been a cause of great scandal and ordered bishops to stamp out all "superstition, ignorance, irreverence and all other abuses" connected with them.

This decree was followed by another short and notably generic decree on "Foods, Fasting, and Feast Days" that imposed on pastors the task of inculcating in the faithful what the church had enjoined regarding such matters without specifying what exactly the church had enjoined. The troubling question of whether the church could or should under pain of sin oblige fasting and abstinence from meat on certain days, a question hotly debated in the era, was completely bypassed.

In a further decree the council acknowledged that the commission working on revision of the *Index* of 1559 had not been able to finish its work and ordered that whatever it had prepared be "presented to the pope" so that it might be completed and published. These materials, which tempered the severity of the earlier *Index,* constituted the substance of the *Index* published by Pius IV on May 24, 1564, in the bull *Dominici Gregis Custodiae.*[87] The decree ended by stating in a single sentence that the council "gives similar orders in the matter of the catechism prepared by those commissioned and of the missal and the breviary."

In the decrees of the council approved up to this time, a catechism was mentioned in passing for the first and last time in canon 7 of the reform decree of the previous Session.[88] The project had, however, been under discussion intermittently and casually from the beginning of the council. Then at Bologna a deputation was formed to compose a catechism but without result.[89] Only in mid-summer of the present year, 1563, was it clear that in this period a deputation (or deputations) for the missal, breviary, and catechism had been commissioned.[90] By this time the catechism had become a special concern of Ferdinand.[91]

Reform of the liturgical books figured in the first draft of Beccadelli's deputation on abuses in the Mass in the summer of the previous year.[92] The document recommended, among other things, that the missal be purged of superstitious elements, but, as mentioned, it never made it to the floor of the council.[93] The problems here were in the first instance the same as for the revision of the *Index*—insufficient library resources and a task too complicated for a large assembly to deal with. Revising the liturgical books was even more complicated than amending the *Index* in that more time and resources were necessary for this undertaking, which required sorting out the many problems embodied in them. It is not surprising that the council was unable to move ahead very far.

The final document was "On the Reception and Observance of the Council's Decrees." It began by deploring the times and the refusal of the heretics, "invited so often," to come to the council. Since there was no hope of their coming and since bishops needed to return to their dioceses, the decision had been made to close the council:

> It only remains for the council to charge all princes in the Lord, as it now does, to give their help and not allow the decrees here made to be abused or violated by heretics, but to see they are devoutly received and faithfully observed by them and by all. But if any difficulty arises over the reception of these decrees, or any matters are raised as needing clarification (which the council does not believe to be the case) . . . the pope will ensure that the needs of the provinces are met . . . either by summoning persons who are suitable for dealing with the matter . . . or even by holding a general council if he thinks necessary, or by whatever means he thinks best.

This document presaged the three-way tug-of-war about the interpretation and implementation of the council that took place afterwards, in which secular rulers, especially Philip II, the popes, and the local bishops each believed the task fell principally to them.

The very last act of the council in Session 25 was a decree of only a few lines solemnly ratifying the closing of the council and requesting confirmation of its decrees from the pope. The latter provision had been discussed back and forth for several weeks. Philip II strongly opposed it because he felt it raised the forbidden question of the relationship of pope and council. Ferdinand opposed it because the council had been conducted under legates of the Holy See, which made papal approval superfluous.

The legates, however, were just as strongly in favor of it and determined to see it through. De Guise and Simonetta suggested having Pius issue a bull approving the decrees and then have the council officially receive it, but the haste at the end precluded putting the plan into operation.[94] Despite the disagreements, the decree passed with only Guerrero voting against it, which prompted three of his old adversaries from the *zelanti* party to intervene during the Session to insist that papal confirmation was not simply desirable but necessary.

The final Session of the council, extending over two long days, proceeded smoothly but left participants exhausted.[95] Finally the great moment came. Once the last decree was approved, Morone rose to his feet and declared the council concluded, and he then bade the council members "to go forth in peace." De Guise immediately stepped forward to lead the assembly in a litany of acclamations celebrating all those associated with the council since its beginning, a litany that began of course with the three popes but included by name Charles V, other rulers, the legates, and so forth down a long list. When he finished the *Te Deum* was intoned and sung by the whole assembly. Present and signing the official record of the decrees were, in order, the 4 legates, Cardinals de Guise and Madruzzo, 3 patriarchs, 25 archbishops, 168 bishops, 7 abbots, and 7 superiors general of the religious orders. After them 19 procurators of absentee bishops added their names. Two days later all the envoys signed except Luna, who awaited word from Philip II empowering him to do so.

In the cathedral after the acclamations, the pent-up emotions broke into the open. Paleotti described the scene in the final entry of his council diary: "I cannot possibly communicate what joy all present felt, and how they blessed God, the author of all good, and gave him thanks. I saw so many grave and distinguished prelates, with tears of happiness flowing from their eyes, congratulating even those with whom they earlier were at odds. . . . There was no one who did not express with his face, his words, and his whole body the very height of happiness, praising God, to whom be honor, power, and glory forever and ever."[96]

Epilogue

In the middle of the sixteenth century the Catholic leaders of Europe decided, under pressure, to play the dangerous game of a council. As the council dragged on for a seemingly endless eighteen years, they came to realize with ever deeper anxiety and frustration what a treacherous game they were engaged in. The fact that of the twenty-five Sessions of the council fewer than half were able to publish decrees of any substance suggests that the course was anything but smooth.

The Council of Trent lurched from major crisis to major crisis, in each of which the stakes were portentous for the future of the West. When it finally concluded on December 4, 1563, none of the players had reason to be perfectly satisfied with the outcome. No one was more aware of this than the legates, especially Giovanni Morone, who reminded the prelates, "We are men, not angels."

Reconciliation with "the Lutherans" was in the beginning a primary
goal at least for the emperor, which explains his insistence that the council be held "in German lands." The council took steps to achieve the
goal, but according to its own principles and with considerable skepticism on the part of many. The experience with Lutheran envoys and
theologians during the second period confirmed the skeptics' intuition.
It dramatized the impossibility of the council's serving as an instrument
of reconciliation. Each side could not help playing according to its own
rules and therefore making demands on the other that required it to
surrender or severely compromise its identity. That was in 1552, but even
before 1545, the year the council opened, the hour was already too late.
The Protestant paradigm of church polity had crystallized. It was incompatible with the Catholic.

The council's decision not to attach names to the positions it condemned was a break with tradition that then as now mitigated the sting
of the anathema. The council condemned teachings, not persons. Protestant leaders could with honesty claim at least in some instances that
the condemned position was not theirs or was a gross misrepresentation
of theirs. But the passions on both sides precluded placid dialogue. Europe was already engaged in *une guerre à outrance*.

For all the sophistication of the theologians at Trent, their approach
suffered from two systemic weaknesses. The first was a penchant for
proof-texting, lifting statements and even ideas of the Protestant Reformers out of context, the result of an underdeveloped skill in textual
analysis that was endemic to Scholasticism. Yet it has to be admitted
that Luther in particular often expressed himself in terms so hyperbolic
and unqualified as to make misunderstanding easy.

The second weakness was an underdeveloped sense of historical
criticism, also endemic to Scholasticism, which resulted at the council
in affirmations of apostolic origins for beliefs and practices where there
were none, or where those origins were much less secure than the council intimated. The Humanists had made important strides in develop-

ing a keener awareness of anachronism, and occasionally their influence made itself felt at Trent. If that influence had been stronger, the council might have been more qualified in some of its assertions.

Although Trent failed at reconciliation with "the Lutherans," it achieved reconciliation among Catholics, symbolized in what happened on December 4 and 6, 1563. On those dates all the players signed off on the council's decrees. After the council, in the bull *Benedictus Deus* dated January 26, 1564, Pius IV, despite strong opposition in the Curia, confirmed and promulgated them in their entirety and thus sealed the relationship between the council and "the head" that during the council had often been badly strained. Further schism had been averted, and Catholic leaders had the satisfaction of knowing that they had brought to conclusion a project of defining importance that had often been at the point of spinning completely out of control.

For the peace that resulted everybody had paid a price in compromises, some of which came back after the council to trouble the church. During the council three centers of authority wrestled with one another—the popes, the bishops, and the great monarchs. After the council each of the three claimed the right to interpret and implement it, and each could find in the council's enactments justification for its claim. No pope and no bishop dictated to Philip II, for instance, how the council was to be implemented in his realm. The rivalry, as well as the cooperation, among these three centers became a mark of Catholicism after the council as it had been before it. The difference was that now interpretation and implementation of the council often became the focal point.

In almost its final enactment the council enjoined "all princes" to see that its decrees were "devoutly received and faithfully observed." Although on December 6 when their envoys signed the final documents the princes vicariously committed themselves to accept and implement them, the matter was not quite that simple. Monarchs reserved to themselves more formal acceptance, which entailed in effect making the council's decrees part of "the law of the land"—no small commitment!

The Italian states fell into line almost immediately. Philip II and Sigismund II of Poland did the same. Morone was sent to win over the Catholic states of the empire, a task which, after considerable difficulty, was accomplished at the Diet of 1566. The Cardinal of Lorraine and the French bishops returned to France intent on seeing the council's decrees made operative, but the deeply troubled political situation precluded an early and easy acceptance. By and large the French clergy rallied behind the council and repeatedly petitioned respective monarchs for formal acceptance. Meanwhile many of them set to work trying to make the decrees operative in their dioceses. Only in 1615, however, did the Assembly of the Clergy on its own initiative but with the crown's implicit support solemnly declare the council received.

On December 4, 1563, the council ended on a note of triumphant jubilation. Once an object of cynicism and derision even among Catholics, it afterwards became a proud symbol of Catholic identity and was invoked as the panacea for the ills of church and society. But of its merit not everybody was persuaded, as is clear from the striking success even in Catholic lands of Paolo Sarpi's *Istoria*. Despite the fact that the book was immediately put on the *Index,* it was translated into the major European languages, in some of which it had numerous editions.

At the council itself the key issue-under-the-issues, of which the final decrees breathe not the slightest suggestion, was the tension and often the conflict among the three centers. The great monarchs, including the papal monarch, put pressure on the bishops to make the council come out the way each of them wanted. The question raised by Sarpi's history of the council inevitably returns: was the council "free"? Certainly not free in the Protestant sense, simply because it was presided over by the papal legates. It was not free even in the sense that the Council of Constance was free, where the prelates' major task was to resolve the scandal of three contenders to the papal throne while, because of that very situation, not being beholden to any one of them.

All three popes who convoked the three periods of the Council of

Trent—Paul III, Julius III, and Pius IV—successfully repulsed every effort by the council to undertake "reform of the head," even though Pius IV finally had to make concessions. In so doing they tried to impose their will on issues, such as episcopal residence, that on the surface seem irrelevant to that reform but that in fact struck at its very heart, the dispensation practices of the Holy See and their financial implications.

After the council Pius IV faced decisions about two issues left in abeyance by the council—the Eucharistic cup and clerical celibacy. The council explicitly passed off to him the decision about the former. Pius, who during the council had indicated his willingness to grant the cup for certain areas, in fact did so for large parts of the empire on April 16, 1564, at renewed requests from Emperor Ferdinand and Duke Albrecht V of Bavaria. By this time, however, the cup had become such a powerful sign of differentiation between Lutherans and Catholics that soon after Pius's Indult went into effect, Albrecht himself began to have second thoughts, and seven years after obtaining the Indult, in 1571, he withdrew it. As the papacy and lay magnates in the empire assumed an ever more intransigent attitude, the cup fell victim to it. Pope Clement VIII did not withdraw it from Hungary, however, until 1604, and the use lasted in Bohemia until 1621.

The council essentially ignored the urging of the same two leaders to mitigate for their realms the discipline of clerical celibacy. After the council the emperor and the duke continued their quest for papal action on their behalf. Ferdinand, for instance, wrote to a number of cardinals who he thought might influence Pius in his favor. After Ferdinand's death his son Maximilian II continued the effort, as did Albrecht. Pius, undecided, in early January 1565 created a deputation of cardinals to deliberate on the matter. Two months later Philip II let the pope know he was utterly opposed to any concession. He argued that, if a change were made for the empire, other nations would demand it, which would result in the end of the church's hierarchical structure. In the few months left him, Pius procrastinated. But when his successor,

Pius V, let it be known immediately after his election that he was adamantly opposed to any concession, the issue died.

On doctrine the popes left the council a virtually free hand.
Charles V did his utmost to prevent, soften, or postpone the council's
action in this area but soon had to yield. On aspects of the reform of the
church the secular monarchs directly and through their envoys brought
effective pressure to bear, but they made their influence most defini-
tively felt in the council's attempt to "reform the princes." Their action
reduced that reform to an exhortation.

The bishops themselves, we must remember, had strong political
allegiances, whether their monarch was the pope, the emperor, the king
of France, the king of Spain, or yet another ruler. In one form or another they owed their presence at the council to them, and some were
beholden to their leaders for financing their time there, which was especially true for the "poor prelates" of Italy. More fundamentally, many
prelates owed their very prelacy to their monarch.

Problematic though these allegiances were, they had the advantage
of ensuring a measure of checks and balances at the council. The different parties had to find ways to proceed through contending priorities.
The most tangible and by far most important outcome of the situation
was the early decision of the council to treat doctrine and reform in tandem with each other and to grant them equal weight. Thus Trent became both a doctrinal council, as the pope insisted, and a pastoral or
reform council, as the emperor insisted.

At the first period of the council the legates rightly saw justification
as the key doctrinal issue. The council labored over the decree for seven
months, which made it the most considered of its pronouncements.
The problem the council faced was to clear the church of the charge of
a save-yourself-by-your-own-efforts Pelagianism while at the same time
affirming a measure of human responsibility in the justification process.
Within the limits of the resources the council had at its disposal, the
decree did perhaps the best that could be done on this extremely difficult issue.

The strength of the decree lies in its measured language, careful to forge a middle course between competing claims. The decree is concerned not to overstate the case one way or another but to forestall possible misunderstandings. It step-by-step develops the basic principles that guide it. Each chapter is a coherent unity, yet the chapters form parts of a coherent whole. As the decree elaborates its points, it makes appropriate qualifications and distinctions. Within its cultural framework, it is therefore intellectually satisfying.

These qualities mean, however, that the decree does not lend itself to sound bites. It was no match for Luther's triad that so brilliantly summarized his position—"Scripture alone, faith alone, grace alone!" The prelates and theologians at Trent approached justification as an intellectual and pastoral problem. Luther approached it as a life-death issue for which he was ready to put his life on the line. Therein lies the major mismatch on justification between Luther and Trent.

The ink was hardly dry on the document when, despite its careful language, disputes broke out among Catholics about how to interpret it. Only a few decades after the close of the council the first major instance of disagreement burst to the surface in the so-called *De Auxiliis* controversy between the Jesuits and the Dominicans in Spain. That conflict served as a prelude to the bitter, prolonged, and destructive conflict between the Jesuits and the Jansenists, centered in France but with repercussions across Catholic Europe. The Jesuits accused the Jansenists of being Calvinists, and the Jansenists accused the Jesuits of being Pelagians.

These conflicts show the limitations of the written word, especially when it touches on matters of deep personal concern—and most especially when it is the product of a committee. For all Trent's insistence on the determining role of grace in justification and for all the later success of the Jansenists, it seems clear that what to a considerable extent prevailed in post-Trent Catholicism was a persuasion that doing one's best was a prerequisite for God to give his grace. Catholics in their own view and in the view of their enemies stood for "good works."

The theologians and bishops at Trent recognized and tried to observe the difference between dogma (or doctrine) and theology. The former consisted in the fundamental teachings of the church, the latter in reflection on them, in explanations of them, and in systems to show their coherence with one another. The council was in principle concerned only with dogma, not with theology. Clear though this distinction was in theory, it was difficult to observe in practice. In the decree on justification, however, the council did so relatively successfully.

It was less successful in the decrees on the sacraments. Scholasticism was the prevailing theological system at the council simply because the theologians had been trained in it. It left its mark on the sacrament decrees. This outcome is not surprising, of course, because during the Middle Ages the Scholastics developed such a thorough theology of the sacraments. That development was nowhere more elaborate than on the Eucharist. Eleven "questions," divided into eighty-four "articles," are devoted to it, for instance, in Aquinas's *Summa Theologiae*.

If the decree on justification had an ambivalent impact on Catholicism, those on the sacraments, and especially on the Eucharist, had an impact much more straightforward. Catholicism emerged from the council more strongly sacramental than ever. The dispute among Protestants over how and whether Christ was present in the Eucharist evoked from the council the resounding affirmation that under the forms of both bread and wine the sacrament contained "truly, really, and substantially the body and blood of our Lord Jesus Christ together with his soul and divinity, and therefore the whole Christ."

Because of the piecemeal fashion with which the council treated various aspects of the Eucharist, the intrinsic relationship between "the sacrifice of the Mass" and the reception of the sacrament during it remained unclear in pastoral practice. This disconnect resulted in the phenomenon of the Eucharist often, perhaps most often, being received by Catholics outside Mass—before it, after it, or at a time with little relationship to it. This situation prevailed well into the twentieth century.

The council encouraged "frequent" reception of the sacrament, seconding a movement already under way for many decades. Frequent might mean several times a year, or once a month, or even once a week. After the council the Jesuits were most notable for promoting with some success weekly reception, which was another issue that in the seventeenth century brought them into conflict with the Jansenists. In any case, after the council more Catholics began to receive the Eucharist more frequently than once a year, the requirement laid down in 1215 by Lateran Council IV. By the nineteenth century, however, due in part to continuing Jansenist influence, once or twice a year had again become the norm for most Catholics.

More frequent reception of the Eucharist meant a higher profile for the sacrament of penance and for the confessors needed to administer it. The council affirmed the apostolic origin of the sacrament in the form it was practiced only beginning in the Middle Ages, that is, as a private self-accusation made to a priest, who imparted absolution. In keeping with that understanding the council affirmed that the self-accusation took place in a tribunal, where the priest was judge, and it required absolution before the penitent could receive the Eucharist if he or she had sinned gravely since last confessing. These determinations of the council were nothing new by the sixteenth century, but Trent's solemn ratification imbued them with new force and prominence.

Trent never mentioned the enclosed piece of ecclesiastical furniture that became known as the confessional because it was scarcely known at the time the council enacted its decree on penance. A few decades later, however, largely due to the influence of Carlo Borromeo, the confessional entered into widespread use and soon became almost ubiquitous. Its consequent prominence in Catholic churches symbolized the greater importance the sacrament began to play in Catholic life and increasingly came to differentiate Catholic houses of worship from Protestant.

Matrimony was the sacrament particular to the laity. The council reaffirmed its sacramental character and its indissolubility. *Tametsi*, which required a priest-witness for the validity of the sacrament, was the council's great innovation. The decree, sometimes criticized as a power-grab by the church, was intended in fact to protect both parties against the abuses of "clandestine marriages." Too often in such marriages one of the spouses, usually the man, later denied vows had been exchanged. The other spouse, bereft of witnesses to validate her claim, had no resources to protect herself. The decree had, however, the further effect of putting matrimony under the aegis of the church to a degree unknown until that time.

Is it true that when the religious spoils were divided in the sixteenth century, Catholics got the sacraments, and Protestants the word? Or Catholics got the altar, Protestants the pulpit? The answer has a ring of truth, as, again, the interiors of their respective churches reveal. Even so, in Catholicism after the council the pulpit entered into almost a golden age. As with all questions of historical influence, it is impossible to say how much of this great outburst of preaching was directly due to the council. Other important factors were at play, including the invigorating influence of the Humanist movement on preaching, the revived vigor of the mendicant orders, which were almost by definition "orders of preachers," and the preeminence the Jesuits gave to preaching among their ministries.

Still, the council insisted in two places that preaching was among the "principal duties"—or was perhaps *the* principal duty—of the bishop. Those stipulations could have remained dead letters had they not been seized upon by reforming bishops after the council, who by their example began to make the ideal a reality, at least in many places, and took measures to train their clergy to do likewise. The council, after all, had insisted on the same responsibility for pastors of parishes, a requirement difficult to implement until the general quality of clerical education improved.

The indisputable fact is that by the early seventeenth century Catholic clergy across the board had never before been engaged in preaching on such a scale, on so many different occasions, and in so many different forms. This enterprise was supported by sometimes massive theoretical treatises, the so-called ecclesiastical rhetorics, which told preachers how to do it. To this phenomenon, the council at least provided an impetus and was, therefore, a contributing cause.

Inseparable from this upsurge in the quantity and quality of preaching, of course, is the decree on seminaries, often touted as the council's most successful enactment. There can be no doubt of its profound long-term impact, which in a few parts of Europe was almost immediate. The year after the council concluded Pius IV founded the Roman Seminary. Other bishops, especially in Italy, followed suit, but the Tridentine stipulation that every diocese have such an institution took a long, long time to be realized. Moreover, though eventually standards rose, the council had set the bar low.

The decree was an expression of the widespread war on ignorance that animated both Protestants and Catholics in the sixteenth century and that led to the founding by rulers, municipalities, and, in Catholicism, religious orders of an unprecedented number of primary and, equivalently, secondary schools. The Humanist movement was of course here once again of crucial importance as its leaders, especially Erasmus, convinced Europe that no one was properly educated unless by the Humanists' standards.

The decree did not make seminary training compulsory for candidates for ordination. It was intended in the first instance for poor boys who otherwise would receive no schooling, or at least no schooling that was morally safe. The upsurge in the quality of Catholic clergy can therefore be attributed not exclusively, or even primarily, to the founding of seminaries but to the general improvement of schooling in Europe, of which seminaries were but one aspect. Young men were happily accepted as candidates for ordination who came from schools other than the seminaries, many of which were far superior to them.

Reforming bishops at Trent set their highest priority on ensuring that bishops reside in their dioceses and pastors in their parishes. They were unable to achieve passage of the stringent measures to effect that goal that some of them believed essential for success. The decrees of the council betray not the slightest hint of the bitter battles fought in this regard. Despite having to accept a solution less than perfect, those bishops, if they lived long enough, would have seen their efforts beginning to bear fruit.

The decrees may have been imperfect, but no bishop at Trent could have missed the point, driven home in so many ways, that residence was more than an ecclesiastical law, more than a canonical requirement from which one could in good conscience easily be dispensed. It was also more than an unrealistic ideal. Although the *zelanti* to the end resisted the idea that the obligation of residence was absolute, required *jure divino*, they finally agreed that it was constitutive of the episcopal office. This was a considerable advance from their original position.

When the more than two hundred bishops returned home from Trent, they knew with a realization that months of wrangling impressed upon them that bishops belonged in their dioceses, just as pastors belonged in their parishes. A process was set in motion that over time resulted in an essentially residential episcopacy in the Catholic church and a residential pastorate. Although the example of great bishops such as Pedro Guerrero in Granada, Bartholomeu dos Mártires in Braga, Gabriele Paleotti in Bologna, and especially Carlo Borromeo in Milan was more responsible for the change in mentality and practice than the penalties the council enacted to ensure compliance, it was the protracted crisis in the council that forced all Catholic prelates and monarchs, including the pope, to face the issue squarely.

The council laid out for the bishops a full job description. They were to preach. They were to found seminaries. They were to visit the institutions of the diocese, over which they had supervisory rights. Although those rights continued to be challenged by different entities, bishops after Trent certainly had a clearer idea of what was ideally expected of them. Extraordinarily important among the expectations yet often overlooked was the holding of annual synods with their clergy and perhaps even some laity. It was in these synods, supposedly, that the general norms found in the council's decrees would be adapted to local circumstances. The council envisaged the synods as the instrument through which the bishops would especially exercise their rightful leadership role in interpreting and implementing the council.

"Trent" after the Council of Trent

The council stipulated that the synods be held annually, which immediately proved impracticable. Even so, bishops set about the task, with greater or lesser success and diligence. Once again, the reforming archbishop of Milan provided the example that surpassed all others. Not only was he zealous in the extreme in this regard (as in others), holding eleven diocesan and six provincial synods during the course of his nineteen-year episcopacy, but his synods achieved a normative status in the Catholic world.

The decisions of his synods were immediately published, beginning with the first in 1566. This publishing enterprise culminated in 1582, when a volume appeared that brought together all the decrees of Borromeo's synods, the "Acts of the Church of Milan" *(Acta Ecclesiae Mediolanensis)*. This edition and especially the superb subsequent edition of 1599 circulated widely in Europe, where it was avidly studied. Further editions followed. Some forty are, for instance, extant in Polish libraries. Borromeo's canonization in 1610 added luster to the *Acta. This* was what a diocese reformed according the Council of Trent looked like. *This* was how it behaved.

The more than seven hundred pages of the *Acta* reflected Borromeo's personality in that they aimed at regulating down to the minutest detail every issue they addressed, in which the deportment of clergy and laity alike played a large role. They thus went far beyond anything legislated by the Council of Trent, to the point of sometimes losing relationship to it. Trent looked upon its reform decrees as essentially disciplinary and in many instances attached penalties to them for noncompliance. The decrees fall, therefore, under the category of social disciplining. But it was social disciplining in a form and to a degree so

much less specified than in the *Acta* as to make comparison almost irrelevant. The bishops at Trent, moreover, turned their most severe discipline against themselves.

In 1577 Borromeo published his prescriptive "instructions" on
church buildings and furnishings, *Instructiones Fabricae et Supellectilis
Ecclesiasticae,* an offshoot of his synods. Like the *Acta* the volume is
minute in its specifications, and, also like the *Acta,* it had a powerful
impact. It prescribed, for instance, that the tabernacle containing the
reserved Sacrament be placed at the center of the main altar, and that, as
mentioned, confessionals be instituted and located in the body of the
church. These measures were not unknown before Borromeo, but his
authority delivered to them a powerful impetus, which in time led to
their almost universal adoption. Less influential but significant, the "instructions" also prescribed that the facade of the church if possible face
east, and, even less influential, that the priest celebrating Mass face the
congregation—"versa ad populum facie."

During the last half of the sixteenth century a wave of moralizing
reform swept over parts of Europe, most notably where Calvinist influence was strong but also where Catholicism prevailed. This "severe morality," as it is sometimes called, was the result of many factors. Not to
be underestimated was the moral imperative at the heart of the Humanist tradition as revived in the Renaissance. Early in the century no one
propounded a strict public morality more insistently than Erasmus, Europe's most esteemed and widely read author.

By its reform decrees, most of which dealt with the proper behavior
of bishops and pastors, Trent added to the moralistic wave. In its procedures the council without question put reform into the hands of canon
lawyers, which unmistakably indicates the mind-set with which the
council approached the problem. But the exacting social disciplining
generally labeled "Tridentine" derived more properly from actions taken
after the council by other agents, most notably by bishops like Borromeo and by Congregations of the Roman Curia, than directly by the
council itself. In that regard the *Acta* stand as exhibit number one.

More obviously related to the decrees of the council (in this case, the doctrinal decrees) than the *Acta* and the *Instructiones* was the new Creed or "Tridentine Profession of Faith" *(Professio Fidei Tridentinae)* prepared by order of Pius IV, drawn up by a deputation of curial cardinals, and published on November 13, 1564, less than a year after the council ended. The pope made swearing to it binding on all priests and teachers, an obligation that remained in force into the twentieth century.

The Creed consisted of three parts: the first, simply the traditional Nicene Creed, accepted by all main-line Christian churches and sung or recited at Mass every Sunday; the second, a summary of specific doctrines decreed by the council; the third, an affirmation that "the holy Catholic Apostolic Church [is] the mother and mistress of all churches" and a profession of "true obedience to the bishop of Rome, the successor of Saint Peter, Prince of the Apostles, and the Vicar of Jesus Christ." (The text of the Creed can be found in Appendix B.)

Condensing council teaching into the simple affirmations of a creed had obvious catechetical, apologetic, and polemical advantages. Lost, of course, was the careful wording of the original decrees, to the point that at least in its first article the "Profession" was misleading. It stated, "I most firmly accept and embrace the apostolic and ecclesiastical traditions and all other observances and constitutions of the same [Catholic] church." For the transmission of the Gospel the council deliberately specified a much narrower scope, namely, apostolic traditions unbroken through the ages. The affirmation of the "Profession" asked more of the person swearing to it.

The article on justification, the council's major doctrinal accomplishment, is especially problematic. Whereas all the other articles in part two are quite specific in what they affirm, this article is vague and all-encompassing in the extreme: "I embrace and accept each and all the articles defined and declared in the most holy synod of Trent concerning Original Sin and justification." Trent's decree was too subtle, it seems, for summary and for public consumption.

Also significant is the fact that among the seven or eight articles in part two, three of them are taken from the hasty measures of the council's final days—Purgatory, indulgences, and the veneration of saints and sacred images. The Tridentine Creed gave those articles a prominence they utterly lacked in the council. The decrees concerning them were, moreover, approved at the council under the rubric of reform, not doctrine.

The stipulation that those charged with the "care of souls" be required to profess their Christian faith and their acceptance of the decisions of the council was set down clearly in the reform decrees of Sessions 24 and 25. In having the profession drawn up, Pius IV gave formulation to that mandate. The participants in the council in the main might well have approved the new profession—no way of telling—but they surely would have amended it and, in particular, tried to give the article on justification more substance. Despite its title, the Creed was in fact neither produced by the council nor approved by it. For many clerics for the next four hundred years, however, it would be as close as they ever got to what Trent decreed. Within a year of the council's closing, the Catholic body-social was thus moving into *Tridentinismo*, that is, into phenomena claiming origin in the council but in fact taking a step beyond it.

The Catechism of the Council of Trent (or *The Roman Catechism*) published under Pius V in 1566 was firmly grounded in the council. At the insistence of Emperor Ferdinand, work on it began during the council itself, and in one of its final acts the council formally commissioned its completion. The resulting text was, however, again the work of a post-Trent deputation. Originally published in both a Latin and an Italian edition in 1566, translations in French, German, and Polish followed soon afterward.

This was a "large" catechism, that is, a catechism intended for pastors, *ad parochos*. In a generic way, therefore, it was modeled on Luther's "Large Catechism," the originator of the genre, and then on the "Large Catechism" of Saint Peter Canisius, the first Catholic venture into that literary form. Such Large Catechisms were thus innovations in the tradition of catechetical literature. They were not intended to drive smaller catechisms out of the market, and, indeed, smaller catechisms proliferated in the Catholic world in the late sixteenth and early seventeenth centuries.

In its fourfold structure, the *Catechism of the Council of Trent* was altogether traditional: (1) the Apostles' Creed; (2) the sacraments; (3) the Decalogue; (4) prayer, especially the Lord's prayer. Until the sixteenth century the sacraments were not included in catechisms, but by the end of the council they had assumed an unquestioned place along with the Creed, Decalogue, and the Lord's prayer. By adhering to the traditional structure the *Catechism of the Council of Trent,* unlike the new Profession of Faith, betrayed no direct relationship to the council. On a deeper level, however, it of course reflected aspects of it.

The relationship was most firmly grounded in part two, on the sacraments. It is difficult to pinpoint specifically any teaching in the *Catechism* on this subject not already common among Catholic theologians before the council, even though some aspects, such as the sacrificial character of the Mass, received greater emphasis than otherwise generally prevailed. With explicit reference to the council's decree, the *Catechism* urges "frequent" communion but goes on to say that "no fixed universal rule" can be given whether that should be "monthly, weekly, or daily."

Although Purgatory is briefly mentioned and the veneration of saints and their images treated at some length, the *Catechism* contains not a word about indulgences. Nor does it treat the biblical canon, translations of the Bible into the vernacular, or, in a professed way, apostolic traditions, even though the term is mentioned here and there in passing. Remarkable for a document intended for pastors, the section on matrimony couches in the briefest and most general terms the stipulations regarding clandestine marriages laid down by Trent in *Tametsi.*

In expounding the Creed the *Catechism* perforce treats of article nine, belief in the "holy Catholic church." In its emphasis on the action of the Holy Spirit in the church and in its use of biblical images to evoke a sense of the church's reality, this section anticipates the first and second chapters of *Lumen Gentium*, the dogmatic constitution on the church of Vatican Council II. It fails, moreover, to mention any distinction between clergy and laity and similarly fails even to mention bishops. It contains, however, a long paragraph arguing from Scripture and the Fathers that the church requires a visible head, the successor of Saint Peter. It goes no further, a stark contrast to the strongly institutional understandings of the "holy Catholic church" that theologians of the era soon constructed and made prevalent.

The *Catechism's* traditional structure precluded the possibility of a section explicitly devoted to Original Sin and justification, with the result that it is easy to come away from the text without a clear grasp of the council's teaching. Original Sin is briefly treated in several places, and in an oblique way justification almost pervades the text through its repeated yet gentle reminders about the abundance of God's love, as, for example:

> [Many of God's actions in the world] are attributed especially to the Holy Spirit, giving us to understand that they arise from the boundless love of God toward us; for as the Holy Spirit proceeds from the divine will, inflamed, as it were, with love, we can comprehend that these effects that are referred particularly to the Holy Spirit are the result of God's boundless love for us. Hence it is that the Holy Spirit is called Gift, for by a gift we understand that which is kindly and gratuitously bestowed, without reference to anticipated remuneration.

In an age in which bitter religious polemic was the order of the day, the *Catechism* maintains a positive tone throughout, not only devoid of polemic but remarkably sparing in threats of hell and damnation. Its pastoral intent shines through on virtually every page, manifesting a concern to help pastors lead their flocks into a heartfelt appreciation of the gifts of God. Although these features characterize the work as a whole, they appear most unmistakably in the fourth part, on prayer.

On March 24, 1564, in the bull *Dominici Gregis Custodiae,* Pius published the new *Index.* The materials sent from Trent had been reviewed and revised in Rome, but they survived more or less intact. This *Index* notably moderated the version published in 1559 by Paul IV. Its most innovative feature was prefacing the catalog of forbidden texts with "Ten Rules," produced by the commission at Trent, that set up general norms for imposing certain restraints on publishers and readers.

The second and third rules dealt with translations of the Bible, and they do what the council refused to do in 1546 by putting restrictions on reading vernacular translations. Though far less absolute than the *Index* of Paul IV, these norms provided the basis for minimizing the Bible in Catholic devotional life and, in some places, making vernacular translations almost impossible to find. The rules also insisted on the normative character of the Vulgate. Catholic scholars continued to study Hebrew and Greek, but their interpretations of the sacred texts were hampered by the ever more sacrosanct authority attributed to that Latin version.

The council had insisted that the Vulgate be revised and corrected. The commission assigned the task after the council worked so slowly that Pope Sixtus V took matters into his own hands and in 1590 published his revision. The text was so heavily criticized that it had to be withdrawn from circulation upon the pope's death later that year, and the task undertaken again. The final revision, published in 1592 under Pope Clement VIII, corrected over 3,000 errors. Since Sixtus had declared his version unalterable, the edition of 1592 bore his name on the title page, but it is commonly referred to as the Clementine edition.

The council would almost certainly not have taken up the subject of an "Index" at all had it not been delivered to it through a peculiar convergence of circumstances. Once the council took it up, however, it perforce made it its own. The subsequent publication of the "Index of the Council of Trent," as it is often called, in effect established that the Roman *Index,* first officially published in 1559, would be an ongoing feature of Catholic life. It remained such for the next four hundred years. The implicit permanence the bull *Dominici Gregis Custodiae* accorded this relatively new institution is the document's greatest significance. When in 1571 the Congregation of the Index, a new papal bureau created by Pius V, held its first meeting, it ensured a long life for papal censorship and banning of books.

All four of these documents—the *Acta,* the "Profession of Faith," the *Catechism,* and the *Index*—can with some justice be called Tridentine. Yet in their relationship to the council they differ considerably among themselves. The *Index* of 1564 substantially represented work done at the council. The other three did not, and they picked and chose what to emphasize, what to qualify, and what to pass over almost in silence. This selectivity, though partly due to the limitations the four different literary forms imposed, was more basically due to the problem of dealing with a phenomenon as densely complex as the Council of Trent. Although they do not professedly claim to be such, these documents are, as mentioned, important interpretations of the council. Borromeo's "instructions" on church buildings and furnishings had an even more tenuous relationship to the council, yet the work's provisions are often attributed to it.

When Pius IV confirmed the council's decrees, he forbade the printing of commentaries or notes on them without explicit permission of the Holy See. In the early seventeenth century Paul V collected into fifty volumes all the materials related to the council and stored them in the Vatican archives under the heading *fondo Concilio.* But the restriction on access to them and on commentary, which remained in effect for the next four hundred years, made comprehensive scholarship and research on the council impossible. Only at the beginning of the twentieth century, after Pope Leo XIII had in 1880 opened the Vatican archives, did the Görres Gesellschaft break the embargo with the first volumes of its magnificent edition of the "acts" of the Council of Trent, the *Concilium Tridentinum.*

At the very time the restriction on the publication of commentaries took force, Pius IV set up a formal and unassailable instrument for interpreting the council. On August 2, 1564, he named Morone head of a Congregation of eight cardinals that was to deal with the council's implementation. Shortly afterward more cardinals were added, and Pius V, Pius IV's immediate successor, explicitly expanded its remit to make it the official interpreter of Trent's reform decrees. This Congregation of the Council, as it was called, continued to function, with expanded responsibilities, for four centuries, until 1966. It emitted official and definitive decisions that eventually constituted a sizeable corpus.

Just how faithfully these responses corresponded to the letter and intent of the council has yet to be studied. In any case, they were by definition something other than the council itself. With the Congregation the papacy staked its claim to the right to control the postcouncil trajectories and not let them slip unmonitored into the hands of bishops and monarchs. Too many forces were in play in the complex politico-ecclesiastical world of the early modern era, however, for the Congregation to be able perfectly to manage those trajectories. Nonetheless, the Congregation's decisions promoted the impression that the council answered all possible questions, even on subjects it in fact never addressed, and that it left little room for change or further development and local adaptation. This impression became an integral element in the myths about the council.

The impression was confirmed and furthered by the publication between 1567 and 1614 of liturgical texts of various kinds. The council specifically mandated only revision of the missal and breviary of the Roman Rite. Its intention was to eliminate superstitions, redundancies, scribal errors, and other inappropriate elements that had crept into the texts over the course of time. Once those revisions got under way, they led to revision of other texts such as the Martyrology, the Pontifical, and the Ritual.

Of these publications the most important of course was the missal of 1570, published under Pius V. The revision, undertaken with the capable supervision of Cardinal Guglielmo Sirleto, resulted in just what the council intended—not a new liturgy in any sense but a reliable text that conformed to the best and oldest manuscripts and printed editions. The text itself is, however, less important than the bull promulgating it, which ordered the universal adaptation of the Roman Rite unless another rite had prevailed in a given region or institution for over two hundred years.

The bull forbade, moreover, that anything ever be added to this edition, removed from it, or in any way changed. The promulgation of the missal, considered part of the "Tridentine corpus," thus implicitly reinforced the impression of a council intent on legislating on all conceivable aspects of Catholic life and belief and on imposing upon them a blanket uniformity and rigidity.

Missing from the bull is any suggestion that a vernacular adaptation might be possible. Despite the opening the council left for such a possibility, no one of any stature later seized upon it or promoted it. It disappeared from the Catholic landscape almost without a trace. The myth took hold that the council forbade it. To be sure, Pius V would be the last person on earth to countenance the introduction of the vernacular, but Latin liturgy had become such a symbol of demarcation that in the religiously belligerent sixteenth century change was unthinkable.

Even more important than the bull in promoting liturgical uniformity were the decisions of the Congregation of Rites, a Roman bureau established in 1588, a quarter of a century after the council, when Pope Sixtus V reorganized the Curia. Beginning in that year, local churches were required to refer to Rome for decision all questions on liturgical matters. The decrees of the Congregation tightly controlled liturgical practice especially as time moved on, and in many people's minds they somehow began to be considered "Tridentine."

Through its publication of the liturgical texts and especially through the newly founded Congregation of Rites, the papacy implicitly but effectively redefined its role regarding Catholic worship. Until that time the pope's role had consisted essentially in handing down ad hoc decisions about liturgical issues such as the creation of new feasts and determining the degree of solemnity with which they were to be celebrated.

Other than that, considerable autonomy rested with local authorities. Even though the Congregation showed sensitivity to local needs and circumstances, by the beginning of the seventeenth century, the papacy had assumed complete and ongoing control over Catholic liturgy. The phenomenon represented a significant expansion of papal oversight.

After the council the popes made good use of their nuncios to various heads of state to press implementation of the council. This development formed part and parcel of the new shot of energy the successful end of the council injected into the papal enterprise. The nuncios represented the pope and served as counterweight to the local hierarchy. As with other institutions in the early modern world, the church, too, moved into patterns of ever greater centralization of authority.

Within a relatively short time after the closing of the council, therefore, Catholicism appropriated and claimed as peculiarly its own certain new institutions and modes of behavior that set it off from the emerging Protestant churches yet did so according to patterns similar to theirs. Those churches, too, developed, for instance, their own professions of faith, liturgical forms, church-state relationships, and instruments of surveillance and punishment. Catholicism thus conformed to the phenomenon of the early modern era known as Confessionalization.

No single institution in Catholicism emerged as more prominent and distinctive than the papacy, for which there was no counterpart in the other confessions. For reasons that should by now be clear, the Council of Trent issued no document on that institution. Reformers at the council wanted to put limits on how the papacy exercised its authority, and the issue of councils' superiority over it, though never formally debated at the council, threatened time and again to raise its ugly head. The history of the Council of Trent and its aftermath is filled with ironies, but none more striking than the refurbished authority the papacy enjoyed for having brought the council to conclusion. The popes made ample use of this new warrant for setting the church's course.

Reformers at the council strove to enhance episcopal authority, not papal, and the council's reform decrees reflect that impulse. Bishops like

Borromeo heard the message and ran with it. Trent issued, however, no update of *Frequens,* a measure meant to ensure for bishops an ongoing role in the governance of the church at large. By 1563 none of the actors in the drama of the Council of Trent was eager to put himself through the ordeal again. The idea in fact was never broached. No outcome of the council could have been more pleasing to the popes. It did not at this point give them exactly a free hand, but it removed from the scene a threat that had bedeviled them for a century and a half. The popes waited another three hundred years, until 1869, before they dared convoke another council. This time they had it meet in the Vatican under carefully controlled conditions.

On the burning question of "reform of the head," the popes from Paul III to Pius IV did everything in their power to keep it out of the hands of the council, insisted without surcease that they were the only instrument to deal with it, and promised time and again that they would do so. Each of them in fact made changes. But they faced heavy obstacles: the threat to the financial base on which their court operated; the challenge to a way of life so long-standing and ingrained as to make change unimaginable; the resistance of the cardinals, whose support the popes needed for ongoing business; and, perhaps most important, the ambivalence or even aversion they felt themselves.

Nonetheless, Pius IV during the severe crisis at the council in the late winter of 1563 once again solemnly professed to Ferdinand and Philip II that he would undertake the task with vigor. In consistory on December 30, 1563, just a few weeks after the council ended, he declared to the cardinals, with considerable exaggeration, that the council's reform decrees were milder than if he had written them himself, but, in any case, he would see to their implementation.

He in fact issued new regulations for several important offices in the Curia, such as the Rota and the Apostolic Penitentiary, and most visibly showed his determination to reform them when in 1565 he placed Carlo Borromeo in charge of the latter. Bit by bit he made it more difficult for cardinals (and others) to hold onto multiple benefices, which resulted for at least some of them in a reduced lifestyle. Although he met with excuses and evasions, several times he ordered bishops resident in Rome to return to their dioceses. His successor, Pius V, a strict and unbending disciplinarian, took the reform of the Curia (and of the city of Rome) even further.

Such efforts were certainly not without success. In 1585, for instance, the Venetian ambassador to the Papal Court, Giacomo Soranzo, painted a picture of a more sober and less ostentatious situation than had earlier prevailed. But ambition and greed did not take flight. In many ways the system resisted or later bounced back. To mention but one notorious example, Cardinal Scipione Borghese, nephew of Pope Paul V (1605–1621), amassed an immense fortune through the ecclesiastical office his uncle bestowed upon him and, according to a later Venetian ambassador in Rome, led a life "utterly given over to pleasures and pastimes."

Systems resisted elsewhere as well, and abuses denounced again and again at the council persisted. The ecclesiastical career of Ernst, the younger brother of Duke Wilhelm V of Bavaria (reigned 1579–1597), successor to Albrecht and a vigorous promoter of the Counter Reformation, flew directly in the face of the council's legislation. Ernst was a notorious pluralist—prince-bishop of Freising, Hildesheim, Luttich, and Münster, prince-archbishop of Cologne, and prince-abbot of Stable-Malmedy. He lived in concubinage for years, and a son from the union succeeded him as prince-abbot of Stable-Malmedy. To Ernst's infractions of the council's legislation a blind eye was turned.

The same blind eye was turned to other abuses and abusers. As late as 1652, for instance, the bishop of Autun complained that clerical concubinage was widespread in his diocese and accepted by Catholics as the norm. The diocese of Autun was not unique. Yet no matter how much systems resisted, the climate in which they operated was changing. A devout personal life, which implied dedication to one's pastoral duties, was now the ideal that prelates, including the pope and his Curia, wanted to project. Again, the example of Carlo Borromeo loomed large, but other high churchmen wanted to make clear to the world by word and example that they took their calling seriously.

The climate was marked more obviously by newly aggressive and intransigent attitudes. Impassible lines of demarcation between Catholics and others not only prevailed but became more absolute. Catholics were separated from others not only by fundamental teachings such as papal primacy and the sevenfold nature of the sacraments but by other matters as well—priestly celibacy, Latin liturgy, wide canon of the Bible, the normative Vulgate, no Eucharistic cup, and so forth. According to the ever more received wisdom, to compromise even on the slightest point threatened to undermine the whole edifice.

How much of the change in climate was directly due to the Council of Trent? A great deal, surely, but greater precision is hard to come by. During the council Catholic leaders of all stripes had their eyes fixed on it, and many were determined or under pressure to make its enactments operative. In the eyes of contemporaries the council stood at center stage.

Trent influenced to greater or lesser degrees all aspects of ecclesiastical life and of the moral climate of Europe, but it also affected specific aspects of culture. Two instances are especially noteworthy. The first regards the visual and plastic arts. Trent's decree on sacred images, even with its warning about possible abuses, resolutely affirmed their legitimacy and usefulness. Let the churches and other places be adorned with them! This message, certainly not unexpected, fell sweetly on the ears of artists and their patrons, and it removed from Catholic lands a threat that had devastated others. It was in keeping with the sacramental principle so distinctive of Catholicism, spirit mediated through material signs. Catholicism emerged as the most sensuous of the post-Reformation churches.

The second, less obvious instance was the implicit but powerful support the council gave to a distinctively Catholic historiographical principle that was just emerging at the time. In reaction to the Reformers' accusation that the church had early on so completely broken with the Gospel that its subsequent history was a distortion of it, Catholic apologists rushed to assert the church's unbroken continuity with the apostolic era. Trent seconded this assertion. No previous council had ever so often and so explicitly insisted on its teaching's continuity with the authentic Christian past. Trent thus helped develop the Catholic mind-set reluctant to admit change in the course of church history, a mind-set that more fully crystallized a little later with works like Cardinal Cesare Baronio's *Ecclesiastical Annals.*

Trent was, therefore, pervasively influential, but, even so, it was not Catholicism. Nor did it intend to be. Not a word did it have to say about the church's missionary activity, and in that regard it betrayed its exclusively Eurocentric focus. Scarcely a word about confraternities, the liveliest venue of religious devotion during this period. Only in passing did the council nod to the network of Jesuit schools that was rapidly expanding in every country of Europe where the Catholic church was allowed to function. Although the council was more directly influenced by the Scholastic style of theology than by the Humanistic, it did not take sides in the rivalry between them. Fully aware though the prelates at Trent were of the Roman, Spanish, and other inquisitions, they did not commend or condemn them, nor did they make any recommendations concerning them. The council forbade dueling (to little avail), but, though it suffered from the wars and threats of war between Catholic leaders, it made no pronouncement about the subject. More surprisingly, it made no pronouncement on the necessity or justice of war "against the infidel," whose armies and navies threatened to overpower the Christian West.

These phenomena did not escape the council's influence, yet they essentially continued to function according to principles peculiar to themselves. They, too, were systems and as such resistant to change from the outside even as they were influenced by it. Within the systems the impact of Trent varied considerably. For Jesuits working in distant Lima or even in Manila it was still palpable, but how palpable, for instance, for those working in Nagasaki or Beijing?

Nonetheless, the Council of Trent made a big difference in the Catholic church and in the modern era in which it occurred. Its enactments surely did not pass pure into the church or into the world at large. They were mediated by the minds, hearts, ambitions, and fears of the human beings responsible for making them operative—popes, other rulers great and small, bishops, preachers, theologians, even painters and their patrons, and many others besides. The myths, misunderstandings, and misinformation about what the council actually enacted proliferated. They have enjoyed a long afterlife, and many are alive and well today, even in the sacred groves of academe.

"Trent" thus took on a life of its own. It derived its authority from the growing prestige the council enjoyed. Although it included the council, it also included the postcouncil phenomena described above. It thus blurred the line between what the council actually legislated and intended and what happened afterward. We should not be surprised. Such blurring and shorthand are hardly unique to "Trent" but are seemingly endemic to the way we understand and talk about any great event: "History with its flickering lamp stumbles along the trail of the past." Myths are inevitable, especially for a happening as complex and controversial as the Council of Trent.

Given the massive amount of documentation that survives from the council and the quality of the scholarship expended upon it over the past hundred years, however, greater precision is in this case attainable. Attaining a measure of such precision is the objective I set myself in writing this book. In working toward that goal I hoped to dispel a few of the myths and misunderstandings that have enshrouded the subject. More particularly, I hoped to make a little clearer the crucial distinction between "Trent" and the closely related phenomenon, the Council of Trent.

Appendixes

Abbreviations

Notes

Acknowledgments

Index

Appendix A

The Twenty-Five Sessions of the Council of Trent

FIRST PERIOD, 1545–1547

Pope Paul III

Session 1 December 13, 1545: Decree declaring the council opened (660)*
Session 2 January 7, 1546: Decree on manner of living (660–661)
Session 3 February 4, 1546: Decree on acceptance of Nicene Creed (662)
Session 4 April 8, 1546: Decree on the "wide canon" of the Bible and on Scripture and traditions (663–664)
Decree on the Vulgate and interpretation of Scripture (664–665)
Session 5 June 17, 1546: Decree on Original Sin (665–667)
Decree establishing lectureships in Scripture and on the obligation of bishops to preach (667–670)
Session 6 January 13, 1547: Decree on justification (671–681)
Decree on residence for bishops and others (681–683)
Session 7 March 3, 1547: Decree on the sacraments in general, on baptism, and on confirmation (684–686)
Decree on reform of the clergy, especially concerning multiple benefices (686–689)
Session 8 March 11, 1547: Decree transferring the council to Bologna (690)

Bologna, 1547–1549
Pope Paul III

Session 9 April 21, 1547: Decree postponing the Session (690–691)
Session 10 June 2, 1547: Decree postponing the Session (691–692)

SECOND PERIOD, 1551–1552

Pope Julius III

Session 11 May 1, 1551: Decree on resumption of the council (692)
Session 12 September 1, 1551: Decree postponing the Session (692–693)
Session 13 October 11, 1551: Decree on the sacrament of the Eucharist
             (693–698)
             Decree on reform, especially concerning bishops' jurisdiction
             and handling of lawsuits (698–701)
             Decree postponing articles concerning the Eucharistic cup and
             children's communion (701–702)
             Decree guaranteeing safe conduct to Lutherans (702)
Session 14 November 25, 1551: Decree on the sacraments of penance and
             last anointing (703–713)
             Decree on reform, especially concerning various aspects of cler-
             ical discipline (714–718)
Session 15 January 25, 1552: Decree postponing publication of further de-
             crees (718–719)
             Decree further guaranteeing safe conduct (719–721)
Session 16 April 28, 1552: Decree suspending the council (721–722)

THIRD PERIOD, 1562–1563

Pope Pius IV

Session 17 January 18, 1562: Decree declaring the council opened (722–
             723)
Session 18 February 26, 1562: Decree agreeing to undertake a review of the
             Index of Pope Paul IV (723–724) (In the General Congrega-
             tion, March 4, 1562, the council renewed the safe conduct.)
Session 19 May 14, 1562: Decree postponing publication of decrees (725)
Session 20 June 4, 1562: Decree postponing publication of decrees (725)

Decree on protocol regarding envoys to the council (797–798)

Decree on the reception and observance of the council's decrees and charging princes to receive and enforce them (798)

Decree ordering the reading during the Session of the decrees passed in the first two periods of the council, 1545–1547, 1551–1552 (798)

Decree declaring the council concluded and request for confirmation of the decrees by the pope (799)

---

* The numbers refer to pages in volume 2 of Tanner, *Decrees.*

Appendix B

The Tridentine Profession of Faith
(Professio Fidei Tridentinae)

Promulgated by the bull of Pius IV, *Iniunctum Nobis,* November 13, 1564

I, [name], with firm faith believe and profess each and every article in the symbol of faith that the Roman Church uses:

[Text of the Nicene-Constantinopolitan Creed]

I [moreover] most firmly accept and embrace the apostolic and ecclesiastical traditions and all the observances and constitutions of the same church. I likewise accept Holy Scripture according to the sense that Holy Mother Church has held and does hold, to whom it belongs to judge the true meaning and interpretation of the Sacred Scriptures. I shall never accept or interpret them otherwise than according to the unanimous consent of the Fathers.

I also profess that there are truly and properly speaking seven sacraments of the New Law, instituted by Jesus Christ our Lord and necessary for the salvation of the human race, though not all are necessary for each individual person: baptism, confirmation, Eucharist, penance, extreme unction, order, and matrimony. I profess that they confer grace and that of these baptism, confirmation, and order cannot be repeated without sacrilege. I also admit and accept the rites received and approved by the Catholic Church for the administration of the aforementioned sacraments.

I embrace and accept each and all the articles defined and declared by the most holy Synod of Trent concerning Original Sin and justification.

I also profess that in the Mass there is offered to God a true sacrifice, properly speaking, which is propitiatory for the living and the dead, and that in the most holy sacrament of the Eucharist the body and blood together with the soul and divinity of our Lord Jesus Christ are truly, really, and substantially present, and that there takes place a change of the whole substance of bread into the body and of the whole substance of the wine into the blood; and this change the Catholic Church calls transubstantiation. I also profess that under each species alone the whole and entire Christ and the true sacrament is received.

I steadfastly hold that there is a Purgatory, and that the souls detained there are helped by the acts of intercession of the faithful; likewise, that the saints reigning together with Christ should be venerated and invoked, that they offer prayers to God for us, and that their relics should be venerated. I firmly declare that the images of Christ and of the Ever-Virgin Mother of God and of the other saints as well are to be kept and preserved, and that due honor and veneration are to be given them. I also affirm that the power of indulgences was left by Christ to the Church and that the use of them is most wholesome for Christian people.

I acknowledge the holy Catholic Apostolic Roman Church as the mother and mistress of all churches. I promise and swear true obedience to the bishop of Rome, successor to Saint Peter, Prince of the Apostles, and Vicar of Jesus Christ.

I likewise receive and profess all other things handed on, defined, and declared by the sacred canons and the general councils, especially the holy Council of Trent. I also condemn, reject, and anathematize all things contrary to them and all heresies that the Church has condemned, rejected, and anathematized.

I do indeed freely profess and genuinely hold this true Catholic faith without which no one can be saved. I promise most constantly to retain and confess it entire and inviolate, with the help of God, to the end of my life. I will make sure, as far as in me lies, that it shall be held, taught, and preached by my subjects or by all who are under my care by virtue of my office. This I promise, vow, and swear, so help me God and these holy gospels of God.

Note. On January 20, 1877, subsequent to Vatican Council I (1869–1870), Pope Pius IX had the following inserted in the penultimate paragraph above, after the word "Trent": "and by the ecumenical council of the Vatican especially concerning the primacy and infallible magisterium of the Roman Pontiff."

Abbreviations

Bäumer, *Concilium Tridentinum*
    Remigius Bäumer, ed. *Concilium Tridentinum.* Darmstadt:
    Wissenschaftliche Buchgesellschaft, 1979.
Bourgeois, *Signes du salut*
    Henri Bourgeois et al. *Les signes du salut.* Paris: Desclée, c. 1995.
Buzzi, *Concilio di Trento*
    Franco Buzzi. *Il Concilio di Trento, 1545–1563: Breve introduzione ad alcuni*
    temi teologici principali. Milan: Glossa, 1995.
CT
    Concilium Tridentinum. Diariorum, Actorum, Epistularum, Tractatuum
    nova collectio. Freiburg i/Br.: Herder, 1901–2001.
DBI
    Dizionario biografico degli Italiani. Rome: Istituto della Enciclopedia
    italiana, 1960–.
Duval, *Sacrements au Concile de Trente*
    André Duval. *Des sacrements au Concile de Trente.* Paris: Éditions du Cerf,
    1985.

Jedin, *Geschichte*
> Hubert Jedin. *Geschichte des Konzils von Trient.* 4 vols. in 5. Freiburg i/Br.: Herder, 1949–1975.

Jedin, *History*
> Hubert Jedin. *A History of the Council of Trent.* Trans. Ernest Graf. 2 vols. London: Thomas Nelson, 1957–1961.

Jedin, *Kirche des Glaubens*
> Hubert Jedin. *Kirche des Glaubens, Kirche der Geschichte: Ausgewählte Aufsätze und Vorträge.* 2 vols. Freiburg i/Br.: Herder, 1966.

Pastor, *Popes*
> Ludwig Freiherr von Pastor, *The History of the Popes from the Close of the Middle Ages.* Trans. F. I. Antrobus et al. 40 vols. St. Louis: Herder, 1899–1953.

Prodi, *Trient und die Moderne*
> Paolo Prodi and Wolfgang Reinhard, eds. *Das Konzil von Trient und die Moderne.* Berlin: Duncker und Humblot, 2001.

Šusta, *Die römische Curie*
> Josef Šusta, ed. *Die römische Curie und das Concil von Trient unter Pius IV: Actenstücke zur Geschichte des Concils von Trient.* 4 vols. Vienna: Hölder, 1904–1914.

Tallon, *France et Trente*
> Alain Tallon. *La France et le Concile de Trente (1518–1563).* Rome: École Française de Rome, 1992.

Tanner, *Decrees*
> Norman Tanner, ed. *Decrees of the Ecumenical Councils.* 2 vols. Washington, DC: Georgetown University Press, 1990.

Notes

Introduction

1. See Jedin, *History*, 1:545–574; Aldo Gorfer, *Trento, Città del Concilio*, 3rd ed. (Lavis: Edizioni Arca, 2003); Roberto Pancheri, ed., *Il Concilio a Trento: I luoghi e la memoria* (Trent: Commune di Trento, 2008); and Douglas W. Freshfield, "The Southern Frontier of Austria," *Geographical Journal* 46 (1915): 414–433.

2. See Hubert Jedin, "Das Gefolge der Trienter Konzilsprälaten im Jahre 1562: Ein Beitrag zur Sozial- und Wirtschaftsgeschichte eines ökumenischen Konzils," in Jedin, *Kirche des Glaubens*, 2:333–347.

3. See Maria Teresa Fattori, "Continuità e discontinuità nel consistorio della chiesa cattolica romana: alcuni momenti della seconda metà del XVI secolo," in *Synod and Synodality: Theology, History, Canon Law and Ecumenism in a New Contact*, ed. Alberto Melloni and Silvia Scatena, 143–172 (Münster: Lit, 2005).

4. See Marc Venard, "L'Église Catholique," in *Le temps des confessions (1530–1620/30)*, ed. Marc Venard, 233–280 (Paris: Desclée, 1992), at 236.

5. See Hubert Jedin, "Die Deutschen am Trienter Konzil 1551/52," in Jedin, *Kirche des Glaubens*, 2:224–236. On the grossly uneven distribution of episcopal sees in Europe, see Joseph Bergin, "The Counter-Reformation Church and Its Bishops," *Past and Present* 165 (1999): 30–73, at 40–43. I am grateful to Simon Ditchfield for this reference.

6. See, e.g., R. H. Heinholz, *The Spirit of Classical Canon Law* (Athens: University of Georgia Press, 1996), especially 394–399. For an analysis of the effect on canon law of the papal prohibition of commentaries on the decrees of the council, see Gérard Franzen, "L'application des décrets du Concile de Trente: Les débuts d'un nominalisme canonique," *L'année canonique* 27 (1983): 5–16.

7. See Jedin, *History,* 2:59–61; and John W. O'Malley, *Four Cultures of the West* (Cambridge, MA: The Belknap Press of Harvard University Press, 2004), 103–115.

8. See Tanner, *Decrees,* 2:723. See also Umberto Mazzone, "Versammlungs- und Kontrolltechniken," in Prodi, *Trient und die Moderne,* 79–106; and his "Giovanni Morone legato al concilio di Trento e la clausula del 'proponentibus legatis,'" in *Il cardinale Giovanni Morone e l'ultima fase del Concilio di Trento,* ed. Massimo Firpo and Ottavia Niccoli, 117–141 (Bologna: Mulino, 2010).

9. Letter of Alvise Mocenigo, Venetian envoy to the council, to the doge, March 29, 1546, quoted in Alain Tallon, *Le Concile de Trente* (Paris: Les Éditions du Cerf, 2000), 26.

10. See Tallon, *France et Trente,* 46–50.

11. See the detailed study by Umberto Mazzone, "Sussidi papali e libertà di voto al Concilio di Trento (1561–1563)," *Cristianesimo nella Storia* 1 (1980): 185–250, at 242; and, for the first period, Hubert Jedin, "Die Kosten des Konzils von Trient unter Paul III," *Münchener theologische Zeitschrift* 4 (1953): 119–132; as well as his *Geschichte,* 4/1:190–204. Mazzone edited CT 3/2, published in 1985, which contains all the financial records pertinent to the council that are extant. The records are extensive and detailed.

12. Hubert Jedin, *Geschichte.* Only the first two volumes have been translated into English: *A History of the Council of Trent,* trans. Ernest Graf (London: Thomas Nelson and Sons, 1957–1961). For a bibliography of Jedin's publications over his long career, most of which pertain in some way to the council, see Robert Samulski, "Bibliographie Hubert Jedin 1926–1975," *Annali dell' Istituto storico italo-germanico in Trento* 6 (1980): 287–359; and Giorgio Butterini, "Bibliographie Hubert Jedin 1976–1980," *Annali dell' Istituto storico italo-ger-*

manico in Trento 6 (1980): 360–367. On Jedin, see John W. O'Malley, *Trent and All That: Renaming Catholicism in the Early Modern Period* (Cambridge, MA: Harvard University Press, 2000), 46–71; and Konrad Repgen, "Hubert Jedin (1900–1980)," *Annali del Istituto storico italo-germanico in Trento* 6 (1980): 163–177. Jedin wrote an informative but notably reserved autobiographical sketch, *Lebensbericht,* ed. Konrad Repgen (Mainz: Matthias-Grünwald Verlag, 1984).

13. Pietro Soave Polano [Paolo Sarpi], *Istoria del Concilio Tridentino* (London: Giovanni Billio, 1619), modern edition, Giovanni Gambarin, ed., 3 vols. (Bari: Laterza, 1935). See David Wootton, *Paolo Sarpi: Between Renaissance and Enlightenment* (New York: Cambridge University Press, 1983), especially 104–117. See also Boris Ulianich, "Il significato politico della *Istoria del Concilio Tridentino* di Paolo Sarpi," in *Il Concilio di Trento come crocevia della politica europea,* eds. Hubert Jedin and Paolo Prodi, 179–213 (Bologna: Mulino, 1979); and especially Ulianich, "Paolo Sarpi nell'opera di Hubert Jedin," *Annali dell'Istituto storico italo-germanico in Trento* 6 (1980): 131–148. See now also Corrado Pin, ed., *Repensando Paolo Sarpi: Atti del Convegno Internazionale di Studi nel 450 anniversario della nascita di Paolo Sarpi* (Venice: Ateneo Veneto, 2006); and Marie Viallon, ed., *Paolo Sarpi: Politique et religion en Europe* (Paris: Éditions Classiques Garnier, 2010). Sforza Pallavicino, *Istoria del Concilio di Trento,* 2 vols. (Rome: G. Casoni, 1656–1657). The literature on Pallavicino is much more limited, but see the critical edition by Mario Scotti (Turin: Unione tipografico-editrice toronese, 1962).

14. Of course, in the meantime other scholars made important contributions to the study of the council. See Hubert Jedin, *Das Konzil von Trient: Ein Überblick über die Erforschung seiner Geschichte* (Rome: Edizioni di "Storia e Letteratura," 1948); and especially Remigius Bäumer, "Das Konzil von Trient und die Erforschung seiner Geschichte," in Bäumer, *Concilium Tridentinum,* 3–48.

15. Tallon, *France et Trente,* especially 10–15, 79–81, 114–115. See also the important studies by James K. Farge, *Orthodoxy and Reform in Early Reformation France: The Faculty of Theology of Paris, 1500–1543* (Leiden: E. J. Brill, 1985); and his *Le parti conservateur au XVIe siècle: Université et Parlement de Paris à l'époque de la Renaissance et de la Réforme* (Paris: Collège de France, 1992).

16. Among the many works in this category are Prodi, *Trient und die Moderne;* Adriano Prosperi, *Tribunali della coscienza: inquisitori, confessori, missionari* (Turin: Einaudi, 1996); Cesare Mozzarelli and Danilo Zardin, ed., *I tempi del concilio: Religione, cultura et società nell'Europa tridentina* (Rome: Bulzoni,

1997); Gigliola Fragnito, *Proibito capire: La Chiesa e il volgare nella prima età moderna* (Bologna: Mulino, 2005); Paolo Prodi, *Il paradigma tridentino: Un'epoca della storia della Chiesa* (Brescia: Morcelliana, 2010), and his "Fourteen Theses on the Legacy of Trent," 40–47, in James F. Keenan, ed., *Catholic Theological Ethics: Past, Present, and Future: The Trento Conference* (Maryknoll, NY: Orbis, 2011). In English, see, e.g., O'Malley, *Trent and All That;* and Wietse de Boer, *The Conquest of the Soul: Confessions, Discipline, and Public Order in Counter-Reformation Milan* (Leiden: Brill, 2001); and now Simon Ditchfield, "Tridentine Catholicism," in *The Ashgate Research Companion to the Counter-Reformation,* ed. Mary Laven et al. (Aldershot: Ashgate, in press, expected 2012). For important studies of liturgical developments after Trent, which had wider significance, see Ditchfield, "Giving Tridentine Worship Back Its History," in *Continuity and Change in Christian Worship,* ed. R. N. Swanson, 199–226 (Woodbridge: Ecclesiastical History Society, 1999); Ditchfield, "Tridentine Worship and Cult of the Saints," in *Reform and Expansion, 1500–1660,* ed. R. Po-Chia Hsia, 203–224 (Cambridge: Cambridge University Press, 2007); and "Carlo Borromeo in the Construction of Roman Catholicism as a World Religion," *Studia Borromaica* 29 (2011): 2–23.

    17. See Giuseppe Alberigo, "Du concile de Trente au tridentinisme," *Irenikon* 54 (1981): 192–210.

    18. See, e.g., Simon Ditchfield, "In Sarpi's Shadow: Coping with Trent the Italian Way," in *Studi in memoria di Cesare Mozzarelli,* 2 vols. (Milan: Università Cattolica, 2008), 1:585–606.

    19. Jedin, *History,* 1:1.

    20. For two works that are also short introductions to the council, see Tallon, *Le Concile de Trente* (2000); and Adriano Prosperi, *Il Concilio di Trento: una introduzione storica* (Turin: Einaudi, 2001). I develop the subject much differently. Franco Buzzi, in *Concilio di Trento,* provides a concise and reliable guide to the "theological themes" of the council. For a recent collection of studies on the council, see Antonio Autiero and Marinella Perroni, ed., *Anatemi di ieri, sfide di oggi: Contrappunti di genere nella rilettura del concilio di Trento* (Bologna: Editioni Dehonlane, 2011).

    21. See, e.g., Ulianich, "Sarpi e Jedin"; O'Malley, *Trent and All That,* 46–71; Iginio Rogger, "Hubert Jedin e la storia del Concilio di Trento," in *Il Concilio di Trent nella prospettiva del terzo millennio,* ed. Giuseppe Alberigo and Iginio Rogger, 13–32 (Brescia: Morcelliana, 1997); Klaus Ganzer, "Hubert Jedin e il concilio di Trento," *Cristianesimo nella Storia* 22 (2001): 339–354; Heribert

Smolinsky, ed., *Die Erforschung der Kirchengeschichte: Leben, Werk, und Bedeutung von Hubert Jedin (1900–1980)* (Münster: Aschendorff, 2001).

22. CT. For the fate of the council's documents through the centuries, see Hubert Jedin, "Fata libellorum im Quellenbestand des Konzils von Trient," in Jedin, *Kirche des Glaubens,* 2:553–564; and Klaus Ganzer, "La conclusione dell' edizione del 'Concilium Tridentinum,'" *Annali dell' Istituto storico italo-germanico in Trento* 29 (2003): 380–403.

23. See Hubert Jedin, "Das Bischofsideal der Katholischen Reformation: Eine Studie über die Bischofsspiegel vornehmlich des 16. Jahrhunderts," in Jedin, *Kirche des Glaubens,* 2:75–117; J. Ignacio Tellechea Idígoras, "El obispo ideal según el Concilio de Trento," in Mozzarelli and Zardin, *Tempi del concilio,* 207–223; and G. G. Meersseman, "Il tipo ideale di parraco secondo la riforma tridentina nelle sue fonti letterarie," in *Il Concilio di Trento e la riforma tridentina: Atti del convegno storico internazionale,* 27–44 (Rome: Herder, 1965). For a more general study of the reforms of Trent, see Klaus Ganzer, "Das Konzil von Trient—Angelpunkt für eine Reform der Kirche?" *Römische Quartalschrift,* 84 (1989), 31–50.

24. See, e.g., J. Absil, "L'absentéisme du clergé paroissial au diocèse de Liège au XVe siècle et dans la première moitié du XVIe," *Revue d'histoire ecclésiastique* 57 (1962): 5–44.

25. On this complicated question, see Bernard Sesboüé, "Les concepts dogmatiques à Trente," in Bourgeois, *Signes du salut,* 151–165.

26. See Piet Fransen, "Réflexions sur l'anathème au Concile de Trente (Bologne, 10–24 septembre, 1547)," *Ephemerides Theologicae Lovanienses* 29 (1953): 656–672. See also CT 6/1: 133–134, 136–137, 137 (lines 29–30), 139 (lines 35–37); and Jedin, *History,* 2:381; and especially Jedin, *Geschichte,* 3:48–49, with n. 19.

27. See CT 9:37.

28. Tanner, *Decrees,* 2:736, canon 9; see also 735, chapter 8.

29. Tanner, *Decrees,* 2:796: "Finally, the holy council declares that each and every matter that has been laid down in this council about reformation of conduct and ecclesiastical discipline, in whatever phrasing and form of words, both under Popes Paul III and Julius III of happy memory and under the blessed Pius IV, are so decreed that the authority of the Apostolic See is and is understood to be intact in all of them."

30. Among implicit and contrasting ecclesiologies some shared ecclesiological principles were therefore operative at Trent. See, e.g., Giuseppe Alberigo, "Die Ekklesiologie des Konzils von Trient," in Bäumer, *Concilium Tridenti-*

num, 278–300; Dorothea Wendebourg, "Die Ekklesiologie des Konzils von Trient," in *Die katholische Konfessionalisierung,* ed.

Wolfgang Reinhard and Heinz Schilling, 70–87 (Münster: Aschendorff, 1995); Klaus Ganzer, "Die Ekklesiologie des Konzils von Trient," in Ganzer, *Kirche auf dem Weg durch die Zeit: Institutionelles Werden und theologisches Ringen: Ausgewälte Aufsätze und Vorträge,* ed. Heribert Smolinsky and Johannes Meier, 266–281 (Münster: Aschendorff, 1997); and Ganzer, "Gallikanische und römische Primatsauffassung im Widerstreit: Zu den ekklesiologischen Auseinandersetzungen auf dem Konzil von Trient," in Ganzer, *Kirche auf dem Weg,* 402–422. See also Hubert Jedin, "Zur Entwicklung des Kirchenbegriffs im 16. Jahrhundert," in Jedin, *Kirche des Glaubens,* 2:7–16.

31. Tanner, *Decrees,* 2:740.

1. The Fifteenth-Century Prelude

1. See Jedin, *History,* 1:210–213. This first volume, though dated, remains the standard introduction to the issues treated in this chapter. See also now, e.g., John Van Engen, "The Church in the Fifteenth Century," in Thomas A. Brady, Jr., Heiko A. Oberman, and James D. Tracy, eds., *Handbook of European History, 1400–1600: Late Middle Ages, Renaissance, and Reformation,* 2 vols. (Leiden: E. J. Brill, 1994), 1:305–330, and Gerald Christianson, Thomas Izbicki, and Christopher Bellitto, eds., *The Church, the Councils, and Reform: Lessons from the Fifteenth Century* (Washington, DC: Catholic University of America Press, 2008).

2. For a splendid survey, see Nelson Minnich, "From Constance to Trent: A Historical Overview," in Christianson, *The Church, the Councils, and Reform,* 27–59, reprinted in the collection of Minnich's articles, *Councils of the Catholic Reformation: Pisa I (1409) to Trent (1515–63)* (Aldershot: Variorum/Ashgate, 2008), n. I.

3. On interpretations of the axiom that the pope is judged by no one, see, e.g., Brian Tierney, *Foundations of the Conciliar Theory: The Contribution of the Medieval Canonists from Gratian to the Great Schism* (Cambridge: Cambridge University Press, 1955).

4. See Tanner, *Decrees,* 1:411.

5. For the complete list, see Tanner, *Decrees,* 1:444.

6. See Tanner, *Decrees,* 1:447–450.

7. See Hubert Jedin, "Vorschläge und Entwürfe zur Kardinalsreform," in Jedin, *Kirche des Glaubens,* 2:118–147.

8. See Tanner, *Decrees,* 1:418–419.

9. Ibid., 1:501–504.

10. Ibid., 1:488–489.

11. Ibid., 1:529–534.

12. Ibid., 1:528.

13. See Jedin, *History,* 1:5, the title of the chapter.

14. See, e.g., Hubert Jedin, "Papst und Konzil: Ihre Beziehungen vor, auf und nach dem Trienter Konzil," in Jedin, *Kirche des Glaubens,* 2:429–440.

15. See Marjorie Reeves, ed., *Prophetic Rome in the High Renaissance Period: Essays* (Oxford: Clarendon Press, 1992).

16. See, e.g., John W. O'Malley, *Giles of Viterbo on Church and Reform: A Study in Renaissance Thought* (Leiden: E. J. Brill, 1968), 100–138.

17. See, e.g., John W. O'Malley, *Praise and Blame in Renaissance Rome: Rhetoric, Doctrine, and Reform in the Sacred Orators of the Papal Court, c. 1450–1521* (Durham, NC: Duke University Press, 1979), 195–237; and Nelson Minnich, "Concepts of Reform Proposed at the Fifth Lateran Council," *Archivum Historiae Pontificiae* 7 (1969): 163–251, reprinted with new appendixes in the collection of his articles, *The Fifth Lateran Council (1512–17): Studies on Its Membership, Diplomacy and Proposals of Reform* (Aldershot: Variorum/Ashate, 1993), n. IV.

18. See O'Malley, *Praise and Blame,* 200.

19. See Nelson Minnich, "The Images of Julius II in the *ACTA* of the Councils of Pisa-Milan-Asti-Lyons (1511–12) and Lateran V (1512–17)," in *Giulio II: Papa, politico, mecenate,* ed. G. Rotondi Terminiello and G. Nepi, 79–90 (Genoa: De Ferrari, 2005), reprinted in his *Councils of the Catholic Reformation,* n. X.

20. As Emily O'Brien makes clear, Julius was not the first pope in the Renaissance to project a military image; see "Arms and Letters: Julius Caesar, the *Commentaries* of Pope Pius II, and the Politicization of Papal Imagery," *Renaissance Quarterly* 62 (2009): 1057–1097.

21. The best account of this complicated scene is Nelson Minnich, "The Healing of the Pisan Schism (1511–13)," *Annuarium Historiae Conciliorum* 16 (1984): 59–192, reprinted with new appendixes in Minnich, *Fifth Lateran Council,* n. II.

22. The studies of Nelson Minnich on the council have completely revised our understanding of it. See the collections of his articles, *Fifth Lateran Council* and *Councils of the Catholic Reformation.*

23. See Minnich, "Images of Julius," 88.

24. See Tanner, *Decrees,* 1:597–598.

25. See Nelson Minnich, "Prophecy and the Fifth Lateran Council (1512–1517)," in Reeves, *Prophetic Rome,* 63–87, at 67, reprinted in *Councils of the Catholic Reformation,* n. VIII.

26. See Tanner, *Decrees,* 1:600–603.

27. See Nelson Minnich, "The Participants at the Fifth Lateran Council," *Annuarium Historiae Pontificiae,* 12 (1974), 157–206, reprinted in *Fifth Lateran Council,* n. I.

28. See Tanner, *Decrees,* 1:606–608 and 609–614.

29. Ibid., 1:638–645, especially 642.

30. See now the Italian translation from the Latin by Geminiano Bianchini, *Lettera al Papa: Paolo Giustiniani e Pietro Quirini a Leone X* (Modena: n.p., c. 1995).

31. See Nelson Minnich, "The Proposals for an Episcopal College at Lateran V," in *Ecclesia Militans: Studien zur Konzilien und Reformationsgeschichte, Remigius Bäumer zum 70 Geburtstag gewidmet,* ed. Walter Brandmüller et al., 2 vols. (Paderborn: Ferdinand Schöningh, 1988), 1:213–232.

32. See Tanner, *Decrees,* 1:614–625. For an English translation, see John C. Olin, *The Catholic Reformation: Savonarola to Ignatius Loyola, Reform in the Church, 1495–1540* (New York: Harper and Row, 1969), 54–64.

33. See Mary Hollingsworth and Carol M. Richardson, ed., *The Possessions of a Cardinal: Politics, Piety, and Art, 1450–1700* (University Park: Pennsylvania State University Press, 2010), 132–152, at 133 and 137. See, more generally, Barbara McClung Hallman, *Italian Cardinals, Reform, and the Church as Property: 1492–1563* (Berkeley: University of California Press, 1985).

34. See Natalie Tomas, "All in the Family: The Medici Women and Pope Clement VII," in *The Pontificate of Clement VII: History, Politics, Culture,* ed. Kenneth Gouwens and Sheryl E. Reiss, 41–53 (Burlington, VT: Ashgate, 2005), at 43.

35. On the council's reform, see Jedin, *History,* 1:127–138.

36. For two contrasting interpretations, both by Catholics, compare Eamon Duffy, *The Stripping of the Altars: Traditional Religion in England c.1400–c.1580* (New Haven: Yale University Press, 1992); and Jean Delumeau, *Sin and*

Fear: The Emergence of a Western Guilt Culture, 13th–18th Centuries, trans. Eric Nicholson (New York: St. Martin's Press, 1990).

37. See Erika Rummel, *Jiménez de Cisneros: On the Threshold of Spain's Golden Age* (Tempe: Arizona Center for Medieval and Renaissance Studies, 1999). For studies of another reforming prelate, see Marco Agostini and Giovanna Baldissin Molli, eds., *Gian Matteo Giberti (1495–1543): Atti del convegno di studi* (Cittadella [Padova]: Biblos, 2012).

38. See, e.g., Guy Bedouelle, *The Reform of Catholicism, 1480–1620,* trans. James K. Farge (Toronto: Pontifical Institute of Mediaeval Studies, 2008), 17–18.

39. See, e.g., John W. O'Malley, *The First Jesuits* (Cambridge, MA: Harvard University Press, 1993), 115–126.

40. See, e.g., James K. Farge, *Orthodoxy and Reform in Early Reformation France: The Faculty of Theology of Paris, 1500–1543* (Leiden: E. J. Brill, 1985); and Paul F. Grendler, *The Universities of the Italian Renaissance* (Baltimore, MD: Johns Hopkins University Press, 2002).

41. See, e.g., Paul Oskar Kristeller, "Thomism and the Italian Thought of the Renaissance," in *Medieval Aspects of Renaissance Learning: Three Essays by Paul Oskar Kristeller,* ed. and trans. Edward P. Mahoney, 29–91 (New York: Columbia University Press, 1992); and John W. O'Malley, "The Feast of Thomas Aquinas in Renaissance Rome: A Neglected Document and Its Import," *Rivista di Storia della Chiesa in Italia* 35 (1982): 1–27; as well as O'Malley, "The Religious and Theological Culture of Michelangelo's Rome, 1508–1512," in Edgar Wind, *The Religious Symbolism of Michelangelo: The Sistine Ceiling,* ed. Elizabeth Sears (Oxford: Oxford University Press, 2000), xli–lii; and Paul F. Grendler, "Italian Biblical Scholarship and the Popes, 1515–1535," in *Biblical Humanism and Scholasticism in the Age of Erasmus,* ed. Erika Rummel, 227–276 (Leiden: E. J. Brill, 2008).

42. For a translation of Ciscernos's dedicatory prologue to Pope Leo X, see John C. Olin, ed. and trans., *Catholic Reform from Cardinal Ximenes to the Council of Trent 1495–1563: An Essay with Illustrative Documents and a Brief Study of St. Ignatius Loyola* (New York: Fordham University Press, 1990), 61–64.

43. See, e.g., Rummel, *Biblical Humanism;* and Jerry H. Bentley, *Humanists and Holy Writ: New Testament Scholarship in the Renaissance* (Princeton: Princeton University Press, 1983).

44. See, e.g., John W. O'Malley, "Introduction," *Spiritualia: Enchiridion, De Contemptu Mundi, De Vidua Christiana,* Collected Works of Erasmus 66 (Toronto: University of Toronto Press, 1988), ix–li; and his *Four Cultures of the*

West (Cambridge, MA: The Belknap Press of Harvard University Press, 2004), 127–162.

45. See O'Malley, *Praise and Blame;* as well as his "Content and Rhetorical Forms in Sixteenth-Century Treatises on Preaching," in *Renaissance Eloquence: Studies in the Theory and Practice of Renaissance Rhetoric,* ed. James J. Murphy, 238–252 (Berkeley: University of California Press, 1983); and his "Erasmus and the History of Sacred Rhetoric: The *Ecclesiastes* of 1535," *Erasmus of Rotterdam Society Yearbook* 5 (1985): 1–29.

46. See, e.g., Paul F. Grendler, *Schooling in Renaissance Italy: Literacy and Learning, 1300–1600* (Baltimore, MD: Johns Hopkins University Press, 1989); and John W. O'Malley, "Paul Grendler and the Triumph of the Renaissance: A Reminiscence and Some Thoughts," in *The Renaissance in the Streets, Schools, and Studies: Essays in Honour of Paul F. Grendler,* ed. Konrad Eisenbichler and Nicholas Terpstra, 323–343 (Toronto: Centre for Reformation and Renaissance Studies, 2008).

47. Pedro de Ribadeneira, in a letter to King Philip II of Spain, 1556, as quoted in O'Malley, *First Jesuits,* 209.

48. Literature on the confraternities is abundant and growing. One of the early books responsible for turning historians' interest to the subject was Brian Pullan, *Rich and Poor in Renaissance Venice: The Social Institutions of a Catholic State to 1620* (Cambridge, MA: Harvard University Press, 1971). For a concise survey of the field, which includes a bibliography, see Christopher Black, "Introduction: The Confraternity Context," in *Early Modern Confraternities in Europe and the Americas: International and Interdisciplinary Perspectives,* ed. Christopher Black and Pamela Gravestock, 1–34 (Aldershot: Ashgate, 2006). See most recently Stefania Pastore, Adriano Prosperi, and Nicholas Terpstra, eds., *Brotherhoods and Boundaries: Fraternità e barriere* (Pisa: Scuola Normale Superiore, 2011). Developments in scholarship can be followed in the serial *Confraternitas.*

49. For the "rule," see Olin, *Catholic Reformation,* 16–26.

50. See John Van Engen, "The Christian Middle Ages as an Historiographical Problem," *American Historical Review* 91 (1986): 519–552.

2. The Struggle to Convoke the Council

1. See Gerhard Ebeling, *Luther: An Introduction to His Thought,* trans. R. A. Wilson (Philadelphia: Fortress Press, 1970), 26–27. The quantity of lit-

erature on Luther is overwhelming. For a recent analysis of his theology, see Oswald Bayer, *Martin Luther's Theology: A Contemporary Interpretation,* trans. Thomas H. Trapp (Grand Rapids, MI: Eerdmans, 2008). For an older, judicious overview, see B. A. Gerrish, *Grace and Reason: A Study in the Theology of Luther* (Oxford: Oxford University Press, Clarendon, 1962).

2. See John W. O'Malley, *Four Cultures of the West* (Cambridge, MA: The Belknap Press of Harvard University Press, 2004), 56–61.

3. See, e.g., Konrad Repgen, "Reich und Konzil (1521–1566)," in Prodi, *Trient und die Moderne,* 43–77.

4. This is the argument of Tallon, who qualifies the unrelieved negative assessment of Francis by German historians, including Jedin; see Tallon, *France et Trente,* 11–15, 57–115.

5. See Tallon, *France et Trente,* 57–65.

6. See CT 12:31, consistory, September 1, 1522.

7. See, e.g., Pastor, *Popes,* 9:114–126.

8. See Robert E. McNally, "Pope Adrian VI (1522–1523) and Church Reform," *Archivum Historiae Pontificiae* 7 (1969): 253–285.

9. The most recent scholarship on Clement is contained in Kenneth Gouwens and Sheryl E. Reiss, eds., *The Pontificate of Clement VII: History, Politics, Culture* (Burlington, VT: Ashgate, 2005). Several authors in the volume point out positive aspects to the pontificate, such as his enlightened patronage of literature, of the papal choir, and of artists, especially Michelangelo. Barbara McClung Hallman writes the most general reevaluation of the pope and his policies, "The 'Disastrous' Pontificate of Clement VII: Disastrous for Giulio de' Medici?" 29–40. She makes, however, no mention of the problem of the council, which is true as well for the other contributions in the volume. Kenneth Gouwens also advances arguments for a less negative assessment of the pontificate, "Clement VII: Prince at War," in James Corkery and Thomas Worcester, eds., *The Papacy since 1500: From Italian Prince to Universal Pastor* (Cambridge: Cambridge University Press, 2010), 29–46. The best overview of the pontiff is Adriano Prosperi, "Clemente VII," DBI, 26:237–259, but as always Pastor, *Popes,* vols. 9 and 10, remains indispensable.

10. For a still useful narrative, see Judith Hook, *The Sack of Rome, 1527* (London: Macmillan, 1972). For more recent studies of certain aspects of the sack, see Gouwens, *Pontificate of Clement VII,* 75–161; as well as his *Remembering the Renaissance: Humanist Narratives of the Sack of Rome* (Leiden: E. J. Brill, 1998).

11. See Gerhard Müller, "Zur Vorgeschichte des Tridentinums: Karl V. und das Konzil während des Pontifikates Clemens' VII," in Bäumer, *Concilium Tridentinum*, 74–112.

12. Jedin, *History,* 1:207.

13. CT 2:402.

14. The full document is translated in John C. Olin, *The Catholic Reformation: Savonarola to Ignatius Loyola, Reform in the Church, 1495–1540* (New York: Harper and Row, 1969), 182–197, at 186–187.

15. Giovan Domenico Mansi, *Sacrorum conciliorum, nova et amplissima collectio,* 54 vols. (Graz: Akademische Druck- und Verlaganstalt, 1960–1962), 32:1095–1140.

16. Ibid., 32:1141–1148.

17. Ibid., 32:1205–1294.

18. Ibid., 32:1149–1202.

19. See James K. Farge, *Orthodoxy and Reform in Early Reformation France: The Faculty of Theology of Paris, 1500–1543* (Leiden: E. J. Brill, 1985), 241.

20. Mansi, *Sacrorum conciliorum,* 32:1151.

21. Ibid., 32:1161. Compare this list with the forty-one articles drawn up by the theologians brought together at Melun by Francis I in December 1541 to prepare for the council, Tallon, *France et Trente,* 134–135.

22. See Tallon, *France et Trente,* 448, 450–451.

23. For the document, see W. Friedensburg, "Aktenstücke über das Verhalten der römischen Kurie zur Reformation 1524 und 1531," *Quellen und Forschungen aus italienischen Archiven und Bibliotheken* 3 (1900): 1–20, at 16–18; English translation in Jared Wicks, ed. and trans., *Cajetan Responds: A Reader in Reformation Controversy* (Washington, DC: Catholic University of America Press, 1978), 201–203. Cardinal Accolti replied in a sharp negative, Friedensburg, "Aktenstücke," 18–20. See Jedin, *History,* 1:274; and John W. O'Malley, *Giles of Viterbo on Church and Reform: A Study in Renaissance Thought* (Leiden: E. J. Brill, 1968), 154, n. 2. For Cajetan as a commentator on the Bible, see the entry by Jared Wicks in Donald K. McKim, ed., *Dictionary of Major Biblical Interpreters,* 2nd ed. (Downers Grove, IL: InterVarsity Press, 2007).

24. For a detailed account of Paul's efforts to convoke the council between 1534 and 1541, Pastor is still valuable, *Popes,* 11:41–132, 359–398.

25. CT 4:2–6.

26. On Contarini, see Gigliola Fragnito, "Contarini, Gasparo," DBI, 28:172–192. He continues to arouse historians' interest. See Elizabeth Gleason,

Gasparo Contarini: Venice, Rome, and Reform (Berkeley: University of California Press, 1993); and Constance M. Furey, *Erasmus, Contarini, and the Religious Republic of Letters* (New York: Cambridge University Press, 2006). See, more specifically, Peter Matheson, *Cardinal Contarini at Regensburg* (Oxford: Clarendon Press, 1972), with a judicious conclusion, 171–181. The fate Contarini suffered through Roman censorship and historians' assessments of him is carefully and amply told by Claus Arnold, *Die römische Zensur der Werke Cajetans und Contarinis (1558–1601): Grenzen der theologischen Konfessionalisierung* (Paderborn: Ferdinand Schöningh, 2008), with an analysis of Jedin's treatment of him, 39–41.

27. On Farnese, see Clare Robertson, "Farnese, Alessandro," DBI, 45:52–70; and, with a more specific focus, her monograph, *"Il Gran Cardinale," Alessandro Farnese: Patron of the Arts* (New Haven: Yale University Press, 1992).

28. The legates' exclusive right to propose was explicit in the bull, *Ad Prudentis Patrisfamilias,* March 20, 1538, for the legates to Vicenza. See CT 4:156–157. See also CT 4:393–394, especially 394 n. 1, and 5:134, 135. For commentary, see Umberto Mazzone, "Versammlungs- und Kontrolltechniken," in Prodi, *Trient und die Moderne,* 79–106, at 101–106; and, more specifically, his "Giovanni Morone legato al concilio di Trento e la clausula del 'proponentibus legatis,'" in *Il cardinale Giovanni Morone e l'ultima fase del Concilio di Trento,* ed. Massimo Firpo and Ottavia Niccoli, 117–141 (Bologna: Mulino, 2010).

29. CT 4:395–396.

30. CT 1:160.

31. See George B. Parks, "The Parma Letters and the Dangers to Cardinal Pole," *Catholic Historical Review* 46 (1960–1961): 299–317. See also CT 4:396 and 394 n. 2.

32. See Jedin, *History,* 1:523.

33. See Hubert Jedin, *Papal Legate at the Council of Trent: Cardinal Seripando,* trans. Frederic C. Eckhoff (St. Louis: B. Herder, 1947); and Alfredo Marranzini, "Girolamo Seripando dopo Hubert Jedin," in *Il Concilio di Trento nella prospettiva del terzo millennio,* ed. Giuseppe Alberigo and Iginio Rogger, 343–370 (Brescia: Morcelliana, 1997).

34. There are two lists of those present, CT 1:4 and CT 4:529–530, with slight discrepancies between them. Jedin says only two of the bishops were Spaniards, but CT 1 lists three, and CT 4, the more precise, lists four. By "Italian" I, like Jedin, include those from the Kingdom of Naples, including Sicily.

35. See Tallon, *France et Trente,* 149–172.

36. On the abbots, see Barry Collett, *Italian Benedictine Scholars and the Reformation: The Congregation of Santa Giustina of Padua* (New York: Oxford University Press, 1985).

37. Massarelli described the ceremony in great detail, CT 1:400–404.

3. The First Period, 1545–1547

1. Unlike the other buildings important for the council, the Palazzo Giroldo no longer exists. It was destroyed by fire in 1845, and in its place is a modern edifice known as the Palazzo a Prato, which houses the municipal post office. The Renaissance portal is virtually the only part of the original edifice that survives.

2. See CT 4:536.

3. See CT 4:540–542.

4. See CT 1:12.

5. See CT 4:542–543. On Martelli, see Hubert Jedin, "Der 'Episkopalist' Braccio Martelli, Bischof von Fiesole: Nova et Vetera," *Römische Quartalschrift* 60 (1965): 153–185.

6. See CT 10:321, 324.

7. CT 4:567.

8. CT 4:568.

9. See Boris Ulianich, "Bonucci [*sic*], Agostino," DBI, 12:438–450; and Robert E. McNally, "Freedom and Suspicion at Trent: Bonuccio and Soto," *Theological Studies* 29 (1968): 752–762.

10. CT 4:572: "Et ita denique decretum fuit, sanctam hanc synodum in materiis pertractandis decidendisque agere simul de dogmatibus et reformatione, adeo ut in qualibet Sessione duo decreta publicari debeant, unum de fide, alterum de moribus."

11. CT 10:321–324.

12. See Tanner, *Decrees*, 1:230–233, 551–552, 570–572.

13. On the procedures at Trent, see Jedin, *Geschichte*, 3:296–297; his "Die Geschäftsordnungen der beiden letzten ökumenischen Konzilien in ekklesiologischer Sicht," in Jedin, *Kirche des Glaubens*, 2:577–588; Johannes Beumer, "Die Geschäftsordnung des Trienter Konzils," in Bäumer, *Concilium Tridentinum*, 113–140; and Nelson Minnich, "The Voice of Theologians in General Councils from Pisa to Trent," *Theological Studies* 59 (1998): 420–441, at 431–434. The primary basis for reconstructing the procedures is the summary of

them prepared after the council by Massarelli, "Ordo celebrandi concilii generalis Tridenti sub Paulo III., Julio III., et Pio IV., Summis Pontificibus observatus," CT 13/2:680–696.

14. From Massarelli's summary of the procedures, CT 13/2:691.

15. See, e.g., Adriano Prosperi, "Lutero al Concilio di Trento," in *Lutero in Italia: Studi storici nel V centenario della nascita,* ed. Lorenzo Perrone, 95–114 (Casale Monferrato: Marietti, 1983); and Vinzenz Pfnür, "Zur Verurteilung der reformatorischen Rechtfertigungslehre auf dem Konzil von Trient," *Annuarium Historiae Conciliorum* 8 (1976): 407–428.

16. See, e.g., CT 7/1:497.

17. See Giampietro Brunelli, "Giulio III," DBI, 57:26–36.

18. See Giampietro Brunelli, "Marcello II," DBI, 69:502–510; William V. Hudon, *Marcello Cervini and Ecclesiastical Government in Tridentine Italy* (De Kalb: Northern Illinois University Press, 1992); and now Chiara Quaranta, *Marcello II Cervini (1501–1555): Riforma della Chiesa, concilio, inquisizione* (Bologna: Il Mulino, 2010).

19. On this aspect of his career, see now Eamon Duffy and David Loades, ed., *The Church of Mary Tudor* (Burlington, VT: Ashgate, 2006), especially 149–200.

20. Pole was a productive writer. His correspondence, for instance, runs to over 2,000 letters, and the literature on him in both Italian and English is extensive. For a recent biography with detailed analysis of his writings, see Thomas Mayer, *Reginald Pole: Prince & Prophet* (Cambridge: Cambridge University Press, 2000). Specifically on the issue of justification, see Mayer, *Reginald Pole,* 153–169; and Dermot Fenlon, *Heresy and Obedience in Tridentine Italy: Cardinal Pole and the Counter Reformation* (Cambridge: Cambridge University Press, 1972). See also the collection of Mayer's studies on Pole, *Cardinal Pole in European Context: A via media in the Reformation* (Burlington, VT: Ashgate, 2000). On the papal conclave of 1549–1550, see ibid., numbers IV and V. The most recent major study is by Vito Mignozzi, *Tenenda est media via: l'ecclesiologia di Reginald Pole (1500–1558)* (Assisi: Cittadella, 2007).

21. See, e.g., Basil Hall, "Biblical Scholarship: Editions and Commentaries," in *The Cambridge History of the Bible,* ed. Peter R. Ackroyd et al., 3 vols. (Cambridge: Cambridge University Press, 1963–1970), 3:38–93, at 48–76. More generally, see Guy Bedouelle and Bernard Roussel, eds., *Le temps des Réformes et la Bible* (Paris: Beauchesne, 1989).

22. See Tanner, *Decrees,* 1:572. More generally on the complicated question

of the development of the canon, see Lee Martin McDonald, *The Biblical Canon: Its Origin, Transmission, and Authority* (Peabody, MA: Hendrickson, 2007).

23. CT 5:8: "De ipsorum autem librorum discrimine, etsi plures rem utilem, minus tamen necessariam iudicarent, maioris nihilominus partis sententia praevaluit, ut quaestio huiusmodi omitteretur et relinqueretur, sicuti nobis a sanctis nostris patribus relicta fuit. In qua sententia cum esset R. Generalis Servorum, addidit hanc rationem, ne in iis, in quibus inter se Augustinus et Hieronymus dissentiunt, synodus iudicium suum, quod ecclesia facere non consuevit, interponeret." For a careful and extended treatment of the general subject, see Guy Bedouelle, "La Bible au Concile de Trente," in *Le temps des Réformes,* ed. Bedouelle, 327–343.

24. See CT 5:18–19.

25. See CT 1:34.

26. See CT 5:19.

27. The question of the precise relationship between Scripture and traditions at Trent took a sudden turn with J. R. Geiselmann's "Das Missverständnis über das Verhältniss von Schrift und Tradition und seine Überwindung in der katholischen Theologie," *Una Sancta* 11 (1956): 131–150. In that regard, see, e.g., Johannes Beumer, "Katholisches und protestantisches Schriftprinzip im Urteil des Trienter Konzils," *Scholastik* 34 (1959): 249–258; Yves-Marie Congar, *La tradition et les traditions,* 2 vols. (Paris: A. Fayard, 1960–1963), 1:207–233; and H. Lennerz, "Sine scripto traditiones," *Gregorianum* 40 (1959): 624–635. More broadly, see, e.g., Paul de Vooght, "Le rapport écriture-tradition d'après saint Thomas d'Aquin et les théologiens du XIIIe siècle," *Istina* 8 (1962): 499–510; de Vooght, "La décretale Cum Martha," *Recherches de science religieuse* 42 (1954): 540–548. Among more recent studies, see Buzzi, *Concilio di Trento,* 23–35; Bernard Sesboüé, "Écriture, traditions et dogmes au Concile de Trente," in Bourgeois, *Signes du salut,* 133–151; and Jeffrey W. Barbeau, "Scripture and Tradition at the Council of Trent: Reapplying the 'Conciliar Hermeneutic,'" *Annuarium Historiae Conciliorum* 33 (2001): 127–146. See also note 38 below.

28. See CT 1:37–38.

29. See Tanner, *Decrees,* 1:632–633, Session 10, May 4, 1515.

30. See CT 1:45–46, and CT 5:71–72. On this interesting personality, who participated in all three periods of the council, see the entry by Wietse de Boer in the DBI.

31. See CT 1:40–42.

32. CT 1:42.

33. See CT 5:42–58, 58–67, 69–72. See also CT 5:76–82.

34. See CT 1:43–44.

35. CT 5:95–101, at 99. See McNally, "Freedom and Suspicion," 752–762.

36. The meetings were on April 12 and 18. See CT 1:525, 535–536, 538. See also CT 2:383.

37. For the full texts in the original Latin with facing English translation, see Tanner, *Decrees*, 2:663–665.

38. Most of the literature on this problem dates from the mid-twentieth century, just before, during, and after Vatican Council II, where it became an extraordinarily difficult issue. See, e.g., Johannes Beumer, "Der Begriff der 'traditiones' auf dem Trienter Konzil im Lichte der mittelalterlichen Kanonistik," *Scholastik* 35 (1960): 342–362; his "Die mündliche Überlieferung als Glaubensquelle," in *Handbuch der Dogmengeschichte*, ed. M. Schmaus et al. (Freiburg im Breisgau: Herder, 1962), 1/4:74–88; and Teodoro López Rodríguez, "'Fides et Mores' in Trento," *Scripta Theologica* 5 (1973): 175–221. Of particular importance is Joseph Ratzinger, "On the Interpretation of the Tridentine Decree on Tradition," in Karl Rahner and Joseph Ratzinger, *Revelation and Tradition*, trans. W. J. O'Hara, 50–66 (London: Burns and Oates, 1966). See also note 27 above. David C. Steinmetz misconstrues the decree, "The Council of Trent," in *The Cambridge Companion to Reformation Theology*, ed. David Bagchi and David C. Steinmetz, 233–247 (Cambridge: Cambridge University Press, 2004), as Jared Wicks points out in his review, *The Thomist* 70 (2006): 289–292.

39. See Robert E. McNally, "The Council of Trent and Vernacular Bibles," *Theological Studies* 27 (1966): 204–227.

40. See CT 10:462–463, 939.

41. CT 10:890–891, at 891, ". . . aspettavamo un bel putto maschio, havete fatta la citta et stroppiata."

42. CT 5:105–108.

43. See Louis B. Pascoe, "The Council of Trent and Bible Study: Humanism and Scholasticism," *Catholic Historical Review* 52 (1966–1967): 18–38.

44. See, e.g., John W. O'Malley, *Giles of Viterbo on Church and Reform: A Study in Renaissance Thought* (Leiden: E. J. Brill, 1968), 155–157.

45. For Martelli's intervention, see CT 5:134–136. For the aftermath on May 10 and 18, see CT 5:143–146. See also Jedin, "Martelli."

46. See Tanner, *Decrees*, 2:667–670. For commentary, see Bedouelle, "Bible," 344–350; A. Larios, "La reforma de la predicacion en Trento (Historia y

contenido de un decreto)," *Communio* 6 (1973): 223–283; and Klaus Ganzer, "Zur Frage der kirchlichen Predigtsvollmacht auf dem Konzil von Trient," *Annuarium Historiae Conciliorum* 7 (1975): 402–416.

47. Jaroslav Pelikan and Valerie Hotchkiss, eds., *Creeds & Confessions of Faith in the Christian Tradition,* 3 vols. (New Haven: Yale University Press, 2003), 2:60–61.

48. CT 10:503.

49. CT 5:163–164.

50. Tanner, *Decrees,* 2:665–667. See Buzzi, *Concilio di Trento,* 47–70. Most of the scholarship on the decree was written in the mid-twentieth century. See, e.g., Jedin, *History,* 2:125–165; A. Vanneste, "La préhistoire du Décret du Concile de Trente sur le péché originel," *Nouvelle Revue Théologique* 86 (1964): 355–368, 490–510; and his "Le Décret du Concile de Trente sur le péché originel: Les trois premiers canons," *Nouvelle Revue Théologique* 87 (1965): 688–726; Zoltan Alszeghy and Maurizio Flick, "Il Decreto Tridentino sul peccato originale," *Gregorianum* 52 (1971): 595–635; and André-Marie Dubarle, "Le péché originel dans la Confession d'Augsbourg et du Concile de Trente," *Revue des Sciences Philosophiques et Théologiques* 64 (1980): 547–560.

51. See Tallon, *France et Trente,* 149–172.

52. CT 1:82.

53. CT 10:531–533, at 532.

54. Summarized in CT 1:82–83. See also CT 5:257.

55. See Jedin, *History,* 2:176.

56. CT 12:613–636. On the difficult question of terminology, see G. R. Evans, "Vis verborum: Scholastic Method and Finding Words in the Debates on Justification at the Council of Trent," *Downside Review* 106 (1988): 264–275.

57. CT 5:294–296, 352–354.

58. I have simply summarized Jedin's detailed description of this famous incident, *History,* 2:190–193.

59. CT 5:663–676.

60. CT 1:116–117.

61. See Tanner, *Decrees,* 2:681–683.

62. Ibid., 2:671–681. Although there is a considerable amount of literature on the subject, relatively little is in English. See, however, H. George Anderson, T. Austin Murphy, and Joseph A. Burgess, eds., *Justification by Faith: Lutherans and Catholics in Dialogue VII* (Minneapolis: Augsburg, 1985); Karl Lehmann, ed., *Justification by Faith: Do the Sixteenth-Century Condemnations Still*

Apply? trans. Michael Root and William G. Rusch (New York: Continuum, 1997); John A. Radano, *Lutheran and Catholic Reconciliation on Justification: A Chronology of the Holy See's Contributions, 1961–1999, to a New Relationship between Lutherans and Catholics and to Steps Leading to the Joint Declaration on the Doctrine of Justification* (Grand Rapids, MI: Eerdmans, 2009); and especially Alister E. McGrath, *Iustitia Dei: A History of the Christian Doctrine of Justification,* 3rd ed. (Cambridge: Cambridge University Press, 2005). For an extensive bibliography of titles from the nineteenth century up to the late twentieth, but almost exclusively in German, see Karl Lehmann, "Das Dekret des Konzils von Trient über die Rechfertigung: Historisches Verständnis und theologische Bedeutung in ökumenischer Sicht. Bibliographie," in *Lehrverurteilungen-kirchentrennend? II: Materialen zu den Lehrverurteilungen und zur Theologie der Rechtfertigung,* ed. Karl Lehmann (Freiburg im Breisgau: Herder, 1989), 368–372. See also Buzzi, *Concilio di Trento,* 71–119.

63. Tanner, *Decrees,* 2:672.

64. See Otto Hermann Pesch, "La réponse du Concile de Trente (1545–1563): les decisions doctrinales contre la Réforme et les consequences," *Irenikon* 73 (2000): 5–38.

65. See, e.g, John W. O'Malley, *Four Cultures of the West* (Cambridge, MA: The Belknap Press of Harvard University Press, 2004), especially 56–65, 103–115.

66. See CT 5:847–848.

67. See CT 5:871–872.

68. CT 1:128, "Illud quod licet et quod expedit hoc est, ut cura animarum a nobis nullatenus negligatur."

69. See CT 1:133.

70. See Tanner, *Decrees,* 2:686–689.

71. See CT 5:844–862.

72. For an accessible and authoritative introduction to the metaphysics of medieval sacramental theology, with special attention to the Eucharist, see Marilyn McCord Adams, *Some Later Medieval Theories of the Eucharist: Thomas Aquinas, Giles of Rome, Duns Scotus, and William Ockham* (Oxford: Oxford University Press, 2010).

73. See Tanner, *Decrees,* 1:540–550. On the decree, see Henri Bourgeois, "Le décret du concile de Florence pour les Arméniens (1439)," in Bourgeois, *Signes du salut,* 119–124.

74. See CT 5:930–931.

75. See Tanner, *Decrees,* 2:684–686.

76. See, e.g., Michael Seybold, "Die Siebenzahl der Sakramente (Conc. Trid., sessio VII, Can. 11)," *Münchener Theologische Zeitschrift* 27 (1976): 113–141; Jared Wicks, "Fides sacramenti—fides specialis: Luther's Development in 1518," *Gregorianum* 65 (1984): 53–87; E. V. Ottolini, "L'istituzione dei sacramenti nella VII sessione del Concilio di Trento," *Rivista Liturgica* 81 (1994): 60–117; Henri Bourgeois and Bernard Sesboüé, "La doctrine sacramentaire du concile de Trente," in Bourgeois, *Signes du salut,* 144–157.

77. See, e.g., Duval, *Sacrements au Concile de Trente,* 11–20; André Gonnelle, "Pédobaptisme, le débat au xvie siècle," *Études théologiques et religieuses* 70 (1995): 191–206; and Jonathan D. Trigg, *Baptism in the Theology of Martin Luther* (Leiden: E. J. Brill, 1994).

78. See, e.g., Paul Turner, *The Meaning and Practice of Confirmation: Perspectives from a Sixteenth-Century Controversy* (New York: Peter Lang, 1987).

79. See CT 1:137–138, 624; 5:1013–1015.

80. For the report, see CT 5:1014–1015. On Fracastoro, see the entry by Bernardino Fantini in *Encyclopedia of the Renaissance,* ed. Paul F. Grendler, 6 vols. (New York: Charles Scribner's Sons, 1999), 2:411–412; and, more specifically, Hubert Jedin, "Laientheologie im Zeitalter der Glaubensspaltung: Der Konzilsart Fracastoro," *Trierer Theologische Zeitschrift* 64 (1955): 11–24.

81. For his letter, see CT 11:113–115. See also CT 11:117–118, 134.

82. See CT 1:144, 625–626.

83. Jedin, *History,* 2:443.

4. The Middle Years, 1547–1562

1. The arrangement was complex and shifting. See Paul F. Grendler, *The Universities of the Italian Renaissance* (Baltimore: Johns Hopkins University Press, 2002), pp. 359, 382–383.

2. See CT 1:646.

3. See CT 1:635.

4. See CT 1:633.

5. See Tanner, *Decrees,* 2:690–691. See also CT 1:145–146, 642–644.

6. See Jedin, *Geschichte,* 3:19–21.

7. See CT 11/2:179–180. For a letter of Charles to Diego Hurtardo de Mendoza, his ambassador in Rome, under the same date, see CT 11/2:180–183.

8. See CT 6/1:74–123.

9. See CT 1:650.

10. See CT 1:657. For some documents that have survived, see CT 6/2:1–28.

11. See CT 1:658.

12. See Tanner, *Decrees,* 2:691–692. See also CT 6/1:184–191.

13. See Hubert Jedin, "Die Bedeutung der Bologneser Tagungsperiode für die dogmatischen Definitionen und das Reformwerk des Konzils von Trient," in Jedin, *Kirche des Glaubens,* 2:213–223.

14. See CT 6/1:7–12. See further, CT 6.1:12–14.

15. See CT 1:672–673. For the few surviving documents, see CT 6/2:31–71.

16. See CT 1:666–675.

17. See CT 1:687; CT 6/1:407–435, and CT 6/2:22–168.

18. See CT 6/1:434–435.

19. See CT 1:692.

20. See, e.g., Pastor, *Popes,* 12:369–383.

21. See CT 1:690–691.

22. See, e.g., CT 1:691.

23. See Tallon, *France et Trente,* 197–211.

24. See CT 1:727–728, and especially CT 6/1:635–648. For Del Monte's letter to Paul III, see CT 6/1:648–651.

25. See CT 1:731.

26. See CT 1:736–738, at 738, and especially CT 6/1:684–704.

27. See CT 6/1:717–727, and Hubert Jedin, "Die kaiserliche Protest gegen die Translation des Konzils von Trient nach Bologna: Neue Aktenstücke aus dem Notariatsarchiv in Barcelona," in Jedin, *Kirche des Glaubens,* 2:202–212.

28. See Jedin, *Geschichte,* 3:162–196. For documents related to the issue, see CT 6/1:717–833, and 6/2:631–719.

29. See CT 6/1:727–728, 739–740.

30. CT 1:864, "Ab hac die cessat concilium Bononiense." See also CT 11:515–516.

31. See, e.g., Frederic J. Baumgartner, "Henry II and the Papal Conclave of 1549," *Sixteenth Century Journal,* n.3 (1985): 301–314.

32. For de Guise, still basic is H. Outram Evennett, *The Cardinal of Lorraine and the Council of Trent: A Study in the Counter-Reformation* (Cambridge: Cambridge University Press, 1930). See now also Tallon, *France et Trente,* passim; his "Giovanni Morone, il cardinale di Lorena e la conclusione del concilio," in *Il cardinale Giovanni Morone e l'ultima fase del concilio di Trento,* ed. Massimo Firpo and Ottavia Niccoli, 143–158 (Bologna: Mulino, 2010); Stuart Carroll, "The Compromise of Charles Cardinal de Lorraine: New Evidence,"

Journal of Ecclesiastical History 54 (2003): 469–483; and, more broadly, his *Martyrs and Murderers: The Guise Family and the Making of Europe* (Oxford: Oxford University Press, 2009).

33. We are very well informed about how the election came about. See CT 2:139–140, including notes 1 and 2.

34. See Pastor, *Popes*, 13: 69–76; the entry, "Del Monte, Innocenzo," in DBI; and Francis A. Burkle-Young and Michael Leopoldo Doerrer, *The Life of Cardinal Innocenzo Del Monte: A Scandal in Scarlet* (Lewiston, NY: E. Mellen, 1997). Massarelli provides a vivid description of Del Monte's affection for the youth. See CT 2:174–175.

35. See CT 11:543.

36. The bull of convocation was not issued until November 14, 1550. For the text, see CT 7/1:6–8.

37. See Tallon, *France et Trente*, 219–247.

38. See CT 7/1:11–12.

39. See, e.g., Ricardo G. Villoslada, "Pedro Guerrero, representante de la reforma española," in *Il Concilio di Trento e la riforma tridentina: Atti del convegno storico internazionale,* 2 vols. (Rome: Herder, 1965), 1:115–155; and Antonio Marín Ocete, *El arzobispo don Pedro Guerrero y la politica conciliar española en el siglo XVI* (Madrid: Instituto "Enrique Flórez," 1970).

40. I base these numbers, which include Madruzzo, on Massarelli's list, CT 7/1:457–458. See Hubert Jedin, "Die Deutschen am Trienter Konzil 1551/52," in Jedin, *Kirche des Glaubens,* 2:224–236.

41. See Tanner, *Decrees,* 2:692–693.

42. See CT 7/1:99–104 for the documents.

43. See Alain Tallon, *Conscience nationale et sentiment religieux en France au XVIe siècle* (Paris: Presses Universitaires de France, 2002); and Jonathan Parsons, *The Church in the Republic: Gallicanism and Political Ideology in Renaissance France* (Washington, DC: Catholic University of America Press, 2004), especially 36–41.

44. See CT 7/1:114–141.

45. See CT 7/1:143–176. For the texts of the theologians' and bishops' interventions, see CT 7/2:97–235.

46. See CT 7/1:144.

47. See CT 7/1:146.

48. See CT 7/1:208–212.

49. See Tanner, *Decrees,* 2:693–702.

50. On the Eucharist, see, e.g., Bernard Sesboüé, "Doctrine sacramentaire," in Bourgeois, *Signes du salut,* 158–165; Josef Wohlmuth, *Realpräsenz und Transsubstantiation im Konzil von Trient: Eine historisch-kritische Analyse der Canones 1–4 der Sessio XIII,* 2 vols. (Bern: Herbert Lang, 1975). Ranging wider but highly pertinent to the council are Miri Rubin, *Corpus Christi: The Eucharist in Late Medieval Culture* (Cambridge: Cambridge University Press, 1991); Paul H. Jones, *Christ's Eucharistic Presence: A History of the Doctrine* (New York: Peter Lang, 1994); and Marilyn McCord Adams, *Some Later Medieval Theories of the Eucharist: Thomas Aquinas, Giles of Rome, Duns Scotus, and William Ockham* (Oxford: Oxford University Press, 2010).

51. See, e.g., John W. O'Malley, *The First Jesuits* (Cambridge, MA: Harvard University Press, 1993), 152–157.

52. Tanner, *Decrees,* 2:697.

53. See CT 11:676–678, 680–684, 692–694, 696–698.

54. See Jedin, *Geschichte,* 3:297.

55. See CT 7/1:259. For the immediate theological background to the Protestants' participation, see Martin Brecht, "Abgrenzung oder Verständigung: Was wollten die Protestanten in Trient?" in Bäumer, *Concilium Tridentinum,* 161–195.

56. See, e.g., CT 7/1:233, 234, 235.

57. For the texts of the theologians' and bishops' interventions, see CT 7/2:239–341.

58. See, e.g., CT 7/1:255.

59. See, e.g., CT 11:699, 700–701, 711, 714–715.

60. See CT 11:742–748, at 743.

61. See CT 7/l:336.

62. CT 7/1:337: ". . . vocando reformationem propositam superfluam et praetensam." On Psaume, see Bernard Ardura, *Nicolas Psaume 1518–1575: Evêque et Comte de Verdun* (Paris: Éditions du Cerf, 1990), especially pp. 121–138, 178–212, and 489–495.

63. We are well informed about this incident and its aftermath. See especially the long account by Francisco Manrique de Lara, bishop of Orense, CT 11:713–714. See also CT 7/1:337–338, 339, and CT 11:709, 710, 717.

64. For the text, see Tanner, *Decrees,* 2:714–718.

65. For the text, see Tanner, *Decrees,* 2:703–713. See Bernard Sesboüé, "Doctrine sacramentaire," in Bourgeois, *Signes du salut,* 170–184. On anointing (extreme unction), see, e.g., Andrew J. Cuschieri, *Anointing the Sick: A Theo-*

logical and Canonical Study (Lanham: University Press of America, 1993). The literature on penance is extensive. See especially R. Emmet McLaughlin, "Truth, Tradition and History: The Historiography of High/Late Medieval and Early Modern Penance," in Abigail Firey, ed., *A New History of Penance,* 17–71 (Leiden: E. J. Brill, 2008). See also, e.g., Duval, *Sacrements au Concile de Trente,* 151–222; Otto Semmelroth, "Das Bussakrament als Gericht," *Scholastik* 37 (1962): 530–549; Carl J. Peter, "Auricular Confession and the Council of Trent," *Jurist* 28 (1968): 280–297; Carl J. Peter, "Integral Confession and the Council of Trent," in *Sacramental Reconciliation,* ed. Edward Schillebeeckx (New York: Herder and Herder, 1971), 99–109; Carl J. Peter, "Dimensions of *Jus Divinum* in Roman Catholic Theology," *Theological Studies* 34 (1973): 227–250; Hans-Peter Arendt, *Busssakrament und Einzelbeichte: Die tridentinischen Lehraussagen über das Sündenbekenntnis and ihre Verbindlichkeit für die Reform des Bussakramentes* (Freiburg im Breisgau: Herder, 1981); Adriano Prosperi, "Die Beichte und das Gericht des Gewissens," in Prodi, *Trient und die Moderne,* 175–197; and, more broadly, his *Tribunali della coscienza: Inquisitori, confessori, missionari,* 2nd ed. (Turin: Einaudi, 2009); and Wietze de Boer, *The Conquest of the Soul: Confession, Discipline, and Public Order in Counter-Reformation Milan* (Leiden: E. J. Brill, 2001). Most recently, see L. Mezzadri and M. Tagliaferri, eds., *La penitenza: dottrina, controversie e prassi tra medioevo e età moderna* (Franzione Pan di Porto: Tau Editrice, 2011); and Paolo Prodi, "Fourteen Theses on the Legacy of Trent," in *Catholic Theological Ethics, Past, Present, and Future: The Trento Conference,* ed. James F. Keenan, 40–47 (Maryknoll, NY: Orbis, 2012).

66. See, e.g., O'Malley, *First Jesuits,* 136–152.

67. See Tanner, *Decrees,* 2:718–719.

68. For the texts of the theologians' and bishops' interventions, see CT 7/2:345–689.

69. See Brecht, "Abgrenzung oder Verständigung"; and Nelson Minnich, "'Wie in dem basilischen Concilio den Behemen gescheen'? The Status of the Protestants at the Council of Trent," in *The Contentious Triangle: Church, State, and University. A Festschrift in Honor of Professor George Huntston Williams,* ed. Rodney L. Petersen and Calvin Augustine Pater, 201–219 (Kirksville, MO: Thomas Jefferson University Press, 1999). See also, e.g., Remigius Bäumer, "Das Trienter Konzil und die Reformatoren: Zum Erscheinung von H. Jedin, Geschichte des Konzils von Trient III," *Catholica* 25 (1971): 325–338.

70. See CT 7/1:500.

71. See CT 7/1:465–475.

72. See Tanner, *Decrees*, 2:718–719.

73. CT 7/1:512, ". . . ab omnibus actibus conciliaribus cessatum est."

74. See CT 7/1:512–513.

75. See Heinrich Lutz, *Christianitas Afflicta: Europa, das Reich und die päpstliche Politik im Niedergang der Hegemonie Kaiser Karls V (1552–1556)* (Göttingen: Vandenhoeck and Ruprecht, 1964).

76. See, e.g., CT 11:853–854, 858.

77. See CT 7/1:518.

78. See Tanner, *Decrees*, 2:721–722. For the deliberations, see CT 7/1:517–554.

79. See Alberto Aubert, *Paolo IV: Politica, inquisizione e storiografia* (Florence: Le Lettere, 1999). This is a second printing of the volume that appeared in 1990 under the title *Paolo IV Carafa nel giudizio dell'età della Controriforma*.

80. The trial has been studied in great detail by Massimo Firpo, *Inquisizione romana e Controriforma: Studi sul cardinal Giovanni Morone (1509–1580) e il suo processo d'eresia*, rev. ed. (Brescia: Morcelliana, 2005). See also Firpo's critical edition of the documents pertaining to the inquisitorial process, *Il processo inquisitoriale del cardinal Giovanni Morone*, 6 vols. in 7 (Rome: Istituto storico italiano per l'età moderna e contemporanea, 1981–1995).

81. See J. M. De Bujanda, ed., *Index de Rome, 1557, 1559, 1564: Les premiers index romains et l'index du Concile de Trente* (Quebec: Centre d'Études de la Renaissance, 1990), especially 325, 331.

82. See Pastor, *Popes*, 14:81–89, 206–232, and CT 15:131–178.

83. On his reform measures, see Pastor, *Popes*, 4:175–205.

84. For a detailed account, see Pastor, *Popes*, 15:1–65.

85. For the capitulations, see CT 8:1–2.

86. For the bull, see CT 8:104–107.

87. See, e.g., Borromeo's letter to the papal nuncio in Spain, May 25, 1561, CT 8:27. See also CT 8:13–14, at 14.

5. The Council Resumes, 1562–1563

1. See, e.g., CT 8:155–157, 190, 220–221, 262.

2. See CT 8:114.

3. See CT 8:142–155.

4. CT 8:197.

5. The pope's letter to Mary Stuart announcing the sending of Floris suggests he had no idea how impossible the situation had become. See CT 8:277–278.

6. For an earlier letter of the pope, May 5, 1560, inviting Elizabeth to send bishops and envoys, see CT 8:17. The same day he sent similar letters to Philip, Ferdinand, and other rulers.

7. See Tallon, *France et Trente*, 249–334; and Wolfgang P. Fischer, *Frankreich und die Wiedereröffnung des Konzils von Trient, 1559–1562* (Münster: Aschendorff, 1973).

8. See CT 8:225–226.

9. See Donald Nugent, *Ecumenism in the Age of the Reformation: The Colloquy of Poissy* (Cambridge, MA: Harvard University Press, 1974).

10. Still valuable is Constancio Gutiérrez, *Españoles en Trento* (Valladolid: Consejo Superior de Investigaciones Cientificas Instituto "Jerónimo Zurita," 1951).

11. See CT 8:176–177.

12. See Paul V. Murphy, *Ruling Peacefully: Cardinal Ercole Gonzaga and Patrician Reform in Sixteenth-Century Italy* (Washington, DC: Catholic University of America Press, 2007), especially 196–244.

13. Cited in Hubert Jedin, *Crisis and Closure of the Council of Trent: A Retrospective View from the Second Vatican Council*, trans. N. D. Smith (London: Sheed and Ward, 1967), 26.

14. Tanner, *Decrees*, 2:723.

15. See CT 8:279, letter of January 14, 1562. For a discussion of the history of the document, see J. M. Bujanda, *Index de Rome, 1557, 1559, 1564: Les premiers index romains et l'index du Concile de Trente* (Quebec: Centre d'Études de la Renaissance, 1990), 51–99.

16. See CT 8:279–281.

17. CT 8:336–337, at 336.

18. For the decree, see Tanner, *Decrees*, 2:723–724.

19. For the twelve articles, see CT 8:378–379.

20. For the dispute over residence, see Hubert Jedin, "Der Kampf um die bischöliches Residenzpflicht 1562–63," in Jedin, *Kirche des Glaubens*, 2:398–413.

21. See Jedin, *Geschichte*, 4/1:114–115.

22. On Beccadelli, see Hubert Jedin, "Das Bischofsideal der Katholischen Reformation: Eine Studie über die Bischofsspiegel vornehmlich der 16. Jahrhunderts," in Jedin, *Kirche des Glaubens*, 2:75–117, at 91–97; and Gigliola Fra-

gnito, "La terza fase del concilio di Trento, Morone e gli 'spirituali,'" in *Il cardinale Giovanni Morone e l'ultima fase del concilio di Trento,* ed. Massimo Firpo and Ottavia Niccoli (Bologna: Mulino, 2010), 53–78.

23. See CT 8:403.

24. See CT 8:418–421.

25. See CT 8:402–463.

26. See CT 8:463.

27. There are discrepancies in the tally. See CT 8:464–465, with n. 5, and CT 3/1:318. See also Jedin, *Geschichte,* 4/1:124 and 325, n. 20. I accept Jedin's calculation. For the letter of the legates to Borromeo on the same day describing the outcome, see Šusta, *Die römische Curie,* 2:86–90, at 88, and also 90–91.

28. See, e.g., Šusta, *Die römische Curie,* 2:89, and especially 92, and 127–131.

29. For three important letters from Rome under the same date, May 11, see Šusta, *Die römische Curie,* 2:132–143.

30. Ibid., 2:143–146.

31. Ibid., 2:150–153, at 152.

32. See Tanner, *Decrees,* 2:725.

33. See CT 3/1:341.

34. See CT 3/1:344, and Šusta, *Die römische Curie,* 2:227–228, 282–284, 487–488.

35. For an extensive and detailed account of Ferdinand's actions regarding church reform, see Robert Trisco, "Reforming the Roman Curia: Emperor Ferdinand I and the Council of Trent," in *Reform and Authority in the Medieval and Reformation Church,* ed. Guy Fitch Lytle (Washington, DC: Catholic University of America Press, 1981), 143–337.

36. For a summary of the theologians' interventions, see CT 8:614–617.

37. For the address, see CT 8:620–626.

38. See CT 13/2:253–256; CT 36–82; and Šusta, *Die römische Curie,* 3:222–223. See also Klaus Ganzer, "Zur Frage der kirchlichen Predigtvollmacht auf dem Konzil von Trient," *Annuarium Historiae Conciliorum* 7 (1975): 402–416; and his "Bayern und die Laienpredigt im 16. Jahrhundert," 18 (1986): 330–333.

39. See CT 8:617–618; and Tanner, *Decrees,* 2:728.

40. See Tanner, *Decrees,* 2:728–732.

41. See Hubert Jedin, "Delegatus Sedis Apostolicae und bischöfliche Gewalt auf dem Konzil von Trient," in Jedin, *Kirche des Glaubens,* 2:414–428.

42. For the decrees, see Tanner, *Decrees,* 2:726–728.

43. See CT 8:719.

44. See CT 8:751–755.

45. For the decree, see Tanner, *Decrees,* 2:732–737.

46. See Duval, *Sacrements au Concile de Trente,* 61–150; Bernard Sesboüé, "L'Eucharistie et le sacrifice de la messe," in Bourgeois, *Signes du salut,* 158–170; Buzzi, *Concilio di Trento,* 136–145; J. F. McHugh, "The Sacrifice of the Mass at the Council of Trent," in *Sacrifice and Redemption: Durham Essays in Theology,* ed. S. W. Sykes, 157–181 (Cambridge: Cambridge University Press, 1991); Erwin Iserloh, "Das tridentinische Messopferdekret in seinen Beziehungen zu der Kontroverstheologie der Zeit," in Bäumer, *Concilium Tridentinum,* 341–381; and David N. Power, *The Sacrifice We Offer: The Tridentine Dogma and Its Reinterpretation* (New York: Crossroad, 1987).

47. For the chapter, see Tanner, *Decrees,* 2:735: "Etsi missa magnam contineat populi fidelis eruditionem, non tamen expedire visum est patribus ut vulgari passim lingua celebraretur." For the canon, see Tanner, *Decrees,* 2:736: "Si quis dixerit . . . lingua tantum vulgari missam celebrari debere . . . anathema sit." See Jedin, *Geschichte,* 4/1:208.

48. CT 8:766: "Et in ecclesia Hierosolymitana sancti sepulchri celebrantur missae qualibet lingua quae est sub coelo."

49. H. J. Schroeder, for instance, in his widely diffused translation of the council's decrees prefaces chapter 8 with, "The mass may not be celebrated in the vernacular," even though he correctly translates the decree. See *The Canons and Decrees of the Council of Trent,* trans. H. J. Schroeder (Rockford, IL: Tan Books, 1978), 148. Bernard Sesboüé, careful scholar though he is, makes the same mistake, "Eucharistie et le sacrifice de la messe," in Bourgeois, *Signes du salut,* 170.

50. Tanner, *Decrees,* 2:734.

51. Ibid.

52. See Hubert Jedin, "Das Konzil von Trient und die Reform der liturgischen Bücher," in Jedin, *Kirche des Glaubens,* 2:499–525.

53. For the draft, see CT 8:916–921. See also CT 8:921–924.

54. Tanner, *Decrees,* 2:737.

55. See CT 8:918.

56. See CT 8:927.

57. For a judicious and comprehensive analysis of the issue, see Craig A. Monson, "The Council of Trent Revisited," *Journal of the American Musicological Society,* 55 (2002), 1–37.

58. For a summary and analysis of the bishops' positions, see CT 8:899–909.

59. See CT 8:942–943.

60. See Tanner, *Decrees*, 2:741. After the passage of this decree, Ferdinand called together a group of advisers to discuss how he should now proceed with the pope to obtain the concession. For the responses from the experts assembled, see CT 13/2:36–82. For the history of the issue after the council, see Gustave Constant, *Concession à l'Allemagne de la communion sous deux espèces: Étude sur les début de la Réforme Catholique en Allemagne (1548–1621)*, 2 vols. (Paris: Boccard, 1923).

61. CT 9:5: "Episcopos non esse presbyteris superiores neque habere ius ordinandi, aut, si habent, id illis esse commune cum presbyteris, ordinationesque ab ipsis factas sine plebis consensu irritas esse."

62. See CT 9:40–41.

63. For Guerrero's development of this argument, occasioned by canon 7, see CT 9:48–51.

64. See Šusta, *Die römische Curie*, 3:39–42, at 40–41.

65. Quoted in Tallon, *France et Trente*, 620, n. 74: "Erano tenuti quasi per heretici et hora respetto alli Francesi paiono santi."

66. See Šusta, *Die römische Curie*, 3:104, 151, 154, 165, 172.

67. See CT 9:242–243, at 242.

68. For accounts of the different positions, see, e.g., CT 13/2:146–252.

69. See CT 13/2:257–261, at 257–258.

70. CT 13/2:275: ". . . sunt duo concilia in ecclesia: nam est unum concilium congregatum Tridenti et aliud concilium congregatum Romae cum papa. Ista duo concilia aliquo modo ex opposito pugnant." For the opinions of the theologians, see CT 13/2:262–285.

71. See CT 13/2:286–287. For the report de Guise gave to the legates after his return to Trent, see Šusta, *Die römische Curie*, 3:250–252.

72. For the letters, see CT 13/2:292–300.

73. See Šusta, *Die römische Curie*, 3:532–534.

74. See Seripando's letter to Borromeo, March 3, 1563, in Šusta, *Die römische Curie*, 3:257–261.

6. The Council Concludes

1. On Morone, besides the works by Massimo Firpo cited above in Chapter 4, notes 32 and 80, pp. 309, 313, see Roberto Pancheri and Domenica Primerano, eds., *L'uomo del Concilio: il cardinale Giovanni Morone tra Roma e Trento nell'età di Michelangelo* (Trent: Terni, 2009); Klaus Ganzer, "Gasparo Contarini

und Giovanni Morone: Das Regensburger Religionsgespräch von 1541 und das Werden einer Freundschaft," *Cristianesimo nella Storia* 30 (2009): 93–132; Massimo Firpo and Ottavia Niccoli, *Il cardinale Giovanni Morone e l'ultima fase del Concilio di Trento* (Bologna: Mulino, 2010); and Adam Patrick Robinson, *The Career of Cardinal Giovanni Morone (1509–1580)* (Burlington, VT: Ashgate, 2012).

2. See Šusta, *Die römische Curie,* 3:526–531.

3. See Umberto Mazzone, "Giovanni Morone legato al concilio di Trento e la clausula del 'proponentibus legatis,'" in *Morone e l'ultima fase,* ed. Firpo and Niccoli, 117–141. For a document of Morone's on the matter produced while he was at Innsbruck, see Gustave Constant, *La Légation de cardinal Morone près l'Empereur et le Concile de Trente, Avril–Décembre 1563* (Paris: H. Champion, 1922), 119–121, and for others much later, 291–299 and 553–555, which demonstrate that the issue remained live and troubling. See the documents, CT 13/2:662–679.

4. For Morone's summary of his response to Ferdinand on the points raised by the two letters, see Constant, *Légation,* 37–44. See also Constant, *Légation,* 128–133, "Summarium eorum quae acta sunt inter Caesaream Majestatem et cardinalem Moronum," and 133–135.

5. See Šusta, *Die römische Curie,* 4:18–21, at 18.

6. See Constant, *Légation,* 157.

7. See CT 9:485.

8. For the document, see CT 9:477–485.

9. See CT 3/1:627. See also, e.g., Massimo Faggioli, "La disciplina di nomina dei vescovi prima e dopo il Concilio di Trento," *Società e Storia* 24, 92 (2001): 221–256; and José Pedro Paiva, "The Appointment of Bishops in Early Modern Portugal (1495–1777)," *Catholic Historical Review* 97 (2011): 461–483.

10. On this canon and its fate, see Robert Trisco, "The Debate on the Election of Bishops in the Council of Trent," *Jurist* 34 (1974): 257–291.

11. Cited by James A. O'Donohoe, *Tridentine Seminary Legislation: Its Sources and Its Formation* (Louvain: Publications Universitaires de Louvain, 1957), v. See also Hubert Jedin, "Domschule und Kolleg: Zum Ursprung der Idee des Trienter Priesterseminars," in Jedin, *Kirche des Glaubens,* 2:348–359; Hermann Tüchle, "Das Seminardekret des Trienter Konzils und Formen seiner geschichtlichen Verwirklichung," in Bäumer, *Concilium Tridentinum,* 522–539; and Kathleen M. Comerford, "Italian Tridentine Diocesan Seminaries: A Historiographical Study," *Sixteenth Century Journal* 29 (1998): 999–1022.

12. See O'Donohoe, *Tridentine Seminary*, 89–120, 134–142.

13. Ibid., 63–87.

14. See CT 9:487–489.

15. See CT 9:489.

16. See CT 9:491.

17. See CT 9:494.

18. See CT 3/1:663. See also CT 9:582–583.

19. See CT 9:587–590.

20. See Tanner, *Decrees*, 2:760, on bishops. For pastors, see 2:770–772.

21. See Tanner, *Decrees*, 2:744.

22. See CT 9:1140–1141.

23. On Foscarari, see Lucia Felici, "Al crocevia della riforma: Egidio Foscarari nella terza fase del Tridentino," in *Morone e l'ultima fase*, ed. Firpo and Niccoli, 79–116.

24. See Šusta, *Die römische Curie*, 4:74–82.

25. The best account of what happened from June 8 to July 15 is Paleotti's, found in CT 3/1:654–692.

26. See Tanner, *Decrees*, 2:742–743.

27. CT 3/1:684.

28. See Constant, *Légation*, 173. See also Alain Tallon, "Giovanni Morone, il cardinale di Lorena e la conclusione del concilio," in *Morone e l'ultima fase*, ed. Firpo and Niccoli, 143–158.

29. CT 3/1:684–685.

30. CT 3/1:688.

31. For the final decrees, see Tanner, *Decrees*, 2:742–753. On the vote, see CT 9:623, 632. An important study that locates the decree in the wide context of the council is Josef Freitag, *Sacramentum ordinis auf dem Konzil von Trient: Ausgeblendeter Dissens und erreichter Konsens* (Innsbruck and Vienna: Tyrolia Verlag, 1991). For a theological analysis, see Bernard Sesboüé, "Le sacrement de l'ordre," in Bourgeois, *Signes du salut*, 184–192; and Duval, *Sacrements au Concile de Trente*, 327–404. For an important analysis, see "The Threefold Ordained Ministry of Bishop, Priest, and Deacon according to the Council of Trent (1545–1563)," in *The Apostolicity of the Church: Study Document of the Lutheran–Roman Catholic Commission on Unity* (Minneapolis: Lutheran University Press, 2006), 103–108. I am indebted to Jared Wicks for this reference.

32. See Constant, *Légation*, 232–233.

33. See CT 9:380.

34. For the text, see CT 9:639–640.

35. See Tanner, *Decrees,* 1:258 (canon 51).

36. See, e.g., Jean-Baptiste Molin and Protais Mutembe, *Le rituel du mariage en France du XIIe au XVIe siècle* (Paris: Beauchesne, 1974); David D'Avray, "Marriage Ceremonies and the Church in Italy after 1215," in *Marriages in Italy, 1300–1650,* ed. Trevor Dean and K. J. P. Lowe, 107–115 (Cambridge: Cambridge University Press, 1998); Anthony F. D'Elia, *The Renaissance of Marriage in Fifteenth-Century Italy* (Cambridge, MA: Harvard University Press, 2004); and Philip J. Reynolds, "Marrying and Its Documentation in Pre-Modern Europe: Consent, Celebration, and Property," in *To Have and To Hold: Marrying and Its Documentation in Western Christendom, 400–1600,* ed. Philip J. Reynolds and John Witte, Jr., 1–42 (Cambridge: Cambridge University Press, 2007).

37. See CT 9:650.

38. For a sampling of arguments against the decree, see CT 9:971–977.

39. See, e.g., Jean Bernhard, "Le décret *Tametsi* du Concile de Trente: Triomphe du consensualisme matrimonial ou institution de la forme solennelle du mariage?" *Revue de Droit Canonique* 30 (1980): 209–234.

40. See Tanner, *Decrees,* 2:755–757.

41. Ibid., 2:753–759. On the doctrinal and theological aspects of the documents, see, e.g., Bernard Sesboüé, "Le mariage," in Bourgeois, *Signes du salut,* 192–200; and Duval, *Sacrements au Concile de Trente,* 281–325. On the decree's wider implications, see Gabriele Zarri, "Die tridentinische Ehe," in Prodi, *Trient und die Moderne,* 343–379.

42. See CT 9:544.

43. See CT 9:589.

44. The most thorough discussion of the pertinent canons is Egidio Ferasin, *Matrimonio e celibato al Concilio di Trento* (Rome: Lateranum, 1970). For a concise discussion, see Georg Denzler, *Das Papsttum und die Amstzölibat,* 2 vols. (Stuttgart: Anton Hiersemann, 1973–1976), 2:207–233. See also August Franzen, *Zölibat und Priesterehe in der Auseinandersetzung der Reformationszeit und der katholischen Reform des 16. Jahrhunderts* (Münster: Aschendorff, 1969), especially 76–88. There is a brief treatment in Helen Parish, *Clerical Celibacy in the West: c.1100–1700* (Burlington, VT: Ashgate, 2010), pp. 191–194. On lay preachers, see CT 13/2:253–256.

45. See CT 9:446–458, at 454–456.

46. See CT 9:463–464, 465.

47. See Šusta, *Die römische Curie,* 4:41–44.

48. Ibid., 4:88–90.

49. See Paolo Prodi, *Il cardinale Gabriele Paleotti (1522–1598)*, 2 vols. (Rome: Edizioni di Storia e Letteratura, 1959–1967), 1:182–192.

50. For the articles, see CT 9:748–759.

51. Paleotti provides a concise summary of the problem, CT 3/1:706–707.

52. For these articles, see CT 9:766–774.

53. See Tanner, *Decrees*, 2:766 and 785.

54. See Jacques Dupuis, ed., *The Christian Faith in the Doctrinal Documents of the Catholic Church*, 7th rev. and enl. ed. (New York: Alba House, 2001), 21–23.

55. See CT 9:841–845.

56. See CT 9:885.

57. For the canons, see CT 9:906–911; for the debate, see CT 9:912–956.

58. On him, see Hubert Jedin, "Die Autobiographie des Don Martín Pérez de Ayala," in Jedin, *Kirche des Glaubens*, 2:285–320.

59. See CT 9:928–930, and CT 3/1:744–745.

60. CT 3/1:712.

61. See Šusta, *Die römische Curie*, 4:263, 303, 337, 569–570.

62. See Constant, *Légation*, 247–248.

63. For the reform decree, see Tanner, *Decrees*, 2:759–773.

64. See CT 9:1008–1011.

65. CT 9:1014.

66. See CT 9:1014–1036.

67. See CT 9:1013–1014.

68. See CT 9:1014–1015. See also, e.g., CT 9:1016, the observations of the patriarch of Aquileia.

69. Tanner, *Decrees*, 2:795–796.

70. CT 3/1:753: ". . . id caput in generalem quandam formulam et fere inanem verborum sonum redactum."

71. Tanner, *Decrees*, 2:784–784.

72. For the decrees in their final form, see Tanner, *Decrees*, 2:784–796.

73. See Giancarlo Angelozzi, "Das Verbot des Duells: Kirche und adeliges Selbstverständnis," in Prodi, *Trient und die Moderne*, 211–240.

74. For the debate, see CT 9:1044–1067. For the final documents, see Tanner, *Decrees*, 776–784. For the background, still basic is Hubert Jedin, "Zur Vorgeschichte der Regularenreform Trid., sess. XXV," in Jedin, *Kirche des Glaubens*, 2:360–397. See also the more widely ranging chapter, "Gli ordini re-

ligiosi," in Paolo Prodi, *Il paradigma tridentino: Un' epoca della storia della Chiesa* (Brescia: Morcelliana, 2010), 169–186.

75. See CT 9:1044–1045, and CT 3/1:755.

76. CT 9:1045.

77. See CT 9:1048.

78. See, e.g., Anne Jacobson Schutte, *By Force and Fear: Taking and Breaking Monastic Vows in Early Modern Europe* (Ithaca, NY: Cornell University Press, 2011).

79. On the ambiguity of the decree, see Anne Conrad, "Das Konzil von Trient und die (unterbliebene) Modernisierung kirchlicher Frauenrollen," in Prodi, *Trient und die Moderne,* 325–341, especially at 331–332.

80. In the past two decades studies of women's convents in the post-Tridentine period have proliferated. For an excellent summary and analysis of the state of the question, with ample bibliography, see Amy E. Leonard, "Female Religious Orders," in *A Companion to the Reformation World,* ed. R. Po-chia Hsia, 236–254 (Oxford: Blackwell, 2004).

81. On Luna's maneuvers during these last days, see Paleotti's account, CT 3/1:758–759. See also Šusta, *Die römische Curie,* 4:410–426, and far beyond these pages.

82. See Constant, *Légation,* 398–399.

83. See CT 9:1069–1076.

84. For the decree, see Tanner, *Decrees,* 2:774.

85. For the decree, see Tanner, *Decrees,* 2:774–776.

86. See John W. O'Malley, "Trent, Sacred Images, and Catholics' Senses of the Sensuous," *The Sensuous in Counter-Reformation Art,* ed. Marcia Hall and Tracy Cooper (New York: Cambridge University Press, 2012). Still fundamental is Hubert Jedin, "Entstehung und Tragweite des Trienter Dekrets über die Bilderverehrung," in Jedin, *Kirche des Glaubens,* 2:460–498.

87. See Carl Mirbt, ed., *Quellen zur Geschichte des Papsttums* (Freiburg i/Br.: Akademische Verlagsbuchhandlung, J. C. B. Mohr, 1895), 190–194.

88. See Tanner, *Decrees,* 2:764. In the English translation the words *in catechesi* are omitted.

89. At Bologna in November 1547, six members were appointed to the deputation. See CT 8:305. For earlier mentions and proposals, see, e.g., CT 1:46, 50; 5:73, 80, 106; 10:864. For a history of the issue during the council, see Pio Paschini, *Il Catechismo Romano del Concilio di Trento: Sue origini e sua prima diffusione* (Rome: Pontificio Seminario Romano Maggiore, 1923), 7–17. For a

listing of the large number of editions and translations through the centuries, see Gerhard J. Bellinger, *Bibliographie des Catechismus Romanus: ex decreto Concilii Tridentini ad parochos, 1566–1978* (Baden-Baden: V. Koerner, 1983). See now the critical edition by a team headed by Pedro Rodríguez, *Catechismus Romanus, seu Catechismus ex decreto Concilii Tridentini ad parochos Pii Quinti Pont. Max. iussu editus* (Città del Vaticano: Libreria Editrice Vaticana, 1989). See also Rodríguez and Raul Lanzetti, *El Catechismo romano: fuentes e historia del texto y de la redacción* (Pamplona: Universidad de Navarra, 1982).

90. See CT 2:689.

91. See CT 9:1013.

92. See Hubert Jedin, "Das Konzil von Trient und die Reform der liturgischen Bücher," in Jedin, *Kirche des Glaubens*, 2:499–525. See also, however, Gottfried Maron, "Die nachtridentinische Kodifikationsarbeit in ihrer Bedeutung für die katholische Konfessionalisierung," in *Die katholische Konfessionalisierung*, ed. Wolfgang Reinhard and Heinz Schilling, 104–124 (Münster: Aschendorff, 1995).

93. See CT 8:917.

94. See CT 3/1:756, n. l; and Šusta, *Die römische Curie*, 4:428.

95. See CT 9:1076–1103, 1105–1110, and CT 3/1:757–762.

96. CT 3/1:762.

Acknowledgments

In bringing this book to conclusion I have been greatly helped and saved from countless errors by the kindness of friends and colleagues. James Coriden and Nelson Minnich responded to my request for their criticism of certain passages for which they had special expertise. Without the extensive bibliography on every aspect of the Council of Trent that Nelson Minnich compiled and to which he, with characteristic kindness and generosity, gave me access, my book would be much the poorer. I am of course especially grateful to the colleagues whose friendship I abused by asking them to read, at different stages of the drafting process, the entire manuscript: Paul Bradford, David Collins, Simon Ditchfield, and Otto Hentz. I single out Jared Wicks for special thanks because of his detailed comments, suggestions, and corrections. James P. M. Walsh double-checked the proofs for me and of course found slips I had missed.

I am grateful to the anonymous readers for Harvard University Press, whose comments helped me considerably. I thank Lindsay Waters, my editor at Harvard, for his enthusiasm for the book and his support. For each of my five books with the press, Christine Thorsteinsson has been my gracious and perceptive copy-editor, and has saved me from many infelicities and mistakes.

Here at Georgetown University, Taraneh Wilkinson checked my citations with a keen eye. Along with his staff, J. Leon Hooper, director of the Woodstock Theological Library at Georgetown University, came to my aid at crucial moments.

For translation of the final documents of the Council of Trent, I have used the text edited by Norman Tanner in the two-volume set *Decrees of the Ecumenical Councils*. To those texts I have, however, occasionally made minor emendations. All other translations are mine unless I explicitly indicate the contrary.

I dedicate the book to Dr. Clare O'Reilly of Dublin. The late Professor Francis X. Martin, O.S.A., introduced me to Clare when I sought his aid as I set out in August 1963 to write my dissertation on Giles of Viterbo. From that first meeting a life-long friendship developed among the three of us that was fostered by the scholarly interest each of us had in Giles, but it was especially furthered by the love we shared for Rome, which included of course its restaurants. What fun we had, even in the archives and libraries!

Index